Gardee les baiguiere

Voite

Frigot

84

GONVEL

P9-CJJ-304

l'appart

ALSO BY DAVID LEBOVITZ

The Sweet Life in Paris

My Paris Kitchen

Ready for Dessert

The Perfect Scoop

The Great Book of Chocolate

l'appart

The Delights

and Disasters

of Making My

Paris Home

David Lebovitz

CROWN

NEW YORK

Copyright © 2017 by David Lebovitz

Published in the United States by Crown, an imprint of the Crown Publishing Group, a division of Penguin Random House LLC, New York.
crownpublishing.com

CROWN is a registered trademark and the Crown colophon is a trademark of Penguin Random House LLC.

Library of Congress Cataloging-in-Publication Data
Names: Lebovitz, David, author.
Title: L'appart : the delights and disasters of making my Paris home / David Lebovitz.
Description: New York: Crown, 2017.
Identifiers: LCCN 2017009159 | ISBN 9780804188388 (hardback)
Subjects: LCSH: Lebovitz, David—Homes and haunts—France—Paris. | Apartments—Remodeling—France—Paris. | Cooks—France—Paris—Biography. | Americans—France—Paris—Biography. | Paris (France)—Social life and customs. | Paris (France)—Biography. | Cooking—France—Paris. | Cooking, French. | BISAC: BIOGRAPHY & AUTOBIOGRAPHY / Personal Memoirs. | TRAVEL / Essays & Travelogues. | COOKING / Regional & Ethnic / French.
Classification: LCC TX649.L43 A3 2017 | DDC 641.5092 [B]—dc23 LC record available at https://lccn.loc.gov/2017009159

ISBN 978-0-8041-8838-8
ebook ISBN 978-0-8041-8839-5

Printed in the United States of America

Jacket design by Alane Gianetti
Jacket photograph by James Roper

10 9 8 7 6 5 4 3 2 1

First Edition

To Romain, who made it all possible.

(Well . . . the good parts, that is.)

1

"Pee in this cup."

The stern doctor sat behind the desk in her dim beige office, under-illuminated by a metal desk lamp fitted with a bulb that cast a dull glow over everything and seemed to have been last changed when De Gaulle was president. She handed me a paper receptacle that felt like it was made of newsprint and averted her eyes—somewhat.

It had been eight exasperating months since I'd signed the first *promesse de vente* and finally, I was close to the day when I would sign the *acte de vente*, the deed to my apartment in Paris. Or as time-pressed Parisians shorten it: *l'appart*.

And here I was. The last *acte* I had to do was . . . just . . . relax . . . Which, considering the circumstances—being vaguely scrutinized by a doctor while standing in the middle of her *cabinet*, anxiously trying to fill a paper cup that threatened to crumple in my free hand—is not an easy task.

Maybe if I'd had a grand café crème *beforehand . . . or better yet, a big glass of rosé,* I thought, while she—and I— waited for me to breathe a shudder of relief, so she could go home and I could get the final approval on my bank loan. We were in the same position (well, not literally), waiting for the same thing. She'd already taken a blood sample and rigorously checked my vital signs to make sure I was in the *bonne santé* required by the French bank to approve my mortgage.

I'd applied for a few mortgages before, in the United States, but a medical screening had never been part of the approval process. I was puzzled, until a banker explained it to me: "Monsieur Lebovitz, we don't want you to die." Which was something I couldn't disagree with—they wanted confirmation that I would live long enough to pay for the place. (Later I learned that they had good reason to worry, because that almost didn't happen.) I urgently needed to complete this final task before they'd release the funds for the loan and I could finally take possession of the apartment I'd spent years looking for.

———

Ever since my arrival in Paris a decade earlier, I had been living in a charming *chambre de bonne*, one of the minuscule top-floor apartments tucked just under the curving roof of a blocky yet regal Haussmannian building in the Bastille quarter of Paris. *Chambres de bonne* are single rooms where the maids (*les bonnes*) once lived. Nowadays, they're sought after by Parisians because they are often the cheapest places to buy, especially the ones in buildings without elevators. (Which is why you rarely see Parisians needing to engage in the unsightly spectacle of *le jogging*—although I'd recently spotted one woman running in the Tuileries, doing her laps in espadrilles.) Other advantages are the spectacular views, and best of all, there are no neighbors in heels clomping around above you.

In Paris, the more high-strung the woman, the higher

the heels, which I know from firsthand experience. And not just from one of the many narrow misses I've had with them playing the Parisian version of "chicken" (not sure if they call it *poulet* . . .) on the sidewalks to see who will move first. (I've learned that holding a baguette and swinging it parallel to the ground, just below waist level, gets anyone you're up against to move first.) But because there was one living below me who was so hyperactive that I could hear her racing around at all hours—most often between one and four thirty in the morning, when her heels resonated so loudly that the noise woke me up a full floor above her.

Another thing that made it hard to sleep in that apartment was the weather, though I didn't mind staying awake, listening to the pounding thunderstorms that lash down on Paris. The pelting rain in the fall and winter drowned out the traffic noises on the busy boulevard below and would eventually soothe me to sleep. But come summer, sleeping—or doing anything else—became impossible, as the temperatures soared under the zinc roof (which I lived directly beneath) to as high as 110°F. The only upside was that I had a lot of premelted chocolate always on hand.

The *chambres de bonne* were built to house the help, so were intentionally Spartan. The apartments didn't have kitchens and some had separate back staircases so the domestics could discreetly slip into the family's apartment without having to pass through the front door. Bathrooms were shared Turkish toilets in the hallways. So next time you're in Paris and lusting over a rooftop apartment listed in a real estate agency window, check to see if there is a bathroom . . . and an elevator, unless you don't mind climbing up seven flights of stairs. More and more of the buildings do have elevators now, but many still share one bathroom with everyone else on the floor. (And speaking of floors, they're often Turkish toilets, which consist of a hole in the floor with two places to stand your ground.) Fortunately, my landlord had previously lived in the apartment, so I wasn't sharing any bathrooms, which was good for my neighbors considering the length of time it was taking for me to finalize my real estate transaction. Sure, the *chambres de bonne* are charming, or "cozy," as they'd say in American real estate lingo, but most are just a single room, 200 to 300 square feet (18 to 28 square meters), or roughly the size of an American kitchen.

I tried to buy the apartment I had been living in, because it was incredibly well situated. My place had been joined with another *chambre* next door, so I actually had two rooms, which made all my other friends who lived in a *chambre de bonne* (singular) jealous. It also had a phone booth–size elevator that I took for granted—until it broke. I was crammed in there when it malfunctioned, and barely managed to crook my elbow to lift the emergency phone to my ear to call the elevator company. Eventually, someone picked up, but the woman on the other end told me to call back in two hours because all the repair people were at lunch. Then she hung up. I broke the door to get out, which I didn't get punished for, but walking up seven flights of stairs for the next four months was definitely punishment enough.

The apartment was in the Bastille, a lively neighborhood adjacent to the Marais and the Place des Vosges, and is a major *métro* hub with lots of connections so I could easily hop to anywhere in Paris. I was just steps from the largest outdoor market in the city. I could grab my market basket, which I kept next to my front door, and be perusing a spectacular selection of French cheeses, wines, pâtés, fruits, and vegetables within minutes. But best of all, it was the unbeatable view of Paris that I didn't think I could ever leave. Each day I'd wake up and unlatch the wooden shutters, and after I adjusted to the barrage of light, I was presented with a spectacular view of the Eiffel Tower and a collage of small and grand buildings in the foreground, with Sacré-Cœur church off to the right and the Seine to the left; a spectacular mosaic of Paris that seemed like it was all mine. At night, just before closing the deteriorating shutters, which I was sure would one day blow off in one of the abrupt storms that whips through the city without notice (during one such storm, I almost lost an arm trying to close a shutter that wanted to play tug-of-war with me), I would take one final gaze at the twinkling lights before climbing into bed. If you've seen the movie *Ratatouille*, I shared the same view that Chef Linguini's apartment had (people even say I resemble the movie's main character—the cook, not the rat). One night, I was lying in bed watching the film on my television, which was just next to that window, when I sat up in surprise—at that moment in the film, my doppelgänger's Pixar-perfect view was an exact replica of my Paris panorama. How could I ever move?

One of the few concessions to modernity in the apartment was the dishwasher (which, to a cookbook author, is *the* most important concession), but with a little polish, the apartment would have been the perfect home for me in Paris. All it needed were new floors, paint, an updated bathroom and kitchen, and air-conditioning (my French friends chided me for being *très américain* when I broke down and bought a portable air conditioner after searing my fingertips on my computer keyboard during one of the withering summer heat waves). Alas, it wasn't to be: the landlord didn't want to sell, and I couldn't blame him. So after seven or eight years of living life at the top of the most beautiful city in the world, it was time to get back down to earth. Unfortunately when you're at the top, there's only one way to go.

I'd moved to Paris from San Francisco, which, like Paris, is a collection of neighborhoods, or little villages, surrounded by water. Paris is a clearly defined area outlined by the *périphérique,* an always-clogged highway that circles the city where tempers flare as people seethe behind the wheel, heady from diesel fumes, lighting one cigarette off the stub of another as they inch forward, moving through the congested highway at the pace of an *escargot. Le périph* separates the city from the inner *banlieues* (suburbs), which are not to be confused with American suburbs, with their lush lawns, kids running through sprinklers, and minivans parked in driveways. These *banlieues* are notorious for their grim housing projects, inhabited by many immigrants and disenfranchised people, known as *les banlieusards.*

Parisians have never made it easy for outsiders to become part of their city, as all of us who have gone through the process of renewing our visas can attest. One year, the folder of documents that I'd spent six months meticulously compiling and organizing to meet the unpredictable demands was folded in half and slid into the garbage can by a poker-faced bureaucrat without a second thought. (I swear I detected a bit of a smirk, though.) Being from California, I probably would have felt better if she had separated the paper clips from the pages and tossed them into their respective recycling bins.

I went through a lot to get to Paris, starting my life over again not just in a new city, but in a new country, plunging into another culture, with a language I didn't speak. (I could see my teacher at the Alliance Française, where I crammed for my move by taking a two-week intensive course before I left San Francisco, crying a little inside every time I tried to form a complete sentence in French.)

People have asked me repeatedly why I moved here, but I could never provide a more satisfying answer than "For the croissants!" But upon reflection, I'd ended a nearly thirteen-year tenure at Chez Panisse in California, a restaurant strongly influenced by market-based French country cooking: *la cuisine du marché*. The climate and ingredients of Northern California were similar to those you'd find in the south of France, whose residents are similarly smitten with the exuberant foods from their region—dewy goat cheeses (back in the '80s, people in Berkeley assumed we were serving them rounds of tofu), olive oils that resonated with the *terroir* of their provenance in each glossy puddle, fresh herbs used liberally, robust wines, crates overflowing in the summer with pulpy, deep-red tomatoes, and a mutual love of aromatic garlic permeating everything, from aïoli to *agneau*. All those ingredients figured heavily into the cuisines of France and the San Francisco Bay Area, two places where people are obsessed with what's on their plate. The transition was natural for me.

Another obsession shared by both San Francisco and Paris is real estate: it's rare that you attend a party or gathering in either city and the subject doesn't eventually become a topic of discussion, with plenty of grousing about the rising prices of homes and apartments. Because of fixed boundaries, including oceans and *périphs*, which won't be changing anytime soon, prices in the highly desirable city of Paris will only go in one direction: up.

Decades in San Francisco made me realize that those who predicted prices were too high and would surely drop were setting themselves up for disappointment. It's wishful thinking, but people have convinced themselves it's going to happen, much like the communists who meet in their Paris offices under posters of tightly clustered workers marching in the streets alongside their comrades with raised fists, in the belief that France will move toward the ideal of communism. I don't want to burst anyone's bubble, but communism hasn't worked out quite as expected elsewhere in the world, and France will likely remain a capitalist country. Few are willing to give up the fashionable black coat they saw in the window of that boutique in the Marais which was *un must* because it looked so good on them, or give up their *maisons secondaires*, the vacation homes that every French family seems to have, where they retreat to every summer. With Paris being such a desirable place to live, rising housing prices are here to stay.

As I learned in San Francisco, if I was going to remain in Paris, the best assurance of staying for the long term was to own a place of my own.

———

So in spite of folder-folding bureaucrats, I decided to stay in Paris. I'd acclimated to life here. I was on a first-name basis with the clerks in my local shops, especially the ones at the office supply store where I replenished the supply of paper and ink cartridges one plows through by photocopying the slew of paperwork that becomes a part-time job. I'd also become friendly with the vendors at my local market, where my life revolved around my twice-weekly rounds of shopping for fruits, vegetables, sausages, pâtés—whatever caught my eye—and stopping off at the bakery on the corner for a *bien cuite* (well-cooked) baguette (which to me are the only kind) on the way home.

The longer I lived in my neighborhood, the better I knew the vendors: Who had the strawberries that would be bright red all the way through when I cut into them later. Whose Comté was aged longer, giving it a sharper, nuttier flavor. Who would give me a better price if I bought several kilos of apricots because I was testing recipes and needed an entire case. And most important of all, who would let me pick out my own fruits and vegetables in a country where picking out your own produce can trigger a blistering reprimand (or even a hand-slapping, as a friend in Provence found out). It's a good thing they retired the guillotine in 1977 before I arrived, because even though I know I'm not supposed to, I can't resist touching and selecting fruit that I'm buying. It's too frustrating for me to order fruit and vegetables by pointing and saying, "I'll take that one of those . . . and three of those, no . . . not *that* one, the lettuce on the left . . . and a few of those nectarines, oh . . . no, wait . . . I want smaller ones. Can you rifle around for some that are riper? Or ones that have a redder blush, for a photograph? . . . Okay, now that I've asked you to do that, can I get four of those pears? I'm testing a recipe and need pears that weigh 125 grams each . . . and two need to be ripe right now, and two that will be ripe for tomorrow. Sure, I can wait . . ."

As I got to know the sellers, I'd banter and chat more freely with them, sometimes to the consternation of those waiting behind me. But the part of being French that I've definitely mastered is that when it's your turn, you don't think about anyone behind you. Lines in France are like the ones for bathrooms on airplanes. When you're waiting, you're impatient: What the heck is taking the person in front of you so long? But when it's your turn, you take all the time in the world and forget about everyone else behind you. If you've ever waited behind *madame* at the market, selecting her two figs as she ensures that each one is free of even the tiniest of scratches, inspecting every cluster to find just the right nine grapes, or wanting only half a head of celery (which they actually do sell), you might swear they're cookbook authors, too.

It took me at least a year, but I became the master of my market. I knew where the ripest *Brie de Meaux* was, which Camembert was primed to give up its gooey center when I sliced it open later that evening. I'd shuffle forward in line, and when it was my turn to speak to the *fromager*, I would stand in our isolated bubble, having a tête-à-tête with her about which particular cheese was *exactly* the right one. If *madame* started nudging me forward with her wheeled shopping trolley (which, I finally figured out, was how I got those skid marks on the backs of my socks), I'd be certain to ask a few additional questions, ones that would provoke thoughtful—and very, very lengthy—answers.

In time, the egg fellow began to give me a discount on the dozens of eggs I cracked my way through testing recipes. And eventually, by unspoken agreement, the fruit sellers conceded to letting me pick my own pears, nectarines, figs, and apricots, once they realized I was more discerning than they were.

As much as I like to pick out my own fruit, and as much as I like to cook, it's hard to replicate the market's spit-roasted chickens, with skin so crisp even after being wrapped up in a stiff paper sack with a 1970s-style black-outlined orange-and-yellow graphic of a chicken bronzing over an open flame. As soon as I got home, I slid the chicken out of the bag, the salty skin so delectably crunchy that if I pulled off even a single piece before I unpacked the rest of my market haul, I was powerless to resist wolfing down the entire *poulet rôti* right then and there. Some people eat peaches leaning over the sink, with the sticky juices running down their arm. For me, it's the *fond de poulet*—the naturally thick *jus* that saturates the meat—that I'm *fou* for.

In France, being *exigeant*, or discriminating, is considered a positive quality, as is complaining: both put vendors on alert that you expect the best. I knew how to time my arrival at the bakery so I'd get there when the baguettes were still warm. The apron-clad clerks were used to my request for a *bien cuite* baguette and would dutifully burrow through the basket of baguettes to find just the right one. Once the clerk found a baguette that met my rigorous standards, they would wrap it with a small square of paper just large enough for my hand to grab the baguette, but no more, as excess is frowned upon in France. (Look what happened to Louis XIV and his wife.) As soon as I got the baguette outside, I'd pinch off the crusty end—*le quignon*—squeezing the tip with just the right grip . . . not too high, because you don't want to end up with a few dry crumbs, but not too low, because you don't want too much of the softer inside of the bread in relation to the crust. Years of experience has taught me precisely where to grab and twist the tip with just the right amount of torque so I end up with a perfect balance of crust and crumb, before popping that bite of warm, supple crunchiness in my mouth as I head home.

I could go on and on about living in a city with streets lined with chocolate shops and *pâtisseries*, where it's perfectly acceptable to enjoy a lengthy, wine-fueled lunch rather than racing back to work. When summer means picnics by the Seine accompanied by icy glasses of rosé, and no meal is complete without a platter of spectacular cheeses, a baguette (or two), and dessert afterward. I could keep going, but I'll stop, because you might start packing your bags and move here, too. Which would jack up apartment prices even further.

DANDELION FLATBREAD
(Pizza aux pissenlits)

MAKES ONE 16-INCH FLATBREAD, SERVES 4

Dandelions are called *pissenlits* in French. Due to their diuretic property, they're reported to have the effect of making someone *pisse en lit*, or wet the bed. (The Swiss call them by the less-graphic name *dents-de-lion*, or "lion's teeth.") But I've eaten a lot of dandelions in my life—I pick them up whenever I happen to see them at the market in the spring— and I haven't had any nocturnal issues. The only issue you might have is that they usually require a good washing. The smallest leaves are the most tender, so I try to find those. (If you can't get dandelion greens, arugula or baby spinach leaves make a good substitute.)

Dandelion's assertive flavor works as the perfect foil to this crispy, cheesy flatbread. Topped with fresh greens, it resembles a bountiful salad piled on bread, with a bonus layer of melted cheese between the two. I toss the greens in a strong dressing, with a heavier emphasis on the vinegar than a traditional vinaigrette and a touch of garlic for extra zip. You can bake some country-style ham, such as prosciutto, on the flatbread, under the cheese, or drape very thin slices over the top. Cooked cubes of crisp bacon could be tossed with the greens in lieu of the ham. Whatever direction you decide to go in, be sure to prepare the salad ingredients before you bake the flatbread, so you can toss everything together shortly after the flatbread comes out of the oven.

The great thing about this flatbread is if you find yourself, um . . . delayed for any reason, it doesn't need to be eaten warm. It's great at room temperature, so you can take your time, and relax . . . and not worry about the wait.

Dough

   ¼ cup (180ml) tepid water

   1 (7g) package active dry yeast (not instant; 2¼ teaspoons)

   Pinch of sugar

   2 tablespoons olive oil

   1½ cups (210g) all-purpose flour, plus more as needed

   ⅓ cup (45g) whole wheat flour (see Note)

   ¾ teaspoon kosher salt or sea salt

Vinaigrette

   1 garlic clove, minced

   1½ teaspoons fresh lemon juice

   1½ teaspoons red wine vinegar

   1 teaspoon Dijon mustard

   ¼ teaspoon kosher salt or sea salt

   1½ tablespoons olive oil

Dandelion Flatbread Topping

   5 cups loosely packed (80 to 100g) dandelion greens (or arugula or baby spinach), torn if large, well-washed, with tough stems removed

   12 cherry tomatoes, halved or quartered

8 to 10 radishes, trimmed and thinly sliced

½ bulb fennel, tough outer layer removed, very thinly sliced

2 tablespoons minced fresh chives

Freshly ground black pepper

Cornmeal, for the baking sheet

2 cups (6 ounces, 170g) grated Fontina, Gouda, or Swiss cheese

3 medium garlic cloves, minced

1. **Make the dough:** In the bowl of a stand mixer, stir together the water, yeast, and sugar. Let sit for 10 minutes to proof the yeast, until it starts to bubble.

2. With the dough hook attached, on low speed, stir in olive oil, then mix in the all-purpose, whole wheat flour, and salt until they're incorporated. Turn the speed to medium-high and knead the dough until smooth and elastic, about 5 minutes. (Alternatively, you can make the dough in a large bowl and mix and knead it by hand.) Cover the dough with a kitchen towel or plastic wrap and let sit in a warm place until doubled in size, about 1½ hours.

3. While the dough is rising, make the vinaigrette: In a large bowl, combine the vinaigrette ingredients and mix well.

4. When you're ready to bake the dough, be sure to have all the ingredients for the topping prepared and in a large bowl so you can toss them with the dressing when the flatbread comes out of the oven.

5. About 20 minutes before the dough is ready, preheat the oven to 500ºF (260ºC) with a pizza baking stone or steel in it. If you don't have a baking stone or steel, put

a sturdy baking sheet in the oven on the lower shelf to preheat it.

6. Scrape the dough from the bowl onto a lightly floured surface. Roll and stretch the dough into a circle about 16 inches (40cm) round (or oval, or to whatever size will fit on your baking stone or sheet), as thin as you can make it. If you have a pizza peel, sprinkle the peel with cornmeal and transfer the dough to the peel.

7. *If using a pizza stone or steel,* sprinkle the dough with the minced garlic, then top it with grated cheese. Slide the flatbread onto the hot stone or steel in the oven. (Use the rack level recommended by the manufacturer of your stone or steel.) If you don't have a pizza peel, you can use a rimless baking sheet or carefully but quickly transfer the dough with your hands to the baking sheet or stone, then top the dough with the garlic and cheese after you've transferred it. Bake the dough until it's crisp on the bottom and the cheese is melted and bubbling, about 10 minutes, but check before that time as pizza stones and steels vary.

   If using a baking sheet, remove the hot pan from the oven and sprinkle it with cornmeal. Transfer the dough to the baking sheet, being mindful that the pan is very hot. Top with the minced garlic and grated cheese. Bake on the bottom rack of the oven for 8 to 10 minutes, then turn on the broiler and place the flatbread dough on the upper rack and broil until the crust is browned and crisp around the rim.

8. Remove the flatbread from the oven and slide it onto a wire rack. Toss the salad ingredients with the dressing and heap them on top of the dough. Cut into wedges to serve.

As any American knows, leftover cold pizza (which this flatbread resembles) makes a great breakfast. For a next-day lunch, reheat the flatbread on a baking sheet in a 350°F (180°C) oven for about 10 minutes. The greens will flatten and become more integrated with the flatbread crust, but *c'est comme ça* . . .

NOTE: If you don't have whole wheat flour on hand, use a total of 2 cups (280g) all-purpose flour.

2

There I was, standing in the doctor's office, finally relieved. I carefully handed over the buckling paper cup. My fate was now in her hands. (And I hoped, for her sake, that the thin paper cup would hold up long enough so nothing else would be in her hands.) I walked out of the dim office, my eyes readjusting to daylight as I joined the fast-paced Parisians crowding the sidewalk, narrowly avoiding being run over multiple times, looking around for the closest bakery where I could grab a baguette to help me clear a path home.

I'd been through a lot in the previous months—no, years—before my full-on medical exam. I was happy that the doctor called off the cavity search, but still, my eager-to-please nature had me worried that I was going to die and upset the people at the bank. A few days later, though, the doctor gave me a clean bill of health. I was, once again, relieved, and ready to sign the papers.

I haven't been a lifelong Francophile, one of those people who kept a poster of the Eiffel Tower by his bedroom window. I never imagined that one day the real thing would be right there. I didn't devour books about how effortlessly chic Parisians are, and never envied how French people could tie a scarf with a certain *je ne sais quoi* that I could never hope to achieve. (Well, maybe I was a *little* jealous.) But I did learn that living in France required some adjustments.

In California, I was used to sloughing through the aisles of the supermarket in ratty sweats, a T-shirt, and flip-flops. Danielle Steel, another San Franciscan who moved to Paris, raised the ire of fellow San Franciscans when she said of the Bay Area, "There's no style ... you can't be chic there ..." before she bid *au revoir* to the City by the Bay. She took quite a bit of flak for that, but if I sold 800 million books, I'd be dressing better, too.

My frumpy Bay Area fashion notwithstanding, I had been cooking in Northern California for so long that it was natural I'd eventually fall for France. My life revolved around my cooking and baking, and in France, everyone seems to be either: 1) talking about what they had eaten, 2) eating, or 3) talking about what they were going to eat. Food is *everywhere*—in the windows of *charcuteries* and *boulangeries*, at the sprawling outdoor markets, and on the tables of the cafés and restaurants that line the sidewalks of Paris.

And after my trial period in Paris, I decided that we were a good fit and it was time to move in together for good. I just had to get Paris to agree.

When you live in Paris for more than a couple of years, you see a lot of people come, and you see a lot of them go. It's a great city to visit for a week, or even a few months, traipsing from museum to café to pastry shop, tearing into baguettes, and capping off the day with *steak frites* in a bistro with a remarkably decent pitcher of *vin rouge maison* that's so cheap, you wonder if you should toss away your return ticket. I lived that way for a couple of years, exploring chocolate shops and lining up at Berthillon for my favorite cone: a scoop of chocolate sorbet paired with a scoop of caramel ice cream. As soon as the scooper, wearing her well-fitted blue uniform, handed it over, I'd race to my special spot on the nearby Pont Marie, where I would luxuriously enjoy my cone, watching life float by on the Seine. But no matter how much we like to imagine ourselves as "living like a local," even if we're just visiting for a week, I was living like a foreigner in Paris. I was a long-term visitor.

Life abroad isn't for everybody. Americans invariably miss customer service the most; not being questioned under a bright lamp in the back room if you want to exchange a shirt for a different size, for example. Or not having to make an appointment in advance to withdraw money from your bank, as I learned when I needed to make a larger-than-normal withdrawal to pay a contractor who wouldn't take a check. I had to go to the bank twice to meet with bank officers so they could get to the bottom of why I wanted to take money out of my own account. (Which tells you why there are so many stores selling home safes in Paris.) They weren't buying my story. After a few rounds of tough questions in a glassed-in cubicle, I finally said I needed the money for a sex change in Thailand, thinking they'd realize their inquiries were a little overly probing. There was silence for a moment as they considered what I'd told them, then they agreed to let me withdraw the money. I was just hoping they weren't going to require post-op proof to verify that I had gone ahead with the procedure.

I navigated the idiosyncrasies of life in France as best I could. I don't want to say that I'd become Parisian, even though like my French friends, one wall of my apartment was lined with bookshelves, each shelf weighed down by three-ring notebooks organized by year and subject, containing every gas and electric bill (which you're required to save for at least five years), bank statement, store receipt, and official document that had ever arrived in my mailbox, which you need to keep for eternity because you never know when someone will insist that you produce an electric bill from exactly four years and eleven months ago. (And trust me, they will.)

In America, your driver's license or passport is the most important document in your life. In France, it's the electric bill. Your *facture d'électricité* is the document that proves that you live in France. You will need to produce a copy of your latest electricity bill to do anything, from getting a visa to opening a bank account or getting telephone service. The catch is that you can't rent an apartment to live in France in the first place if you don't have a bank account, but if you're not already renting an apartment, then you wouldn't have an electric bill to open a bank account. (And if you don't have a phone, how can the landlord reach you to let you know if you got the apartment or not?) It's a *cercle vicieux*, and if you're confused, don't feel bad. The French are, too. It's part of living like a local.

VANILLA ÉCLAIR PUFFS WITH BITTERSWEET CHOCOLATE SAUCE

MAKES 35 BITE-SIZE PUFFS

One thing I've learned from the French is that not everything needs to be reinvented. Sometimes, what already exists doesn't need to be improved upon. (But I *am* keeping a list of a few things that could stand a little improvement, just in case they ever ask me.) Young Parisian chefs trying to break away from classic French cuisine attempt to make statements by spewing foam onto square plates and dusting plate corners with powdered mushrooms. And no matter how much I want to dive into a slab of juicy *côte de bœuf,* I'll never get used to the sound of a steak knife screeching across the slate plate underneath it. I'm happy with a (round) plate of fish or vegetables, properly sauced, or a steak presented on a wooden board, ready to be devoured.

I feel the same way about pastries: sometimes, it's best to stick with the classics, and there's nothing I love more than a good éclair. For home bakers, though, éclairs can be tricky to pipe and fill, so I call these mouthfuls éclair puffs and douse them with warm chocolate sauce, which I like better than the usual chocolate *glaçage.* (So I guess I am guilty of a little tradition-tampering, too.)

French bakers use vanilla beans, while Americans favor vanilla extract in their desserts. Like my life as an American in France, I straddle two cultures, appreciating the qualities of each. In this case, the bean adds an earthy, floral vanilla flavor, and extract introduces a brighter vanilla note to the pastry cream filling, so you can get the best of both worlds in one perfect bite.

Vanilla Pastry Cream

    2 cups (500ml) whole milk
    1 vanilla bean, split lengthwise
    2 large eggs
    3 large egg yolks
    ⅔ cup (130g) sugar

6 tablespoons (50g) cornstarch

2 tablespoons unsalted butter, at room temperature

½ teaspoon pure vanilla extract

Pâte à Choux

1 cup (250ml) water

8 tablespoons (4 ounces, 115g) unsalted butter, cut into cubes

2 teaspoons sugar

¼ teaspoon salt

1 cup (140g) all-purpose flour

4 large eggs, at room temperature

Chocolate Sauce

1 cup (250ml) water

½ cup (100g) sugar

½ cup (160g) light corn syrup, rice syrup, or golden syrup

¾ tablespoon (75g) unsweetened cocoa powder

2 ounces (55g) bittersweet or semisweet chocolate, chopped

Toasted sliced almonds (optional)

1. Make the vanilla pastry cream: Have ready a clean medium bowl with a mesh strainer set over the top.
2. Pour the milk into a medium saucepan. Scrape the vanilla seeds from the beans. Add the vanilla bean seeds and pod to the milk and heat over medium-high heat.
3. In a medium bowl, whisk together the eggs, egg yolks, sugar, and cornstarch. While whisking continuously, gradually pour the warmed milk into the egg mixture, then scrape the mixture back into the saucepan. Cook the custard, stirring continuously with the whisk, until it comes to a boil, then cook, whisking continuously, for 1 minute, until the custard is quite thick.

4. Pour the custard into the strainer and press it through with a flexible silicone spatula. Stir in the butter and vanilla until the butter is well incorporated. Press plastic wrap directly against the surface of the pastry cream and refrigerate until cool.

5. Make the pâte à choux: Preheat the oven to 400°F (200°C). Line two baking sheets with silicone baking mats or parchment paper.

6. In a medium saucepan, combine the water, butter, sugar, and salt and heat over medium-high heat, stirring occasionally, until the butter has melted.

7. Add the flour all at once. Reduce the heat to medium and stir vigorously until the mixture pulls away from the sides of the pan and forms a smooth ball. Remove from the heat and let rest for 2 minutes, stirring it once or twice to help it cool.

8. Add the eggs, one at a time, stirring quickly to make sure the eggs don't cook. (You can also do this step in the bowl of a stand mixer fitted with the paddle attachment . . . as long as your mixer hasn't been buried when you're packing up for a move.)

9. Scrape the mixture into a pastry bag fitted with a wide plain tip and pipe the dough onto the prepared baking sheets in thirty-five 1-inch (3cm) rounds, evenly spaced apart. (If you don't have a pastry bag, fill a zip-top freezer bag with the dough, snip off a corner, and squeeze the dough out through the opening. Or use a spring-loaded ice cream scoop to shape the dough.)

10. Bake the choux puffs until deep golden brown on top, 25 to 30 minutes, rotating the baking sheets in the oven halfway through baking. Let cool on the baking sheets.

11. Meanwhile, make the chocolate sauce: In a medium saucepan, combine the water, sugar, corn syrup, and

cocoa powder and heat over medium heat, stirring continuously with a whisk, until the mixture comes to a boil. Remove it from the heat, add the chocolate, and stir until it has melted.

12. Scrape the pastry cream into a pastry bag fitted with a small plain tip. (If the pastry cream is very stiff, you can beat it by hand or in the bowl of a stand mixer fitted with the paddle attachment, to smooth it out.) Poke a round hole in the bottom of each puff by inserting a paring knife and rotating it. Fill the puffs with the cream. You can also split them horizontally and spoon the cream in the puffs.

13. Serve the puffs, three per plate, doused with warm chocolate sauce. Scatter toasted sliced almonds on top, if desired.

3

When I began searching for an apartment, I had no idea what I was doing, or what I was getting into—kinda like how I decided to move to Paris. I just did it, then learned the steps along the way, aka, the hard way. I'd never left my home country before, except for an occasional vacation, and hadn't considered all that was involved in making a definitive move overseas. To say that I was unprepared would not be an exaggeration. The learning curve was so steep that I often fell off with a thud. And I have the bruises to prove it.

As much as Americans envy the French way of life—from a health care system that is one of the best in the world to the lengthy vacations—few actually think about everything else that comes with it, namely steep social charges (that pay for the health care), waiting for hours in disorganized lines to throw yourself at the mercy of *les fonctionnaires* (bureaucrats) whose job description begins with telling you *non* right off the bat, bidding *à bientôt* to being able to do errands quickly, and saying *au revoir* to returning anything you bought.

And then there's the eternal question: Are Parisians rude? On one hand, online travel boards are filled with visitors exclaiming how friendly and kind Parisians are, but Parisians see themselves rather differently. *Le Parisien* newspaper brought up the subject of whether its citizens were friendly to visitors, prompting one Frenchman whom they interviewed to laugh, then reply, "Rude to tourists? Why don't they talk about how rude Parisians are to other Parisians?"

To the best of my knowledge, the city hasn't launched a guide with tips for how Parisians should treat one another, but the Paris Chamber of Commerce did launch an initiative called "Do You Speak *Touriste*?" to make sure they were nice to tourists. The pamphlets they published (I don't know if they were ever *distributed*) included guidelines for taxi drivers, salesclerks, and others on how to properly treat visitors. (After what I went through, I would suggest they add guidelines for real estate agents, too.) In the guide, the spectrum of foreign visitors was classified according to their likes, dislikes, and peculiarities, to help Parisians better understand them.

Italians were characterized as "exuberant and spontaneous" . . . but also "impatient." Germans were said to be "precise." The favorite activities of Japanese visitors are luxury shopping and not complaining. Americans expect "full service" and like "nonsmoking spaces." We also "appreciate Wi-Fi" and "easily call each other by first names." I'd have to agree about appreciating Wi-Fi, especially after mine went dead for three months and the company refused to come and fix it, which is particularly challenging when you work online. (I almost went broke calling their customer service line and waiting on hold for twenty minutes, only to be cut off and have to call back again, and again, and again, for months . . . at 34 cents a minute.)

After living in the same building with my keep-to-themselves Parisian neighbors for nearly ten years, we still addressed one another as "Monsieur" or "Madame," which

I actually found easier since I didn't have to remember their names, first or last. Although no one in the building ever introduced themselves, or offered up either one of theirs.

I do, however, politely disagree with the Chamber of Commerce's overall sentiment that Parisians could use some help in dealing with visitors. Shopkeepers have told me that they love Americans (with Australians pulling up a close second), saying we're polite and appreciative, which could have something to do with the fact that we arrive ready to spend. Our high approval rating is partly due to the fact that it's been drilled into us to be extra polite when we come to France so we don't risk the ire of the fastidiously polite French.

Just like so many Americans dream of packing it all up and moving to Paris, the *rêve* of many Parisians is to live in the United States. Specifically, in "Brook-*leen*," as they call it. But as much as we admire the French and they admire us, each of us ultimately thinks our way is the best way, and the majority of us stay in our respective countries. Having lived in both places, I've seen that each country does some things better than the other. (Exhibits A and B: the French health care system; American customer service.) But I'll say one thing with absolute certainty: the American way of finding an apartment is better.

I wasn't one of those who only *rêve*'d about living in Paris. I did it, and somehow it worked out. It was even going well. My life had turned out pretty sweet. I was renting, so my roots weren't deeply planted. I could have left at a moment's notice on the next flight home. But instead, I decided to buy an apartment.

Aside from an expanding waistline from all the cheese, chocolate, and wine, a few other things had changed after my first
few years. Most important, I met my partner, Romain, a native
Parisian, who I continue to suspect may actually be Italian.
(Exhibit A: His name means "Roman" in French.) He smiles
frequently, is quick with a laugh, and fits the Paris Chamber
of Commerce's description of someone who's "exuberant and
spontaneous." A short, slender-waisted Frenchman with a
round face and a bristly moustache framing his prominent
lips, he was nothing like the kind of person I thought I'd be
with when I packed up my life in San Francisco.

When we met, he spoke eleven words of English, four of
which were "Can I help you?" possibly learned from a school
filmstrip highlighting common American expressions. (For
some reason, we didn't learn that same phrase when I was
learning French.) But who was I to talk? My French was ap-
pallingly bad at the time. A lot of it was me using my high-
school Spanish and Frenchifying Spanish words, rolling my
R's, lisping my C's, and enunciating in staccato tones, thinking the French would get the gist. They didn't. Many, in fact,
assumed I was Italian, due to a habit I developed of talking
with my hands to fill in gaps in my vocabulary.

On our first date, I made the classic Anglophone mistake of saying "*Je t'aime*," which translates literally to "I like
you." But in one of those language quirks designed to make
non-natives feel like nitwits, it actually conveys "I love you."
(Just in case you ever find yourself in the same situation, "*Je
t'aime bien*" means "I like you.") The poor guy was alarmed
by the suddenly stalkerish American sitting across the table.
Fortunately, he's not only exuberant and spontaneous, but
understanding and patient with my faults, and we've been
together ever since.

Thanks to Romain, I saw Paris from an insider's perspective. We'd walk by buildings that I normally would have brushed past, rushing to the chocolate shop down the street, and he'd remark on the iron fence or the doorknob, noting what century it was made in and how unusual it was to find one from that material, from that particular era, in that specific neighborhood. Wooden floorboards we walked over in lobbies took on historical provenance—I was charmed. A stroll through the Marais, where he was born and where I'd normally be bounding by monuments to get to Pierre Hermé's macaron shop, or to Jacques Genin for a bag of mango-passion fruit caramels, turned into a history lesson. I also learned, as one does when one dates a Frenchman, that he wasn't afraid to express his views. Americans will politely say, "It's okay," even if it's not. The French don't mince words. They'll not only tell you that they don't like something, but why—with a frankness that takes adjusting to. They consider it "helpful" to you, to let you know that the new shirt you're wearing proudly makes your stomach look like you've eaten too much Camembert, or how the dinner you've spent all day gathering the ingredients for and cooking was *pas terrible*—which literally means "not terrible" ... but is the French way of letting you know there's room for improvement. To the French, there's always room for improvement. Although I wasn't sure how hearing my *sexe* was *moche*—or ugly, because I was circumcised—was particularly helpful to me. Nor did I want to take any steps to "improve" it. (A point which was moot, since I'd already used up my goodwill at the bank, and couldn't go back and ask for money for any restoration work.)

Romain is especially frank (which confirms that yes, he's definitely French), and will go into situations with an abruptness that startles me. The French don't mind provoking others, which isn't considered a fault, but part of the *jeu* (game) of everyday life. I'm an easygoing Californian and not used to quarreling with others. But you never know how an interaction will go in France. Of course, there are things you do to pave the way for success before entering into one, like saying *"Bonjour, madame"* when walking into the *boulangerie* to pick up your baguette, or beginning a request with *"Excusez-moi de vous déranger"*—"I'm sorry to bother you"—leading off with an apology, letting a salesclerk or receptionist know that you recognize their importance over yours. But the politesse doesn't necessarily guarantee that things are going to go your way.

So the French enter into situations assuming things aren't going to go well. When things do go well, you could not ask for more wonderful people to help you. When they don't, like when you've interrupted a salesclerk's important conversation with a coworker about their weekend plans because you want to pay for a new shirt (which you pray your partner will like), or used a staple rather than a paperclip to attach two pages together when presenting your dossier to a bureaucrat, well . . . you'll understand why it's important to always be ready for anything.

Parisians also have a reputation for not being overly enthusiastic. A sticker you'll sometimes see around the city reads: *J'♥ rien. J'suis Parisien,* "I love nothing. I am Parisian," a self-acknowledgment of their reputation for dissatisfaction with everything. Appearing enthusiastic can come off as unseemly, often construed as being *très américain.* If you do like something, it's *pas mal* (not bad), which also works in the other direction: if you don't like something, it's *pas terrible* (not terrible). But while the Parisian penchant for *modération* keeps things centered, one thing Parisians don't feel neutral about is real estate agents. Partially because agents charge money for their services, which puts them in the distasteful category of someone who makes money, but also because of their reputation of not doing such a great job.

Unlike in the United States, there's no MLS, or multiple listing service, in Paris that features all the available apartments in one central (and extremely convenient) place. In France, only sellers have agents, who only represent their own listings. (And, as such, are only looking after their own client's interests, not yours.) If you want to buy something, such as a one-bedroom apartment in the Marais or a three-bedroom overlooking the Seine, you'll need to find it on your own.

Paris is often referred to as the City of Light, thanks to its status as one of the first cities to introduce gaslights, which they use to such great effect. But the evening illumination that captivates Parisians these days comes from real estate agency windows that highlight apartments for sale. Walk down any street or boulevard in the evening and you'll see Parisians pulled like moths toward the bright lights, drawn toward apartments for sale, then shaking their heads before walking away. "*C'est trop cher!*" they'll groan ("It is too expensive!"). "*C'est ridicule . . .*"

Coming from San Francisco, I'm used to *crise cardiaque*-inducing prices. What amazes me more is that people sometimes don't bother tidying up their apartments before the photos are taken. I've seen pictures in real estate listings with underwear and bras dangling from drying racks, bathrooms with towels piled up on the floor, kids' toys spilling out of a crammed-in closet, coffee tables with half-empty glasses of the previous night's red wine (accompanied by last night's dinner plates) still on the table, and kitchen sinks loaded with pots and pans in need of scrubbing. Romain told me those pictures were better than staged photos because they give buyers a more accurate idea of what it would look like if you actually lived in that apartment. I haven't worn a bra since I tried on my mom's when I was seven, and would not leave my undies in the middle of a living room for all to see (even though I've gotten used to the changing rooms at yoga and fitness facilities in Paris and mingling with others—men and women—in various states of undress).

Because real estate agents in France only represent sellers, and only their own listings, you have to go from agency to agency as part of your search. The properties lit up in the windows at agencies across Paris are only for places in that particular neighborhood, listed by that particular agency. The agency next door will have a completely different list of apartments for sale that no other agency will have any knowledge of. Or will say they have no knowledge of.

In their defense, they have no reason to know about them: their job is to sell the places they've got listed; they get zero commission for helping you buy a place from anyone else. But even if they do have the listing, selling it doesn't always seem to be their priority, as anyone who has left multiple unreturned calls to a Paris real estate agent can attest.

Unlike in America, where the real estate agent handles some of the legal work, once the first round of papers are signed in France, the rest of the work is passed on to the *notaire*. Then the agents are free to go outside for cigarette breaks and wait for their check.

And thus, I started my own multiyear search for an apartment. From the moment I circled the pen back, looping the slash from the final *Z*, back over the *T* in "Lebovitz" to complete my signature on the apartment that I finally found, I was committed to shelling out *beaucoup de* bucks for the seller's agent, which was especially distressing because by the day of the final closing, none of us—the seller, the agent, or me—were on speaking terms. We were on yelling terms.

THAI CURRY WITH LAMB AND HARICOTS VERTS

Curry d'agneau aux haricots verts

SERVES 4 GENEROUSLY

Although the French can be fiery at times, Thai food, with its heady mixture of heat, is elusive in Paris. The day I realized Romain was a keeper was when he took a bite of authentic Thai curry. His face turned a rosy shade of red, and with beads of sweat moistening his forehead, he declared Thai cuisine to be his favorite in the world. My friends who have French partners and spouses say I lucked out, because theirs won't eat anything spicier than a buttered potato. Anything with even a hint of spiciness always comes with a reassuring note on a menu that it's *légèrement pimenté!*, lightly spiced, to warn that it's okay.

Spicy foods may not be their thing, but the one food the French rally around more than any of the others are *haricots verts*, or green beans. They can't imagine them *not* being available. When they're not in season, the popular frozen-food chain Picard, which has nearly a thousand stores in France (and has everything from *framboises* to foie gras), carries them. I wasn't surprised when I learned that green beans are their bestselling product.

I'm someone who likes to cook with things that are locally sourced, or in season, although as an expat, I do know the joy of a bag of Texas pecans or a roll of heavy-duty American aluminum foil, so I don't have to struggle with the tissue-thin sheets of French *alu* that tears into silvery wisps whenever I try to pull a piece off the roll.

If you can't find the vegetables I suggest, don't worry; you needn't rely on frozen. If round Thai eggplants aren't available, slender Japanese ones work fine. If baby corn (canned or otherwise) isn't available, you can substitute a peeled, cubed sweet potato. Other swap-outs include fresh pineapple chunks; peeled, cubed turnips or butternut squash; and perhaps fresh spinach; use your intuition as to when to add them so they'll all finish cooking at about the same time. Hard vegetables will take 10 to 15 minutes to cook. Pineapple and softer vegetables will take less time. A handful of spinach can be added at the last minute.

The curry will also be fine without the lemongrass or galangal: many Thai curry pastes include them as an ingredient. But be sure to buy good-quality curry paste. Cock Brand is a favorite, even if I worry my Frenchman might find it ugly.

> 1 tablespoon vegetable oil
>
> 1 pound (450g) boned lamb shoulder, cut into 1-inch (3cm) cubes
>
> 1 (13.5-ounce/400g) can coconut milk
>
> 2 tablespoons good-quality Thai red curry paste
>
> 1 teaspoon dried shrimp paste (optional)
>
> 2 lemongrass stalks, cut into thirds, crushed with a mallet or the bottom of a cleaver handle to release their fragrance

3 slices galangal, rapped gently with a mallet or the bottom of
   a cleaver handle to release their fragrance, but kept whole

1 cup (250ml) low-sodium chicken stock

5 or 6 Thai eggplants (8 ounces/240g), unsliced, or 2 slender
   Japanese eggplants, unpeeled, sliced ¾ inch (2cm) thick

8 ears baby corn (8 ounces/240g), preferably fresh (if using
   canned, drain before using), halved on an angle

4 ounces (120g) fresh green beans, trimmed and sliced into
   2-inch (5cm) pieces

2 tablespoons fish sauce

1 tablespoon palm sugar or dark brown sugar

2 or 3 long Thai chiles, sliced into rings

1 cup (25g) loosely packed fresh Thai basil leaves

Cooked Thai rice, for serving

1. In the Dutch oven or similar-sized pot with a lid, heat
   the oil over medium-high heat. Add the lamb pieces and
   cook, stirring frequently, until they are seared on all
   sides, about 5 minutes. Remove the pieces of lamb from
   the pot and set aside on a plate. Add one-quarter of the
   coconut milk, the red curry paste, and the shrimp paste
   (if using) to the pot. Stir continuously until the coconut
   milk comes to a boil, then add the remaining coconut
   milk, the lamb pieces, lemongrass, and galangal. Bring
   to a boil, reduce the heat to low, cover, and simmer, stirring occasionally, for 15 minutes.

2. Add the stock to the pot. If using Thai eggplant, quarter
   them (if sliced in advance, they'll turn brown) and add
   them to the pot, giving them a stir right away to coat
   them with the curry liquid. Cover and cook, stirring
   occasionally to keep the eggplants submerged, until the
   eggplants are partially tender, about 6 minutes.

3. If using sliced Japanese eggplant, add them to the curry,

along with the baby corn, green beans, fish sauce, and brown sugar. Cover and simmer gently until the corn and green beans are cooked through, about 10 minutes. Add the chiles during the last few minutes of cooking. Remove from the heat and stir in the basil leaves.

4. Serve with Thai rice, alerting guests not to eat the batons of lemongrass or disks of galangal. They can be plucked out before serving, if you wish.

4

I started and stopped my hunt for an apartment more times than a terrified American driver behind the wheel of a Citroën (who shall remain nameless) attempts to enter the chaos of traffic encircling the Arc de Triomphe, the famed (and feared) roundabout that caps off the Champs-Élysées where all bets are off, and so is your automobile insurance: Many policies have an exclusion if you drive there. I've stopped pushing my luck and avoid the traffic roundabouts in Paris, but Romain just steps on the gas and goes for it without a second thought. I don't know how he does it, but as soon as he accelerates to enter, I close my eyes, and sometimes hit the floor until we're safely out of it.

Apartment hunting in Paris is just as stressful, but at least they make it easier by not making a lot of listings available for you to look at. You have to patch together a mélange of methods to see what's out there, because there's no user-friendly MLS that shows all the available apartments in one convenient place.

Real estate agency windows are one place to start. But when I started my search, newspaper classified ads were one of the primary places to sell an apartment, along with *De Particulier à Particulier*, which means "From Person to Person" and is efficiently abbreviated to *PAP*. Like a Pap smear, reading it could also be considered a test for something potentially hazardous. The weekly catalog of real estate listings, in which individual sellers listed their places without the use of an agent, was printed on no-nonsense newsprint. It was imperative that you picked one up as soon as the tied-up bundles were dropped off at the newsstands first thing Thursday morning, because anything good would be snatched up between the time the stack hit the pavement and the moment the string holding the bundle together was snipped open.

When I moved to France, it was almost unheard of to have Internet access at home. "It will steal your soul!" people in Paris warned me, and I chuckled at their naïveté. (Who knew that later they'd be right?) As the rest of the world rushed online, France eventually followed, and classified ads have now moved to the Internet. Whether they're listed on paper or online, nearly a third of the places in Paris get sold by their owners, *sans* agent.

Adding to the challenge, many of the best apartments in Paris are sold without ever having been listed anywhere at all. So as part of one's search, you should include the time-honored *bouche-à-oreille*, or "mouth to ear." (The American idiom for the same idea, "ear to the ground," alarmed Romain when I explained how I was going to search for an apartment by pressing my ear against the pavement. He was especially concerned because of what's left behind by so many dogs on Paris sidewalks.)

The French proclivity for discretion, especially when it comes to discussing anything that has to do with money, extends to not being so gauche as to put a sign on your apartment window, which would let others know that you are willing to take something as distasteful as money for it. If you do see a "For Sale" sign, consider it an indication that the owners are having a hard time unloading the place.

Pavement-ear-pressing aside, it's not uncommon to walk around a neighborhood you're interested in and ask in cafés and shops, stop people on the street, and even query the vigilant *gardiennes* of buildings to see if they know of anyone selling their place. It's the *gardiennes'* business (or they think it is) to know everything about everyone in their building. Since they keep such good tabs on the goings-on of their building's inhabitants, they can likely guess—based on, say, a spouse who has a frequent midday visitor who slips away, down the stairs and out of the building, with wet hair from a hasty shower before returning to work—whether an apartment might be available in the future.

During my search, exasperated by the system and fearful of an angry ex showing up at my front door if I went the *gardienne* route, I asked a real estate agent why they don't just use a multiple listing service, where everybody could see all the homes that were available in one convenient place. It would benefit both buyers and sellers; agents would split their commission, which would eventually even out because there would be twice as many agents who got work. Which probably should have been my first clue as to why it wasn't that way already: twice as much work.

"Why would I want to share a commission with someone?" an agent remarked, startled at the idea. I explained that not only would it be easier for everyone, but there'd be a lot more business to go around, which, as expected, further confused her. I left her office to continue my search, and she went back to her desk to not answer phone calls.

Real estate agents in France don't fill the same role as they do in America. You don't have the same relationship with an agent, where you might go out for coffee to discuss your dreams and goals for finding the perfect place. You don't share family stories or swap cooking tips with someone who is helping you, whether you're dreaming about a nice balcony to have your morning coffee on or looking for a place with a nice kitchen to bake in. There are no smiling headshots of well-groomed agents, ready to do anything to make sure you get just the right place to call home. French people avoid real estate agents as much as possible, viewing them with suspicion. I soon learned why.

————

As with any major purchase, the first thing one needs to do is to figure out a budget. But for the Paris apartment hunter, it's just as important to start off deciding which neighborhood you want to live in. Each arrondissement has its own personality, and Parisians are defined by their *quartier*.

I'd been living in the 11th since moving to Paris. Though it's one of the city's most popular neighborhoods, it's less known elsewhere: While speaking at an event in the United States, I was asked where I lived. When I answered, "The eleventh," the woman who'd asked looked confused, then followed up with, "So . . . do you take the train into Paris every day?" I didn't want to sound like a wise-guy, so I let her know . . . "I usually just walk."

Many visitors stay in the upscale 6th and 7th arrondissements, close to the Saint-Germain-des-Prés area on the Left Bank, but it's become prohibitively expensive to buy there and the neighborhood is not a *quartier populaire*, as they say in French. That doesn't mean it's not "popular," but that it's not where a cross-section of people live, and I wanted to live like a local. (Minus the bureaucracy and paperwork.) The Left Bank is historically mesmerizing and sumptuous, but if you live on one side of Paris—say, on the Left or Right

Bank—you rarely cross the river to visit the other side. Once you're in a neighborhood, that's where your life is. It helps to think of Paris as a collection of small villages bundled together, each one offering its own butchers, markets, bakeries, pharmacies, and even its own city hall. When you get to know everyone, you don't want to leave.

Whenever the annual winner of the Best Baguette in Paris competition is announced, visitors will ask me if that's where I'll be going to get my baguette from now on. No one in Paris would ever dream of getting on a *métro*, or even stepping out of their neighborhood, to pick up a baguette. I do enough walking just going to Paris every day—which is just outside my front door, literally.

I hoped to stay in the 11th arrondissement, one of the largest in Paris, spanning from Père Lachaise Cemetery to the Place de la République, as well as bordering the Marais. It's considered hip, or *bobo*; *les bobos* are the upscale Parisian version of a hipster—although none are knitting bonnets, like they do on the subways in Brooklyn; or raising chickens in their henhouse, like they do in Oakland; or building smoking and curing sheds in their backyards, like they do in Portland. Their primary activities are smoking (not the kind that flavors artisanal bacon) and drinking beer, not making it. Still, it's a very diverse neighborhood that has a lot going for it; it borders the multicultural Belleville quarter and is a short walk to the 10th arrondissement, where many of the best new chefs in Paris have opened their restaurants. And because the 11th is quite vast, parts of it are (or were) affordable because there are so many apartments there.

The single-digit arrondissements, including the Marais, are certainly more familiar to visitors, but are very, very expensive. The Île Saint-Louis in the 4th is another stunning area that's popular with visitors—so popular that they've scooped up most of the places there as they've become available. While most of us think we could live on Berthillon ice cream, the streets are packed with tourists checking out the shops selling jewelry and Eiffel Tower–shaped staplers, and there are few, if any, restaurants or cafés of note. The last time I ate at a famed *bistro* on the island, my dining companion was dismayed by her soggy onion quiche, which was obviously baked in a store-bought crust and then microwaved. I can't even remember what I had, which isn't a good sign, either. I didn't want that place to be my neighborhood *cantine*.

The double-digit arrondissements are more diverse, and each has a distinct feel. Being more working class, there's a greater sense of community. Some are certainly less polished than the single-digit arrondissements, with narrow streets and passages instead of grand avenues, but they have a more neighborhood feel. And while the chicest chocolate and pastry shops are in the more upscale areas, young chefs and bakers have opened places in the outer arrondissements that are casually inventive, and less expensive.

I like the 20th, perched high above Paris. The Parc de Belleville has an unparalleled view of Paris (second only to the view I had from my rooftop apartment), and I could have easily imagined living there amid its rough brick streets and the human scale of the architecture. There are no imposing Haussmann buildings and many old storefronts have been turned into studios by artists. There's a flourishing community of specialty food shops on the crest of the hill. But it is only served by one *métro* line and is a very steep walk home if you miss the last train. (And riding one of the city-owned Vélib' bikes up that steep hill is impossible, although a good way to work off all those *frites* and Côtes du Rhône.)

The Butte-aux-Cailles in the 13th is charming (and flat),

and resembles a mini village far removed from a big city. Few buildings are taller than three or four stories, and the cobbled streets wind their way around sweet little sidewalk cafés and low-key restaurants, shaded by trees. Flowering vines cover ornate iron gates in front of apartment buildings and houses, and best of all, to beat the summer heat, there's an art nouveau building that houses one indoor and two outdoor pools to cool down in, all filled with water sourced from artesian wells, and open to the public. It's truly *très charmant*, but insanely expensive, although you can get a little bit of respite from the high prices at the communist restaurant, Les Temps des Cerises, a quirky place that offers inexpensive, serviceable food and cheap wine by the carafe—along with the all-caps slogan LA LUTTE CONTINUE!!! (The Fight Continues!), in case you want a helping of politics with your *poulet rôti*. (Personally, though, I don't choose a restaurant based on how ready the staff is for a fight.)

———

Paris offers so many special places, but like most Parisians, I didn't like the idea of leaving my neighborhood. I wanted to avoid the *bizutage* (hazing) of adapting to a completely different community: going through the process of becoming acquainted with a new set of shopkeepers, market vendors, and—the most important friend you can have in Paris—your pharmacist, who might look aside and fill a prescription for you without an *ordinance* (prescription), or will diagnose that curious rash on your back right in their pharmacy. (As long as you're not shy about taking off your shirt in front of everybody in the store.) Mine in the Bastille had a freezer for storing drugs, so they were the recipients of a lot of ice cream when I was testing recipes for a book. I saved hundreds of euros in doctor's bills by dropping off ice cream, which worked quite well for both of us. So I decided to focus on staying in my neighborhood; it had a good location, a burgeoning pastry scene, and convenient (and reasonably priced) health care.

The mouth-to-ear method of searching for an apartment didn't work for me. I'm too timid to walk up to a stranger and ask them if they'd like me as a neighbor. But being French, Romain likes to talk—and is one of the few Frenchmen who also listens—and will happily spend forty-five minutes chatting up someone at a flea market about a cracked plate that he has no intention of buying, with the seller responding, even though he doesn't seem to care if he sells it or not. They'll spend fifteen minutes discussing the color, the era the plate was made, how it differs from other plates of that era, where the dealer obtained it, and what it was used for (a big point of discussion in France, where putting things in their own specific category is important; each plate, piece of cutlery, bowl, or glass, has its own specific purpose). I keep making the mistake of calling an *assiette à soupe* (soup plate) a soup bowl (*bol*) because it has sides to hold in soup. Before I moved here, I had always thought plates were flat and bowls were rounded. There aren't just one or two forks in France: there are salad forks, melon forks, oyster forks, fruit forks, cornichon forks, snail forks, fish forks, meat forks, dinner forks, dessert forks, and even *cuillères-fourchettes* (sporks). And then there are all the knives, and spoons.

Romain's conversation with the seller might then lead to a discussion of the highlights of the region where the plate was made, the food that might have been served on that kind of plate (and the right wine to accompany it), as well as the topography of the region, then, finally, what kind of plates their respective families used. By the time their conversation is over, I'll have combed the entire flea market and returned loaded up with starched ivory-colored French linens, a copper ice cream mold, several sizes of enameled gratin dishes, a few bistro wine glasses, a well-used wooden bread board, and a set of vintage pastry utensils, and he'll be surprised he came away from the market with nothing.

———

I don't use dating apps, but friends who do tell me when they meet someone and know it's not going to work, they say good-bye and leave right away. I used to think, *How cruel! I could never do that to someone.* Until I started looking at strangers' apartments and wanted outta there as fast as possible.

It's hard to look at places with the *propriétaire* present, which is the case when the apartment you're looking at is being sold directly by the seller. I found it impossible to walk around someone's place and not to ask things like "It must have been a great party last night. Look at all those empties!" or "Those are some gray skivvies you got there. Have you ever tried washing your whites separately?"

In the United States, sellers and agents host open houses. If you don't like a place, you can quickly move on. I wanted to tell Romain, "I don't like this place. Let's go," but he wandered around and took the owners up on their offer to sit on the couch (after moving a pile of laundry that needed folding and a little bleach) and settled in for a *p'tit café* with them. While the owner was busy preparing the coffee, I'd frantically motion toward the door, trying to wordlessly transmit a message that I was ready to scram, which was ignored. Or he'd say, out loud, "Why are you gesturing toward the door, *Daveed*?"—while I tried to figure out how I could disappear into the folds of the sofa, in spite of my concern about what might be buried in them.

I tried coming up with a code word, like couples in America use if one of them is ready to leave a party or gathering. My favorite French word is *pamplemousse* (grapefruit), so I explained to Romain that when I said "pamplemousse," it was a signal that I was ready to split. I don't think I described the concept well enough, though, and was stuck on many sofas, wondering how many times I could weave the word *grapefruit* into a conversation, hoping he'd remember why I was talking about grapefruit juice (and grapefruit varieties, and desserts made with grapefruit, and grapefruit cocktails, etc.) when we were supposed to be discussing the apartment.

It never worked, and I had no choice but to sit and listen to the sellers talk, and talk and talk and talk, which is the downside of being with a Frenchman who doesn't mind listening.

———

Like most Parisians, my decision as to which *quartier* to live in was heavily influenced by which outdoor markets were nearby. If I told someone I was interested in a certain neighborhood, they'd pause, then brighten up, "*Bien sûr!* There is a very good *marché* there. The *poissonnière* has excellent Belon oysters at Christmas," or "Oh, the Bastille market—they have superb Brie on Sundays. And that farmer who brings the leafy Swiss chard . . . it makes a gratin that's truly *pas mal*."

Of (almost) equal importance to living close to a good

Brie de Meaux was living on the top floor of a building with an elevator, which is what I had at the time. I had tons of light, spectacular views, and no manic neighbors clomping around above. Since I dislike *le jogging* as much as the French, having an elevator so I didn't have to walk up seven flights of stairs meant I'd just had to live with the *poignées d'amour* (love handles) I had developed from all the cheese and chocolate. But I was willing to live with them.

Unfortunately, I discovered early on in my search that 98 percent of the people in Paris looking for an apartment were also hoping to live on the very top floor, the ultimate *étage élevé*.

Whether it was the lack of a multiple listing service, awkward visits with people selling their apartments, gray unmentionables, agents uninterested in selling you the apartment they're representing, an exchange rate that I kept praying would get more favorable, or confusing Romain (who by now thought he'd ended up with an American who not only started off as a possible stalker, but was also weirdly obsessed with grapefruits), I spent a couple of years starting and stopping my search. The process was frustrating and overly time-consuming because it was impossible to filter places—you had to first find the apartment, then go through the arduous task of trying to make an appointment to see each and every one, leaving messages and waiting for a response, then trying to find a time that was agreeable to the seller, and doing that over and over and over again. It took forever. And unfortunately, most of what I saw wasn't worth the wait.

The first apartment that seemed like it might be the right place for me was a short walk from the Marché d'Aligre, which I think is the most exciting market in Paris. It's a lively mix of French and North African vendors selling just about anything you could imagine: white-tipped French breakfast radishes (which no one in France eats for breakfast); Iranian dates, squat pumpkins as large as a Michelin tire, sold by the wedge; nutty Argan oil (made from nuts pooped out of goats, which tastes better than it sounds); oysters offered up by the platter and eaten on the sidewalk chased with a bracing glass of Sancerre—this market has it all.

On the ground floor was a place that sold homemade pasta, and three of the best bread bakeries in Paris were within a two-block radius. Like most apartments in Paris, the kitchen wasn't large, but had more counter space than my current *demi*-kitchen. I was poised to make an offer on the duplex with no upstairs neighbors and just a short hop to the market. It was almost perfect . . . except for the hula hoop–size concrete post in the middle of the modest kitchen and dining area, holding up the floor above. Although the owner had already moved out and the space was empty, I found myself having to swerve around it every time I walked anywhere in the apartment. No amount of baguette swinging would have moved it out of the way.

The next apartment with potential was near the Buttes-Chaumont, a bucolic, lushly wooded park with grottos and a scenic man-made lake. The apartment was a loft: huge, wide-open, and *brut* (unfinished), a big plus, so I could create exactly the big kitchen I wanted, without having to worry about walls, or concrete pillars. The downside was that it was directly above a rap recording studio (which, oddly, wasn't mentioned in the listing). The seller assured me that it was so well insulated you couldn't hear a thing, despite disquieting thumps and vibrations coming from below as he told us otherwise. When we were leaving, we passed a few of the rappers, taking a break. Romain (naturally) started talking to them, and they casually dropped that they really enjoyed the neighborhood, liked recording there and did their best work after two A.M.

Next I went to look at a place beyond the Canal Saint-Martin in the northern part of Paris, which I didn't consider to be a particularly treacherous part of town ... until I turned the corner onto the street where the apartment was and surprised a pair of *gendarmes* in full-on riot gear, standing their ground in front of a building next door to the apartment I was there to look at. Each held a machine gun, pointed, cocked, and ready. They fixed their gaze on me as I hesitantly walked to the front door of the apartment building careful not to make any sudden moves. Once safely out of the neighborhood after I'd looked at the place, I called to tell the sellers I wasn't interested, although I couldn't have imagined a safer place to live. As long as I never left the house.

I grew excited about the possibilities of a place just off the up-and-coming Rue de Belleville, which Fox News determined to be a "no-go zone" in a rather odd *reportage* on the dangers lurking in Paris. Unlike the other neighborhood with machine-gun-ready *gendarmes*, this is one area where I'd spent a lot of time, and as far as I could tell, the biggest danger would be living close to stores selling sacks of bright green pistachios and dried apricots from Turkey, luscious figs and candied tangerines from North Africa, tins of Provençal and Tunisian olive oils, and fresh sheep's-milk cheeses bobbing in vats of milky brine—and buying more than I could carry home.

The Belleville apartment close to all those shops had been transformed from an old print shop, and one of the photos in the *annonce* for the apartment showed a small patio, a big plus in Paris, where light and outdoor space command a premium.

The agent met me there at nine A.M., smelling as if he'd

just spent the night at one of the nearby clubs in the gentrifying area. The place had looked nice in *l'annonce*, but
the secluded courtyard ended up being tighter than the
expansive-looking one in the photo. (Looking at apartments
in Paris, I quickly learned the transformative powers of a
wide-angle lens.) But still, it could be a nice place for a breakfast table for two . . . as long as you didn't need to back your
chair away from the table, or move sideways. We entered
through the galley kitchen to the main space. The place had
been listed as having a *chambre* (bedroom), which I found
hovering over the living room; it was a bed held up by four
cords on pulleys that needed to be moved up and down if you
planned to eat, sit, work, watch television, or do anything
other than sleep in the apartment. The agent looked like he
would kill for a cup of coffee and another cigarette (he'd already gone out for two during the short time I was looking
at the apartment), and he seemed just as happy to get out of
there as I was.

Still hoping to find something around the Marché
d'Aligre, I looked at another apartment on the top floor of a
gorgeous corner building near Rue Paul Bert, a street lined
with excellent restaurants and one of my favorite pastry
shops in Paris. The rooms weren't very spacious, but were
bathed in warm natural light thanks to its *triple exposition*,
which meant I could wean myself off the vials of vitamin D
my doctor prescribes to me and 95 percent of her other patients, she told me, due to *la grisaille*, the gray skies of Paris
that keep everyone in the city lining up at the pharmacies all
winter.

During my visit, direct sunlight was already creeping
into the apartment as the sun rose overhead that morning.
When the sun hits a café terrace, sun-starved Parisians cluster at the tables where the strongest sunlight is, drawn to the

light, and I imagined myself doing the same while enjoying my first coffee of the day on my own private balcony. To get a better look, I took a step outside without much thought. Fortunately, before I thought more about taking a second step, I looked down and saw that the only thing between me and a fourteen-story drop was a shin-level railing. The upside to moving into that apartment would have been that I wouldn't have to answer the frequent interview question I'm inevitably asked about what my last meal on earth would be: it would be a café au lait.

After passing up the apartment with the death-drop terrace, I came upon what seemed like the perfect loft in an industrial building with a wall of windows. The large factorylike space was perfect and already had a workable open kitchen, and even built-in air-conditioning, unheard of in Paris.

The other units in the building were workshops occupied by artists, writers, and other creative types, who I figured would be great to have as neighbors. Since owners and agents in Paris are reluctant to disclose any flaws, it's a good idea to talk to any neighbors for intel. Complaining comes easy to the French (which is why I didn't have that much trouble adapting to life in France), especially on the subject of neighbors. When I took the language test for a visa, the proctor had to choose a scenario for us to discuss, based on something typical of everyday life. "*Imaginez,* monsieur," she began, "that I am a friend who is having trouble with a neighbor." Of course, I aced it, since that's such a frequent topic of discussion.

On the way out, I ran into the woman from downstairs in the stairwell; she was talkative, and said it was a very nice building and that she was very happy there. She was also kind enough to invite me to see her apartment. She was an artist who had some of her work on the walls, which I glanced at but didn't take the time to examine too closely—I was in apartment-hunting mode, not perusing art. After a look around, we parted with smiles and *bisous*, and exchanged cards. Finally, I'd found a great place with the perfect neighbor! I was so ready to take it that I could barely sleep that night and was prepared to make an offer the next morning. A place like that was sure to go fast.

The next morning, I opened my in-box to see she'd sent me a message. I clicked it open, expecting an invitation for a glass of Champagne to welcome me to the building. Instead, it was one of the most startling messages I've ever received (and having a blog, that's saying something . . .), about how I didn't appreciate her artwork, how rude I was, and how my behavior was absolutely a disgrace. I let that place go.

This went on for several years. I'd start looking, see a few places, get discouraged, and stop. I gave up on finding a top-floor apartment—not just because I learned that sometimes problems can come from below, but the competition for top-floor places was fierce and the scarcity of them was limiting my search.

I decided to expand my hunt to include *espaces créatifs*, thinking that I might find something more unusual or "creative" than the standard Parisian apartment. In a country where "thinking outside the box" isn't always encouraged, I reasoned that it would help me score a place if I found one that was *atypique*, which would put others off. When I arrived in Paris in 2004, lofts and open-plan apartments weren't very popular. Some had a hard time thinking that you could live in an apartment that didn't have a separate kitchen (*cuisine*) with a door, where you prepare the cuisine; and a proper dining room, a *salle à manger*, specifically for eating. An eat-in kitchen? *C'est pas possible . . .*

Kitchens in Haussmannian apartments were separate from the family quarters to keep the help, and the smell of cooking, as far away as possible. When I moved to France, I found it odd that the smell of food cooking was considered intrusive to Parisians, whether coming from another room or a neighboring apartment. But then the odor of fried fish pervaded my hallway, lingering for days and days and days (not to mention a neighbor who smelled like very ripe Camembert), and I realized the French were right.

When I started looking at apartments, I'd also said to myself, *I don't want to buy an apartment that I have to do any work on.* That was wishful thinking. There isn't an apartment in Paris that isn't in need of some sort of work. You don't even need to look deeply to see what needs to be done. Minerals from the calcified water clogs pipes and leaves a heavy, impenetrable crust around the joints. *Serpillières* (tattered floor rags) are laid out on kitchen floors and in bathrooms to sop up the water that sprays from ancient spigots and showerheads. Walls in older places may be stained nicotine-yellow, and dark rooms are not brightened up by low-wattage wall sconces with burn marks surrounding the bulbs. And all the gray hair I've acquired since moving to France isn't from frustration with the bureaucracy, but from plugging my stand mixer in to the wall and getting zapped by a jolt of ungrounded electricity every time I wanted to mix up a batch of cookies.

———

Then, at long last, I found it: *l'appart*. I had given up again and again, coming back with revised expectations, and still returned empty-handed. Juggling writing cookbooks, maintaining a blog, and keeping up with all the paperwork that I never seem to get ahead of, I had less and less time to go traipsing around town, hoping I'd eventually come across the right place. Dispirited, I engaged a search company, a type of business that's sprung up in Paris due to the absence of a multiple listing service. Frustrated Parisians are starting to use them more and more, but it's foreigners who've turned to search companies after pulling out most of their hair trying to find a place. I'd lost a lot of my hair for other reasons here, and what little I had left, I wanted to hold on to, so I hired one.

Within a few weeks, I'd seen a couple of apartments with Catherine, a confident, casually cool Frenchwoman who worked with the company I used. She would arrive on her scooter, remove her helmet, and let down her blond hair so we could exchange *bisous* on both cheeks. Because we were in France, we began on more formal terms, using *vous* as we spoke, but soon we were *tutoyer*-ing each other, meeting at cafés over lunch to discuss what I was looking for or having afternoon *apéros* after looking at places she thought would be of interest to me. We made an odd couple—a pretty Parisienne, full of youth, breezing through the convoluted traffic on her *moto* with a hapless American clinging to her back (and losing more of his hair with every harrowing turn she made through traffic.) But we clicked. Every few days, she'd e-mail me listings with notes. Some we'd go look at, others I'd nix right away. She also kept her ear to the ground, so to speak, and we looked at a couple of places that were being offered under the radar (an expression that required an explanation to Romain, who didn't understand how one used a radar to find an apartment).

My new best friend, Catherine, sent me a text one day in the early spring to let me know she'd seen a place that was *un peu atypique*, but might be worth looking at. It was a bit *spécial*, she added, with some hesitation in her voice when I called her back, but she thought it was still worth a visit. *Spécial* is one of those elusive French words that means something (or someone) is . . . peculiar. The use of it is one of the rare times that the French are noncommittal about their opinion. It's a nebulous designation, so you need to decide for yourself if whatever pluses something has will outweigh the minuses. It's usually not bad, but a warning that a heads-up is in order. We made an appointment with the seller's agent to take a look. And as soon as I walked in, I saw how *spécial* it was.

CHERRY FLAN
(Far aux cerises)

MAKES ONE 9-INCH (23CM) ROUND FLAN; ABOUT 8 SERVINGS

There's a French expression, *les temps des cerises* (cherry season), which was the title of a song that originally had revolutionary overtones, something still very dear to the French, who take pride in their ability to rise up in protest. Many Americans express admiration about that *spécial* quality, although I think if a subway or train strike happened and disrupted their commute, or vacation, they'd be a little less sympathetic to their comrades.

Les temps des cerises is sometimes a reference to springtime, similar to "everything's coming up roses." I like roses, but I prefer bringing home bags of deep-red cherries when they're piled up at the markets in Paris come spring and summer to bunches of flowers.

When I gave cherries a try in *far*, a classic Breton custard that's normally studded with prunes, French friends were beside themselves because I had been so bold as to—*gasp*—replace one fruit with another. *"C'est . . . c'est . . . c'est pas possible, Daveed!"* You would have thought I asked them to eat it with a fork *à escargots*, rather than a *fourchette à far*, which probably exists somewhere in the pantheon of French *fourchettes*.

To add to the confusion, *far* means "flan" in the Breton language, which surprises Americans, thinking they're going to get served a soft custard sitting in a pool of caramel, rather than a sturdy wedge, often studded with fruit. Regardless of the controversy a cherry-studded custard can cause (welcome to my life!), everyone open-minded enough to take a bite of this *atypique* custard likes it very much.

¼ cup (60ml) butter, melted, plus more for the pan

2 cups (300g) fresh pitted sweet cherries

½ cup (60g) dried sour cherries (optional)

2 cups (500ml) whole milk

3 large eggs, at room temperature

¾ cup (110g) all-purpose flour

⅔ cup (130g) sugar

3 tablespoons dark rum

1 teaspoon pure vanilla extract

¼ teaspoon pure almond extract

¼ teaspoon salt

1. Preheat the oven to 375ºF (190ºC). Brush a 9 by 2-inch (23 by 5cm) round cake pan (not a springform pan,

which will leak) with melted butter. Line the bottom with a round of parchment paper cut to fit and butter the top of the parchment paper.

2. Distribute the fresh and dried cherries (if using) evenly over the bottom of the prepared pan.

3. In a blender, combine the milk, eggs, flour, sugar, melted butter, rum, vanilla and almond extracts, and salt. Blend until smooth.

4. Pour the custard over the cherries and bake until the center is completely set and the top is browned, 45 minutes. It may puff up a bit when it's done. Remove from the oven and run a knife between the cake and the pan to help it release from the pan. Let cool completely.

5. When cool, set a large plate over the pan and, holding them together, turn them upside down to release the flan. (You might need to lightly rap the plate and pan on the counter to help it release.) Carefully peel off the parchment paper. Set a serving plate over the bottom of the flan and turn the flan and the plate right side up. Remove the top plate.

6. Serve at room temperature. The flan will keep in the refrigerator for up to 2 days.

5

The wooden door with murky glass panels swung open. Its fragile condition gave me pause, as it would only be a matter of time—as in, perhaps the next time it was opened—before it fell off its hinges. We walked inside.

The apartment was an old metal shop that had been transformed to a living space. (Although not quite as livable as we thought, I later learned.) Catherine had forwarded me some photos, and while they were the typically not-so-great interior shots I'd become accustomed to in local real estate notices, they showed a few features that piqued my interest: large windows; high ceilings; an open, loftlike floorplan; and space for a home office, another thing on my dream list. Working at home has its obvious advantages; namely, you don't have to brave the crowds on the morning *métro* to get to work, and you're home to accept packages, a boon in Paris, where getting deliveries can turn into a second full-time job.

The downside to working at home is that you can't get anything done. Still, I reasoned, *If only I had a door between me and my kitchen, I'd spend a lot less time foraging for sweets and chocolate when I should be writing. I'd get a lot more done.* Apparently it takes a lot more than a door to keep my hands out of the chocolate, because I've never been able to successfully prove that theory. Next time I'll add "electrified fence" to my kitchen plans, although it probably isn't wise to joke about anything as serious as electrical issues—as I found out later, too.

Both the seller and his agent were there to meet us. The owner was a lanky man in his sixties with long black hair whose thinning tips barely grazed his collar. Like most French men, he hadn't shaved in a few days and had a classic Gallic nose, which he kept slightly lifted, as if he were constantly appraising everything around him. A lit cigarette burned in his hand and billows of smoke escaped from his mouth as he inhaled, filling the room.

The suited-up agent had an overjoyed smile on his face, perhaps because Catherine had mentioned the words "*client américain*" when she called for an appointment, but the owner looked uncomfortable. We went through the usual pleasantries. I took in the owner, who, within the first few minutes of meeting me, had gone off on several tangents, none of which I was able to follow. From the look on her face, Catherine wasn't following them, either. His agent continued to focus his smile in our direction.

Fortunately, by this point, I'd learned to simply nod when apartment owners talked . . . and, in many cases, talked and talked and talked. More so with agents, who usually had nothing of value to add to my apartment visits, except for having the key to the front door. No matter how much they might try to convince me a rap studio, a bedroom dangling on pulleys, or a neighbor who already hated me even before I moved in were *pas de problème*, I knew better.

When we finished with the required rounds of French politesse, I broke away to take in the apartment. It was one large room with a partitioning wall slicing it nearly in half. Behind that wall was the bathroom. Wedged in next to it, by another clouded-over window, was a slim galley kitchen with a stainless-steel countertop, a menacing German black sink, a college dorm–size refrigerator, and a surprisingly delightful enameled French oven with a pretty crimson door. The only issue was that right at the top, set between the heavy brass oven knobs, was a prominent digital clock with glaring blue numbers that blindingly, and continuously, presented the time. I leaned in to see if there was a gap next to it, where it could be pried off.

Above the kitchen counter was a labyrinth of pipes coated with flaking paint, attached to the wall with bent, sagging brackets. One of them led to the hot water heater. Unlike American hot water heaters that keep a giant tank of water warm (which runs out if you're the last one to get a shower in the house), European hot water heaters provide unlimited hot water, since it's heated to order. Or so they say. I never got to experience that in my previous apartment; with its decrepit *chaudière*, I hadn't had a hot shower that lasted more than 35 seconds in nearly a decade. Which also may have explained why my neighbors were avoiding me.

The gas and electric meters took up the rest of the usable space on the kitchen wall. They're always inside Paris apartments, and it's unthinkable to put them in common areas; I'm told that people are worried their neighbors are going to tinker with them. Considering the relationship some people have with their neighbors, I guess no one wants to take any chances.

As I walked around the apartment with Catherine, the agent followed us with a big grin still plastered across his face. Catherine and I looked at each other, wordlessly communicating our mutual unease. Parisians don't habitually smile, and they especially never walk around grinning for no reason. People who walk around with smiles on their faces are either trying to pick someone up, or they're American.

Meanwhile, the owner meandered. He'd sit down, only to get back up a few moments later and pace the room for a minute, mutter something to himself, then sit back down, open a magazine, close it, and stand up again. He repeated that a few times. On the side table was an ashtray that looked like it hadn't been emptied in two weeks—although, watching him blow through half a pack of cigarettes while we were there, the buildup of butts was probably just from that morning.

The volume of the room was impressive, especially with the high ceilings. Large, vertical windows increased the sense of space, and although the frosted windows were riddled with cracks (which had been patched over with papery, dried-out duct tape) and a patina of grime, I imagined if they were cleaned and replaced, the space would be spectacular.

I went behind the wall to check out the bathroom, which took up a substantial portion of the main living space. Less-than-a-minute showers aside, I don't spend all that much of my time in the bathroom, so figured I could downsize it and devote the extra space to expanding the kitchen, where I do.

Like the other real estate agents I had dealt with, this one didn't seem to be the best option for obtaining accurate information, so I asked the owner a few things. A simple question, like, "Do you have the missing knob that came with this cabinet?" would provoke a moment of pensive thought, his face contorting as he thought deeply about it, searching for the right answer. It didn't seem like a challenging question. A simple *oui* or *non* would have worked, but instead he went on a lengthy pronouncement that he didn't know where it was, finally ending with "*Oui, oui,*" he recalled, the kitchen had come with knobs when he bought the cabinets, but how could he be responsible for knowing where everything was now?

After his speech about the knob, he went back to busying himself with rearranging the ashtray's position on the table and finding another magazine not to read.

The tanned agent hovered with a folder under his arm, clutching a cellphone in the ready position, surely waiting to call his office the minute I was ready to sign. I later learned that an American accent translated either to "pushover" or "someone with money," which gave him the incentive to be so attentive. Catherine kept a respectable distance from him.

As a former metal shop, the place included a garage, which had been enclosed and turned into a bedroom. *That's my office*, I thought. There was a heavy metal roll-up door affixed to the ceiling, which didn't bother me, and a concrete planter just outside filled with empty soda cans and cigarette butts, which did.

We followed the stairs down to the *cave*, which is found under every building in Paris. Most *caves* are used for storage, although there's been a recent interest in converting them to living spaces. The two-level apartments are similar to a *duplex*, but because they're partially *sous-sol* (underground), they're cleverly called a *sousplexe*.

Stone *caves* can be cold and damp, but this one was nice and warm, and even toasty. I assumed the owner, who wasn't young, got chilly down there and kept the heat on. It was dim, too, with the only illumination provided by a lone bulb dangling next to the bed. I stood in the middle and took in the cavernous space under the spectacular stone arch, the bare bulb casting lengthy shadows, giving a sense of drama to the curved vault. The floors were covered with rugs worn down to their threads, but I imagined this space would make a perfectly quiet bedroom, barricaded from noises coming from above by the thick stone walls. (And there definitely wasn't anyone below, either.) It would be the opposite of sleeping in my rooftop aerie, but the peaceful calm fit the bill for the kind of private haven I was seeking. Another bonus: What better place to store wine than in my very own *cave*?

I assumed that time had buffed the stones of the arch to a Louvre-like patina. But I had to guess at that, because I couldn't see it. The entire arch had been papered over and hidden, except for a few places where the glued-on paper was peeling away. While the old is generally celebrated in France, over the years, things like ancient stone walls, historic marketplaces (like the bulldozed glass-and-steel Les Halles market, once considered the Belly of Paris), and even certain styles of kitchen sinks got furloughed because they reminded people of tougher times. It's known as *la cache-misère;* hiding the misery of the past.

There was a wall closing off the *cave* from the upstairs so any natural light or fresh air that might want to enter into it didn't stand a chance. I imagined that with the help of a sledgehammer and a sandblaster, I could be responsible, in my own little way, for restoring one small part of the glory of France.

The apartment checked off most of my boxes. There was the potential for a big open space and windows that could, someday, let in plenty of light. It wasn't far from where I was currently living, with another excellent outdoor market nearby (that shared some of the same vendors as my current market), and the price was within my modest budget, likely due to its condition and its *atypique* configuration. And it didn't need all that much work: I could move that wall in the main room and redo (and reduce the size of) the dowdy bathroom with a new bathtub, sink, and toilet. Ripping the paper off the walls of the *cave* would be a pleasure and take me ten minutes, max. I could extend the kitchen by replacing the existing slender counter with a larger one, find a way to *cacher la misère* of the oven clock, and put in new appliances. I had found my apartment.

————

The owner was still mumbling to himself on the sidelines, pacing back and forth as we finished poking around the apartment. I smiled politely, rather than pointing out anything I didn't like. A French friend later told me one thing you should never do is show enthusiasm when you find a place you want. One should point out everything that's wrong right off the bat and act like it would be a great imposition to even consider living in such a place.

"This kitchen is way too cramped for me. I wouldn't even make toast in it!"

"I'm not sure this bathroom is usable. Just look at this towel bar. I couldn't possibly hang my beautiful towels on it."

"Those light switches . . . that shade of ivory is definitely unacceptable . . ."

You should point out each and every shortcoming, regardless of how inconsequential they are, to put the seller in the position of defending their fault-filled apartment against your impeccable standards, letting them know what an imposition it would be for you to live there. But, *sigh*, you could be convinced . . . perhaps . . .

I didn't do any of that and couldn't wait to tell Romain I had found my apartment. When I mentioned that I had told the seller and his agent that I was very interested in the place, he was naturally skeptical, as the French are, and I told him that I hadn't pointed out anything I didn't like about the place. (Including the *moche* oven clock.) "*Tu as ouvert la porte d'opportunisme,"* he told me. I had opened the door for opportunity—for them, but not for me.

Concerned that someone else might get to it before I did, I took Romain to the apartment the next day. He looked around, but didn't see what I saw, or at least saw some things I should have noticed on my previous visit, and expressed his concerns. But I shook it off as French pessimism, even though he's the least pessimistic person in perpetually pessimistic Paris. I decided to put in an offer and see what happened, opening the *porte* of opportunity.

6

After a few more visits—including a late-night one to make sure there were no recording studios nearby or that I would need an armed escort to get home—I put an offer in on the place.

In France, if you've listed your property with an agency, you're not permitted to sell it for more than the listed asking price. Coming from a country where real estate values are determined by what people will pay for a place, this was a strange concept. It's like putting something up for auction and setting a maximum amount you'll take for it.

If you offer the asking price, the seller is obligated to accept it. I didn't want to take any chances on losing it, so that's what I did. Coming from San Francisco, where offers start at 20 to 50 percent above the asking price and get bid upward, auction-like, from there, it seemed like a deal to be able to buy an apartment at the actual asking price. And making an offer at the listing price meant all other offers were blocked, reassuring me that the apartment would be mine.

The year that passed between when I initialed the first round of papers, and when I signed the final *acte de vente* and got the keys, proved to be one of the toughest years of my life.

I'd gotten used to things that should normally take a few minutes taking much, much longer, like going out to buy a bag of sugar and spending most of the afternoon going to every grocery store in my neighborhood, because each was mysteriously out of stock, or embarking on a two-week odyssey to open a bank account. I learned to allocate extra time for things that I took for granted. Americans are results-oriented, and when we want something, we find the easiest and quickest way to make it happen. If there is a problem, we figure out how to make it work.

In France, the process takes precedence. Things first begin with working on understanding existentially *why* the problem exists. Once all the declarations are made, then it's on to lengthy discussions, paperwork, meetings, phone calls, signatures, more phone calls, more meetings, photocopying, official notary stamps, more photocopying, fees, taxes, registered letters (requiring multiple trips to the post office), bills, copies of bills, all of which generates stacks of paperwork and receipts, which need to be categorized, filed, and archived for eternity. And even though France is a pioneer in technology, and things have changed a bit since then, very little can be done online or by computer. Nothing was digitized, and paperwork needed to be submitted on paper, not scanned or e-mailed.

The process leading up to the closing wasn't made any easier by the seller, who seemed to be doing whatever he could to thwart the process, as well as his agent, who didn't make it easier, either. For a results-oriented American like me, it was difficult for me. I just wanted to buy the place and move in.

In addition to the time involved in the purchase, I learned about a laundry list of costs and expenses that needed to be factored in. As is customary in France, the buyer is responsible for paying the seller's agent's entire commission, about 5 percent. I, the buyer, also had to pay all the taxes and the fees for the work of the *notaire*, the legal entity who handles the paperwork, an additional 7 percent. (But at least the bank paid for the urinalysis.) The presence of a *notaire* is required for any real estate transaction in France. There are good *notaires* and not-so-good *notaires*. Fortunately, I had an amazing one: Madame Bernachon, who, perhaps taking pity on me for bravely taking on the purchase of my first apartment in Paris, looked out for me.

My conversational French is fine: I can order chocolates like no one's business, and I have no problem letting *madame* inching around me in line at the apple stand understand that her position behind me means she has to wait for my turn to be over, before it's hers. But wading through pages and pages of legalese in French (or even in English) isn't my specialty. I was relieved that Madame Bernachon spoke good English and was happy to explain things to me clearly, and patiently, making sure I understood what I was agreeing to. Which was essential, because I have a tendency to nod and just say, "*Oui*," as one learns to do when living in a foreign country, to avoid looking like a dolt. Romain once told me about a restaurant that was *incroyable*. It was *calme* yet absolutely *extraordinaire*. I kept nodding in agreement while he described the wonderful food served at this place he'd been fortunate to find. When he was done describing the meal to me, I said, "That sounds great! Let's make a reservation for dinner there this weekend." He looked at me, baffled. He was talking about Zidane, a French soccer player.

I had signed the *promesse de vente*, the initial round of

paperwork, which obliged the seller to sell the apartment to me but allowed me a brief window of time to change my mind without any consequences. When you put in your offer on a property in America, it's customary to have an inspection done. You hire someone with expertise to poke around, making sure the beams holding up the place haven't been ravaged by a team of famished termites, that the electricity isn't going to give you the shock of your life, and that water won't come bursting through your ceiling, an occurrence so common in Paris due to the ancient plumbing that if you mention *les dégâts des eaux*, you'll be subjected to a vitriolic rant about the leaky pipes of upstairs neighbors, the kind that's usually reserved for bankers, *notaires*, real estate agents, and, as I later found out, contractors.

Even though inspections are uncommon in Paris, Catherine suggested having an architect friend come over the look at the place, as a favor to her overly enthusiastic American friend. And it was a good thing she did. If the architect had charged me €50,000, it would have been the best €50,000 I'd ever spent.

Catherine and I met Aurélie, the architect, outside the front door, along with the real estate agent who had the keys. Thankfully, I was told Monsieur Legrand, the seller, would be away; his constant pacing and copious fretting made it hard to focus on my own issues, which I needed to pay attention to, since they were all in French, and from this point on, I needed to make sure I understood what was happening. Having him as a distraction was extra stress I didn't need.

Monsieur Legrand surprised us all by being at the apartment when we arrived. And I think if the judges for the Césars had been present, he might have won the French equivalent of an Oscar for his performance that day. The agent had his collar wide-open at the neck to expose a caramel-colored chest, which matched his coffee-colored complexion, no doubt obtained at one of the many *centres de bronzage* in Paris. He smiled broadly as we walked in, to find Monsieur Legrand already worked up, agonizing externally about something unspecified, but hovering close to his ashtray. As we walked through the apartment, the agent followed. Aurélie didn't say much, but looked closely at things, stopping to rap on walls with her knuckles, often tilting her head in to listen closer. She kept moving, pausing to press her foot down on the floor in various places, and opening cabinets and closets to check out what might be lurking behind closed doors before continuing.

A few minutes into the visit, she stopped next to a wall and didn't move. She furrowed her brow as she leaned toward a tangle of wires poking out of a hole near the baseboard. She stood back up, not saying anything, and moved on. Catherine glanced at me. I nonverbally let her know that it had been a good idea to have her friend come by. Aurélie was in competition with Madame Bernachon for the position of my new favorite person in Paris.

Aurélie clicked the light switches, which were from a different era, and wrinkled her nose faintly, suggesting disapproval. She hadn't said much during her perusal, but when she came upon an especially knotty tangle of wires coming out of another wall, she kneeled down to give them a gentle tug, which caused the plaster around them to crumble into a pile of dry shards, and the handful of wires fell out with barely any effort. She sighed loudly, glancing at the agent.

"Oh, *non . . . non, non, non . . .*" she said, wiping the dust off her hands, *tsk-tsk*ing and shaking her head from side to side. "This . . . *this* is very bad. Very, very bad." The agent didn't say anything, but continued smiling, cocking his head in an attempt to show concern. For once, Monsieur Legrand didn't say a word, and continued to turn through the pages of a magazine that looked to be thirty or forty years old.

Aurélie beckoned me closer to the wall and ran her hands over it, then rapped on it a few times. Her brow furrowed deeply. "There is a big problem here," she said, drawing "big" out to "*beeeeg*." "Right here, underneath this wall. *Daveed*, come closer." I don't think anyone else noticed the barely perceptible glint of terror in the agent's eyes, which only managed to look a little worried, thanks to a pair of professionally arched eyebrows. (And perhaps a touch of Botox.)

She tugged slightly on another electrical wire dangling nearby, which also came off in her hands with barely any effort. "*Très dangereux!*" she declared, waving the broken wire in her hand for all to see. "*C'est pas bon . . .*" she added, shooting a disapproving glare at the seller and his agent, which failed to elicit much of a response from either. Monsieur Legrand seemed even more engrossed in his magazine now, remaining quiet but releasing little bursts of air from his pursed lips and rocking his head side to side. None of the problems were his fault—*C'est pas ma faute*, he was surely thinking. The architect said she was surprised there hadn't been a fire yet. The agent just smiled and said, "*Ah bon?*" and Monsieur Legrand turned another page, exhaling another cloud of cigarette smoke.

Aurélie continued walking, shaking her head as she tried out some of the light switches and outlets. She said she was very concerned about the electricity, and whatever else might be going on behind the aged plaster walls, and her look had me worried, too. The hot water heater in the kitchen tried its best to shoot tepid water out of the kitchen faucet when she turned it on, but was clogged with too much calcium from never being serviced. Having someone look at the hot water heater, or replacing it, would need to go on my list of things I'd have to do in the apartment, in addition to replacing the clock on the stove and updating some of the electrical wires, I thought to myself.

Monsieur Legrand stayed put (which was wise), but the rest of us walked downstairs to the *cave* where the owner had his bed and a full-size grand piano. There was no bathroom down there, just a small hand sink fitted with a pump, similar to the one that had been attached to my aquarium filter when I was in the fifth grade. I told Aurélie I was planning to knock down the wall that sealed off the *cave* from the rest of the apartment and was going to put my bedroom down there, where it was so nice and cozy. The weather had gotten much warmer in the last few weeks, and it was still warm and cozy down there. It didn't bother me, but it bothered her.

"Why is the heat on . . . when it's so warm out?" she said, to no one in particular. The agent didn't volunteer any explanation. Based on buckling she'd noticed in some of the walls, she suggested a humidity problem in the apartment. I pulled a few books from his shelves to see if there was any mold on them, since, as a cookbook collector, I've learned books are particularly susceptible to mold, and there wasn't any. So I returned them to the shelf and we all marched back upstairs, the agent stepping aside and graciously making a sweeping gesture with his hand for Aurélie, for her to go first. *"Après vous, madame."* She didn't seem impressed by his chivalry, nor by what she had seen.

———

Aurélie announced her verdict. The apartment needed a complete overhaul, beginning with redoing the electricity, including all the wiring, which was completely shot. Not only was a new hot water heater needed, but every plumbing fixture and pipe needed replacing. The electrical heaters were outdated and needed to be replaced, and the walls and ceilings would need to be replastered and repainted after they were torn down to access the wires and plumbing behind them. I knew the windows would have to be addressed, which she pointed out was going to be a considerable—and expensive—prospect, and she also recommended having a professional come in to test the *santé* (health) of the *cave* and assess the questionable condition of the stones.

When I put in my offer on the apartment, I had thought it only needed to be *rafraîchit*, merely "refreshed." I had been concerned with oven clocks, removing paper from the wall, and the toilet paper holder I found on Pinterest that I became obsessed with, a no-nonsense, utilitarian curve of white porcelain where the roll rests, and the paper hangs perfunctorily through a slot in the bottom. She was now telling me the apartment needed to be *rénové . . . complètement.* My stomach felt as if it had suddenly turned to lead, dropping in disappointment.

My idea of moving the main bathroom downstairs so I could have more kitchen space was a possibility, she said. But that would require building and attaching an entirely new water line to the main of the building. To do that, I'd need to get permission from the others in the building. "That shouldn't be a problem. I never had an issue with neighbors in any apartment I owned in San Francisco," I said confidently. "I'm sure everyone in the building will be happy I'm fixing up the apartment." I assumed they'd be happy I was replacing the dilapidated windows, certainly a real boon to the building. Still, I decided to stop rePinning my toilet paper holder, just in case.

———

Aurélie, seven months pregnant yet faultlessly balanced in heels, put on her gloves ready to hop onto her scooter to head to her next meeting, and I thanked her for coming over. Before she sped off, I asked if she could give me some sort of estimate how much the work she was talking about would cost. She tossed out the number, and I froze in place. When I put in my bid for the apartment, I had budgeted in what I assumed the renovations would be. The amount Aurélie gave me was much, much more than I had originally thought it would cost—three times more.

Thud.

After Aurélie had given me the bad news, she didn't add *"Bon courage!"* ("Good luck!") before speeding off. She just puttered away.

Another way to say "good luck" is to say *"Merde!,"* a custom that goes back to a time when the French took horse-drawn carriages to the theater. A sign that a show was a success was an abundance of horse *merde* piled up around the theater. (I assume dog doo didn't count; otherwise, success would be harder to determine in Paris.)

The owner and his agent were still on speaking terms at this point, but once I was back inside with them, they were not convinced that the apartment had any of the problems Aurélie had listed. The French have a peculiar way of ignoring things; even when a handful of electrical wires comes crumbling out of a wall, that's still not proof that there's an issue with the electricity. Troubling water stains on the walls and ceiling? Those were *grains de beauté*, or "beauty marks," on an otherwise pristine apartment. All the walls need to come down to replace the water pipes? *C'est exagéré!* —Now you're just exaggerating. That one in the back of the cabinet can surely stay.

The whole deal suddenly seemed like a very bad idea. And now I was standing in a big pile of *merde*, and didn't feel like much of a success.

PAIN PERDU CARAMÉLISÉ

SERVES 4

This recipe makes good use of something you might think is beyond redemption. *Pain perdu* takes lost (*perdu*) bread and turns it around, creating something marvelous. I was hoping to do the same to the apartment, until I got the bad news and wasn't sure I was up to such an extensive, and expensive, task.

Rather than just frying the bread until it's browned on each side, like "French toast" (as we call it) is traditionally made, I sear the bread with sugar until it's deeply caramelized and lacquered, giving it a crunchy, crackly surface. To make it even better, I serve it with an extra drizzle of salted butter caramel. *Pourquoi pas?*

This *pain perdu* is best made in a nonstick or cast-iron skillet, two pieces of bread at a time, unless you have a skillet large enough to fry all four slices in a single layer at once. (I don't mind doing them in two batches; it makes my guests extra appreciative that they're getting a dessert made *à la minute*.) Either way, I have the ice cream and warm caramel sauce ready to go before I start.

6 tablespoons (90ml) whole milk

2 tablespoons (30ml) heavy cream

2 large eggs, at room temperature

½ teaspoon pure vanilla extract

Big pinch of ground cinnamon

Small pinch of salt

Unsalted butter, for frying the bread

4 slices brioche or challah bread, ½ inch (1.2cm) thick

8 teaspoons granulated sugar

Vanilla ice cream or whipped cream, for serving

Salted Butter Caramel Sauce (recipe follows), for serving

1. In a shallow bowl or baking dish, use a fork to vigorously stir together the milk, cream, eggs, vanilla, cinnamon, and salt.

2. Heat a good-size pat of butter in a skillet over medium-high heat until it starts to sizzle.

3. Dip a slice of bread in the milk-and-egg mixture, pressing it in a bit and encouraging it to soak up the liquid. Turn it over and soak the other side. Place the first piece of bread in the pan and quickly do the same to a second slice of bread.

4. Fry the slices of bread until they are well browned on the bottom, about 2 minutes. When they are close to being done, sprinkle each piece of bread evenly with 2 teaspoons of the sugar, then flip the slices and cook until the sugared sides (the sides against the pan) are caramelized, about 2½ minutes.

While they are cooking, press down on the slices with a spatula a few times to encourage them to caramelize, and move the pieces of bread around in the pan so they cook evenly and can sop up any gooey caramelized sugar that may collect in the bottom of the pan. (Resist the urge to not cook them enough. When the caramelized slices of bread look close to being too dark, but not burnt, that's the moment when I remove them from the pan. You can flip them over to get a better look at the bottom, then flip them back over to continue caramelizing them.)

5. Transfer the slices of bread to plates, caramelized side up, and serve with a scoop of ice cream, or some whipped cream, and a drizzle of warm salted butter caramel sauce. Wipe the skillet clean, melt another pat of butter in the pan, and cook the remaining two slices of bread the same way.

SALTED BUTTER CARAMEL SAUCE

MAKES ABOUT 1 CUP (250ML)

2 ounces (55g) salted butter
½ cup (100g) sugar
½ cup (125ml) heavy cream
½ teaspoon pure vanilla extract

1. Melt the butter in a saucepan with a capacity of at least 4 quarts (3.5l). (The caramel will bubble up when the cream is added, so it's a good idea to use a larger pot.)

2. Add the sugar and cook, stirring frequently with a heatproof utensil, until the butter and sugar begin to turn a light amber color. Keep a close eye on the caramel and

cook, stirring, until it turns a deep amber color and begins to smoke.

3. As soon as it's as dark as an old centime, or copper penny, turn off the heat and immediately stir in the cream; be careful, as it will bubble up and sputter. Stir until smooth, then add the vanilla.

4. The caramel sauce can be made ahead and will keep in a jar in the refrigerator for up to 2 weeks. It will thicken as it stands but can be rewarmed over low heat and thinned with milk, if desired.

7

France doesn't really do discounts. Sales (*les soldes*) are limited to twice-yearly dates mandated by the government. Stores and supermarkets are allowed to have promotions, but you take your chances buying something *en promo*, because even if the flyer advertises an item on sale, my experience has shown that more often than not, it'll ring up at the full price at the register. Getting a cashier to verify and honor the discount is such a protracted experience that I now just pay the regular price; my sanity is worth more than saving 30 centimes on a jar of Dijon mustard.

Nevertheless, the owner of the apartment search company that I used also happens to be an attorney, and likely forgot about the no-discounts policy in Paris: she told me to retract my offer and lower it by the amount the architect told me the construction would cost, nearly 20 percent off the purchase price. They had already accepted my offer and I knew they would never take it.

"What's the worst the seller can say?" she replied. "*Non?*"

After his performances at the showings and the walk-through with the architect, I was certain the seller had spent his life absolving himself of any responsibility, as in the frequently uttered French phrase: *C'est pas ma faute.* But as my non-French mother used to say, with the backseat of her car piled high with Loehmann's bags and a trunk filled with bargained-for treasures from flea markets, "If you don't ask, you don't get."

So I heeded her advice, retracting my offer and submitting a new one, minus the amount Aurélie said the renovations would cost. (I didn't include the double-door, stainless-steel refrigerator I already had my eye on. Or the German toilet paper holder.) The agent kept his grin wide as he removed the paper from the envelope, doing his best to avoid registering any sort of reaction as he took in the revised offer. I watched his eyes take an extra moment to reread the final number, then he folded the paper up and proclaimed that he couldn't possibly show it to his client.

Clients aren't obliged to work with their agents in France and can list their apartments with multiple agents at the same time, even at different prices. However, agents *are* obligated to show their clients offers—if not professionally, then at least ethically. So I said I was taking it to Monsieur Legrand directly. No doubt concerned about the loss of his commission, the agent reluctantly agreed to present it to the owner.

The next day, the agent rang me up. "*Désolé*, Monsieur Lebovitz," he began, "but we now have another offer on the apartment from a buyer offering the full asking price." Since my offer had been accepted first, I could still have it—at the full price, he said, but warned me that I needed to act very fast if I wanted the apartment. So it wasn't possible to lower the price, *malheureusement*.

Something about the whole thing sounded off. I wasn't sure why. He said he would send me a copy of the other offer so I could see for myself. Shortly after, an e-mail arrived with a scan of the other offer, along with a note that I needed to respond quickly if I still wanted the apartment, because the other party was ready to move forward and take it.

I have an odd tendency to believe people are telling the truth. So I wanted to think there was another buyer for the place, ready to pounce. Considering all the work the place needed, and that it was an *espace atypique*, I wasn't sure who else would want it at the full price. With the renovations, it was far more expensive than anything else in that neighborhood. And if you've ever watched how carefully the French dole out money to pay for purchases at the market and carefully scrutinize the change, you'll know they keep an eye on every euro. But good for the owner, I thought, if he had someone who was willing to pay such a heady price for a place that needed so much work. To people in Paris, having to do construction is like being asked to spend the weekend at traffic school: an ordeal that ends with a required *psychotechnique* test, confirming that you are mentally able to drive again. (Next time someone tries to run you over in Paris, you'll wonder what kinds of questions are part of that particular *psychotechnique* test.) It's hard to sell a place that needs a major renovation, and an apartment that needs any sort of *travaux* is always priced lower than a place that's ready to move in to.

Looking at the other offer more carefully, there was something off about the handwriting, which looked like it had been drawn up in the backseat of a taxi. Even though I liked the place a lot, the idea of taking on the work it required was just too much, especially at that price. Reluctantly, I decided to give it up.

"Fine, let the other people have it. Thank you for sending the other offer, and thank you for your time," I politely wrote, and hit the "Send" button. About a minute after I sent

the response, my phone rang. It was the agent, who told me—
with a lilt of surprise in his voice—that the other party had
unexpectedly decided that they were going to move abroad
instead, and no longer wanted the apartment. So I could
have it.

I don't exactly remember how long it took me to decide
to uproot my entire life and move to another country, but I
know it took longer than one night. And I certainly wasn't
putting in offers on apartments while I was making that decision.

Miraculously, he told me, the owner decided to accept my
new offer, and even though the apartment needed more work
than I'd initially thought, that was something I'd deal with
later. For now, I just needed to make sure the apartment was
mine. I'd think about the renovations later. So we made an
appointment with the *notaire* to sign a round of paperwork,
and I put down a deposit, being aware that there was a *clause
pénale* which didn't have anything to do with what would
happen later in the doctor's office, but meant that I could lose
my substantial deposit if I didn't complete the sale within a
certain period of time.

I was well on my way to owning my very own place in
Paris, which was scary and exciting at the same time. The excitement was short-lived. The scary part was about to begin.

8

"*C'est pas ma faute!*" he insisted, pushing the paperwork away as if he had been presented with a plate of sole meunière that was well past its prime. Monsieur Legrand resumed his pacing around the *notaire*'s office, while Madame Bernachon read through the paperwork with both of us present, as required by law, before we signed it.

She had started at the top of the very first page, reading each part of the document aloud, then looking in both my and the seller's direction for confirmation that we both understood what each section meant and how it affected us. I'll have to admit, there were probably a few other things I'd rather be doing, like drinking a Kir royal at one of the cafés I could see through the windows of the drab conference room where we were sitting, where the rest of Paris seemed to be enjoying the lovely weather on the terraces. Listening to a bunch of French real estate legalese in a conference room under a halo of unflattering fluorescent lights wasn't my idea of a good time, either. But we were obliged to be there and listen if the owner wanted to sell his apartment and I wanted to buy it.

As we sat around the table slogging through the documents, Monsieur Legrand seemed startled by every point as she mentioned it, even if it was something as simple as

I hereby declare that these two people are in the same room with me. He felt it necessary to add something to every single point, piping up that yes, he agreed that we were all in the same room, when a simple nod of approval would have sufficed.

As Madame Bernachon made her way down the first page, he added commentary to every point, or made some gesture—like clearing his throat loudly or dramatically pushing back his unkempt hair, which kept sliding back down over his face. For most of them, a simple "*Oui*" would have sufficed. It was rote legalese she was reading, nothing either of us had any say over. In addition to thinking about how nice a sparkly *apéritif* would taste, I was also thinking how fortunate I was that *notaires* aren't paid by the hour.

By the end of the first page of the contract, Monsieur Legrand was unable to stay seated in his chair. He stood up and exhaled little bursts of air, shrugging his shoulders up to his ears, wondering what was taking so long, hoping for some sympathy, perhaps, for what an inconvenience this was to him. By the beginning of the second page, when Madame Bernachon looked again in the seller's direction for confirmation on a particular point, he began saying that he wasn't sure, it was all too much, and it was taking too long, etc. . . . Behind her thin wire glasses, Madame Bernachon was starting to look a little worried, and cast a sidelong glance at me.

She diplomatically explained that she was required by the Republic of France to read this aloud so he could sell his apartment. I got the feeling his agent had seen this before and knew it was best to just keep on grinning and bearing it. Perhaps he was sharper than I thought. Once this meeting was over, he didn't have much else to do but wait for the day when he could breeze in, pick up his check, and get out of there.

Madame Bernachon finally reached the end of the document, the page describing the usage of the apartment. In Paris, apartments are *résidentiels* and commercial spaces are *commerciaux*. She suddenly stopped reading and stared at the paper. Her head tilted slightly, then she reached under the pile of paperwork for the pages showing the layout of the apartment, then looked back at the document.

She straightened herself in the chair, removed her glasses, and, with the authority bequeathed on her by the Republic of France, announced, "I am obliged to tell you this, Monsieur Lebovitz: you may not live in this apartment."

BUCKWHEAT CHOCOLATE CHIP COOKIES

Cookies au sarrasin et aux pépites de chocolat

MAKES 20 TO 22 COOKIES

When something goes wrong—say, a frustrating administrative snafu that I might write about, or a meeting with a seller seemingly doing everything he could to hold up a sale—a reader might write, "Just go have a croissant!" If it were only that easy to solve problems, the bakeries in Paris would be overwhelmed with orders for croissants.

I love croissants, and their cousin, *pains au chocolat*. But patriotically, my allegiance will always be to chocolate chip cookies, or as the French call them, *les cookies*. Having one always cheers me up, and *les cookies* are showing up in more and more bakeries in Paris—perhaps as a backup for when they run out of croissants?

I'm always looking for ways to dial up my chocolate chip cookies, and these boast the earthy taste of buckwheat, a popular ingredient often found in crêpes (in which case they're called *galettes*). The hearty flavor of *sarrasin* pairs well with the generous amount of mix-ins I pack into my dough. The copious chocolate chunks and nuts may cause the dough to crumble a bit when you shape the cookies, like a real estate deal may crumble when extra things are suddenly tossed into the mix. But you should be able to push them all back together, like I had to do with my deal.

To avoid that with your cookies, it helps to squeeze the balls of dough together with *notaire*-like authority to get everything to stay in place. Once baked, when you remove the cookies from the oven, each one gets rapped with a flat metal spatula or pancake turner to compact them slightly, resulting in chewier cookies. If too many melty chocolate bits get stuck to the spatula, wiping them away will keep the appearance of the cookies as presentable as possible, and keep what's hidden under the surface a surprise. In this case, though, the surprise is a good one.

½ cup packed (90g) light brown sugar

⅓ cup (65g) granulated sugar

8 tablespoons (4 ounces/115g) salted butter, melted and cooled to room temperature

1 large egg, at room temperature

1 large egg yolk

1½ teaspoons pure vanilla extract

¾ cup (110g) all-purpose flour

½ cup (75g) buckwheat flour

½ teaspoon baking powder, preferably aluminum-free

½ teaspoon baking soda

½ teaspoon kosher salt or sea salt

1½ cups (230g) coarsely chopped bittersweet or semisweet chocolate

3 tablespoons toasted buckwheat groats, sometimes sold as kasha

¾ cup (75g) walnuts, almonds, or pecans, toasted and coarsely chopped

Flaky sea salt, such as fleur de sel or Maldon, to finish the cookies

1. In a large bowl, mix together the brown sugar, granulated sugar, and melted butter. Add the egg, egg yolk, and vanilla.

2. In a separate bowl, whisk together the all-purpose flour, buckwheat flour, baking powder, baking soda, and salt. Stir the dry ingredients into the butter-sugar mixture.

3. Mix in the chopped chocolate (and any small bits of chocolate), buckwheat groats, and nuts. Cover the bowl and chill overnight.

4. Remove the dough from the refrigerator at least 30 minutes before you plan to scoop the cookies.

5. Preheat the oven to 350°F (180°C). Line two baking sheets with parchment paper or silicone baking mats.

6. Use a spring-loaded ice cream or cookie scoop (or a tablespoon and your hands) to form the dough into 1½-inch (4cm) balls, and place them 2½ inches (6cm) apart on the baking sheets (you will likely need to bake the cookies in batches). Slightly flatten the tops with damp fingers and sprinkle with flaky sea salt.

7. Bake the cookies until light golden brown on top, about 12 minutes, rotating the baking sheets on the oven racks midway through baking. Remove the cookies from the oven and using a flat metal spatula (also called

a pancake turner), tap the top of each cookie to flatten it, so each is about ½ inch (1.25cm) high. The bottom of the spatula may pick up some sticky chocolate, which can be wiped clean so the finished cookies have a neater appearance. Let cool on the baking sheets.

8. Once the cookies and baking sheets are cool, remove the cookies from the baking sheets and finish baking the rest of the cookie dough.

NOTE: Buckwheat flour and toasted buckwheat groats are available at natural foods stores and well-stocked supermarkets. Toasted buckwheat (kasha) is sometimes sold in the kosher aisle, or in the tea aisle at Asian markets. A good substitute for the toasted buckwheat is roasted cocoa nibs.

9

The *notaire* shook her head *"C'est pas possible . . . c'est pas du tout possible . . ."* glancing over the rim of her glasses to get a clearer look at the floorplans. The seller looked like a teakettle that had been left on the fire too long and was ready to blow.

And then, he did. He jumped out of his seat in one last round of histrionics, saying that this was ridiculous and everything was taking way too long. Whatever it was she was talking about, he didn't know anything about. *"C'est pas ma faute!"* he said, throwing up his hands one final time, before he headed for the door and left.

We all looked at each other—the *notaire*, me, and the real estate agent, who probably should have left with his client before an incensed Madame Bernachon turned to him. French people don't like authority figures. At this very moment, I saw why.

After she dispensed some choice words for the agent, he managed to slither out of there, assuring her that he would "look into it." She had just dropped a room-clearing bomb. And it was my mess to clean up.

The apartment was zoned as a commercial space, so it could only be used as an office or a similar business. The "bedroom" in the apartment had been incorrectly listed as such: you can do whatever you want in a commercial space—except sleep there or live there full-time. And as much as Monsieur Legrand protested that he didn't know anything about it, the *notaire* didn't seem so sure.

It's hard to believe that someone could own and live in an apartment for ten years and not know that it wasn't legal to live in. It was also odd that I, a foreigner with zero experience in French real estate, understood that as soon as the *notaire* pointed it out. And even odder, that a real estate agent, whose job it is to know these kinds of things, was completely unaware of it.

After the agent left, she told me I could get out of buying the apartment if I wanted to, to just let her know and she'd take care of it. I was filled with disappointment, or *déception*, in French, which is not necessarily about being deceived. Nonetheless, I felt both.

10

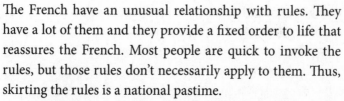

The French have an unusual relationship with rules. They have a lot of them and they provide a fixed order to life that reassures the French. Most people are quick to invoke the rules, but those rules don't necessarily apply to them. Thus, skirting the rules is a national pastime.

The obligatory reading through the real estate contract was understandably just too much for Monsieur Legrand. Most real estate transactions have problems. This wasn't the first time I'd bought a place, and in my previous experiences, I was motived to buy and the sellers were motivated to sell. (That sounds so simple, doesn't it?) When there was a problem, we worked to find a solution, then moved forward to the closing. But then again, I had been in a results-oriented culture, not one where prolonging the process and stirring up drama was par for the course. I thought about how fortunate the people who had put in the other bid for the apartment were, and hoped they were happy, wherever they had decided to move. Or not.

The seller and his agent insisted they weren't responsible for the oversight, so it was on me to find a solution. All I wanted to do was wake up the next morning and hit the market, buy whatever produce looked beautiful that day, and bring home a selection of cheeses to enjoy with the fresh baguette I'd pick up at my bakery on the way home.

But instead, my new life began, working to convince the city of Paris to change the *destination* of the apartment, a term I found odd, until I realized I was, indeed, responsible for determining the destiny of the apartment. (So perhaps I should have consulted Voltaire, rather than a lawyer?) Never mind that the apartment wasn't even properly mine yet. Nor were the owner or his agent willing to help in any way, or admit they knew anything about it. All *I* knew was that I was doing a lot more fretting than cooking. My own destiny was becoming less clear . . .

———

As someone who is frugal, I'm jealous of how the French are intricately careful with their spending. Money is never handed over until it's absolutely necessary. Americans are ready and willing when it's time to pay; we've got our credit cards out of our wallets even before the cashier has finished ringing up our order.

One thing Americans do admire about the French is that the French "take time to enjoy life." I don't know if the time French cashiers spend making us rifle through our pockets and purses scavenging for change counts toward the time spent enjoying the finer things in life. If it does, the French are the happiest people in the world.

The city of Paris required a petition, including a drawing of the apartment, to change the apartment's "destiny," which was now linked to mine. Or vice-versa. Just broaching the subject with Monsieur Legrand of chipping in for the architect to do the drawing brought on an apoplectic bout of nervousness, provoking him to massage his forehead with his fingers, pull with extra concentration on his cigarette, and talk about how he was surprised by all of this, etc., which was his roundabout way of saying "*Non.*" Had I backed out, he would have had to do it regardless, if he planned to sell it to someone else, now that the *notaire* had made sure it had been brought to his attention. But I don't have the same patience for protracted negotiations and wanted to move forward. So I caved. Meaning I got stuck taking care of the architect's fee, several thousand euros to do the drawings of his apartment to submit with the application to make my apartment—I mean, *his* apartment—residential.

While I worked with another architect on the plans (Aurélie had taken her maternity leave), with my sizable deposit in escrow with the *notaire*, Monsieur Legrand started a campaign of calling me frequently, sometimes at six in the morning, to ramble on about how long the process was taking. I shared his pain, I really did—I wanted to complain to him about exactly the same thing (and a few other things), but decided it was a waste of my time. I was trying to be more European and take time to relax, and enjoy life, two things I was sure were just around the corner.

———

Summer was now in full swing in Paris, which meant that by mid-July, almost everybody would be closing up their apartments, offices, and shops for the annual exodus, when Parisians go on *les vacances*, which happens en masse, hence the use of the plural. (Or because there are so many of them.)

Government workers get the longest vacations, and that would include the people at my local *mairie* (city hall), to whom I'd be submitting the plans and application. They'd be gone for at least six weeks, so I wanted to get the drawings and application in quickly, before they took off. While café and bakery owners taped signs on their doors, noting that they'd be back in September, locking the doors behind them, I canceled my own summer vacation plans so I could finish the application. I watched everyone go, as I headed back to OfficeMax (which kept American hours) for yet another ream of printer paper and more ink cartridges to tackle this unexpected round of paperwork. I was sure the people at city hall wouldn't have time to review my application before their vacations, but I wanted it to be at the top of their pile when they returned in the fall.

Proof that not only the beauty—and pastries—of Paris continue to astonish, a few days later, I received a response: the city would approve the conversion if the windows in the apartment were replaced. Everything else was in perfect order, which made me realize that all the time I'd spent on *la paperasse* over the years had finally paid off. I've gotten pretty good at it.

In Paris, residential properties must have transparent windows, which would make sense. I certainly wouldn't want to live in a place where I couldn't see out of the windows either (although the current resident didn't seem to mind). I contacted the most reputable window company in Paris to get an estimate for changing them. They quoted an astonishingly high price: just shy of 20,000 euros. I wasn't going to spend close to that to change the windows of an apartment that wasn't mine . . . That would be crazy.

At least I thought so. But there was something (or some-

one) even crazier I'd have to deal with before I could move in
to the apartment.

CROISSANTS AUX AMANDES

MAKES 4 CROISSANTS

It had been a tough few months, negotiating with banks for
a mortgage, getting entangled with an obstinate seller and
a shifty real estate agent, going cross-eyed from reviewing
lengthy documents in French that I understood about 4 percent of, and petitioning the folks at city hall. There weren't
enough croissants in Paris to make it all better—especially
in August, when all the bakeries were shut down.

The French are a frugal lot, which is one reason I fit right
in. I hate throwing things away, especially anything edible.
Bakeries do their part, too, giving a second life to leftover
croissants by stuffing them with a velvety smear of rich *frangipane* (almond cream) and baking them again. I've often
warned visitors not to try them, because once you do, you
are on a slippery slope and will always crave them. (Trust me
on that one . . .)

Fortunately, these can be made with frozen or good-
quality store-bought croissants, in case you really need one
and your favorite bakery happens to be closed. I've seen
some really giant croissants outside of France, especially in
America. If yours are larger than a reasonable person would
eat in one sitting, you may want to double the frangipane

filling and the syrup. (Extra frangipane can be frozen for your next batch.) Be sure to saturate the croissants with the syrup more than you think is necessary. I keep the syrup on the less-sweet side, but if you like things a little sweeter, you can add 2 more tablespoons of sugar to it.

Frangipane

½ cup (50g) almond flour (also called ground almonds)
¼ cup (50g) sugar
1 large egg, at room temperature
3½ tablespoons (50g) unsalted butter, at room temperature
A few drops of pure almond extract
Pinch of salt

Syrup

½ cup (125ml) water
¼ cup (50g) sugar
2 tablespoons dark rum, amaretto, or kirsch (optional)

4 croissants, preferably day-old
4 tablespoons (20g) sliced almonds
Powdered sugar

1. Preheat the oven to 375°F (190°C). Line a baking sheet with parchment paper or a silicone baking mat.
2. Make the frangipane: In the bowl of a stand mixer fitted with the paddle attachment, beat the almond flour, sugar, egg, butter, almond extract, and salt on low speed until combined. Turn the speed to high and beat the almond cream for 3 minutes, until very light and fluffy. (You can also beat it by hand in a bowl with a wooden spoon or flexible silicone spatula.)

3. Make the syrup: In a small saucepan, heat the water and sugar until it comes to a boil. Stir to dissolve the sugar, remove from the heat, and add the liquor.

4. Starting at one side, slice each croissant in half horizontally, stopping just before you reach the other side, leaving it closed as a hinge. Brush the inside of each croissant liberally with the syrup on both sides, making sure each side is completely saturated. It may seem like a lot, but the finished croissants benefit from the moisture.

5. Smear the inside of each croissant with 2 tablespoons of the frangipane. Put them on the prepared baking sheet and press each down firmly. Divide the remaining frangipane over the top of each croissant and smear it over the top. Sprinkle each croissant with 1 tablespoon of the sliced almonds, then bake until the tops are golden brown, about 15 minutes. Let cool a few minutes, then sprinkle with powdered sugar.

SERVING AND STORAGE: The almond-filled croissants are best served the same day they are made, either warm or at room temperature, but they can be kept in an airtight container overnight.

11

While in the process of buying the apartment, I was also in the midst of working on a cookbook proposal. One of the pleasures of living in Paris is shopping the markets: gathering apricots, tangerines, or whatever was in season, for tarts and sorbets, and buying olives and capers to mash together for a briny tapenade. I wanted to share what I learned sorting through the never-ending varieties of French cheeses at the *fromageries*, paring them down to the ones I liked the best (a tough task, indeed), and exploring the different Parisian *pâtisseries* to get my hands on the best *financiers*, croissants, and chocolates (another challenge—but someone had to do it).

The food in Paris had evolved quite a bit since I'd arrived. Parisian cooking had become a mix of French classics, but also included dishes from other cultures that have assimilated here, infusing the city and its restaurants and markets with new flavors that included "forgotten" French ingredients (like root vegetables and regional liqueurs), now being rediscovered by a new generation, and couscous, kebabs, and even *les hamburgers,* which were adopted by Parisians. Just as France was changing, so was I: my cooking had changed since moving to Paris too, and I wanted to share recipes and stories from my kitchen, even if I wasn't quite sure where that kitchen would be.

Writing a book isn't something you just up and decide to do. It takes months to work on a detailed proposal; then you need to find the right publisher who will buy the book, along with an editor who shares your vision and will nurture you and your book through the publishing process. After signing the contract, there's writing the book and developing the recipes, then on to editing and taking the photographs, before all those words and recipes become a reality: a finished cookbook. Most books take about a year to write, and I started planning in my mind, and in my calendar, how I'd work on mine while moving in to my new apartment.

Then there was my blog, which had developed a wide readership and was a more casual way to share recipes and stories about my life in Paris. As it increased in popularity, I also needed to keep up with the evolving technology, and found myself learning how to code recipes for the Internet, engaging in tech talk with web designers and developers, practicing food photography so the food would look as good on the screen as it did in my kitchen, and tackling beyond-my-comprehension photo-editing software so I could make the photos look good when published online.

I'd started my blog back in 1999, well before the word *blog* was coined, and it blossomed over the years, eventually attracting an admirable number of visitors from around the world. I loved sharing stories and recipes, and the engagement with a wide variety of people helped me broaden not just my culinary horizons, but my cultural ones as well. It also helped me understand France and French culture, writing about quirks and differences, usually through the lens of something I was eating, while touching on other things about life in France that intrigued or baffled me.

It became a full-time endeavor, which I didn't mind. But I soon realized that I had three full-time jobs—the cookbooks,

my blog, and living as an expat—and now was taking on a
fourth: buying an apartment. If that worked out, I'd soon be
taking on my fifth: renovating it.

———————

I was ruminating on what to do about the windows, because
I was (understandably) extremely reluctant to invest tens
of thousands of euros in an apartment I didn't even own.
Buoyed by my success in getting such a rapid response from
city hall, I wrote back and noted that I was preparing to
change the windows since they were in such bad shape, but
didn't want to do it right away because I wasn't the owner yet.
But hoped that soon, I would be.

During one of my daily phone check-ins with the up-
standing Madame Bernachon, I joked that maybe I should
just Photoshop clear glass panes on the current apartment
windows, send those in to the folks at city hall, and replace
the windows later. There was silence on the other end of the
line for an uncomfortable moment, then "Oh, *non, non,
non . . .*" she said, with alarm in her voice. "That is *complètement* unthinkable, Monsieur Lebovitz!" The French have a
robust sense of humor, but they don't do sarcasm (they don't
need to—they say what they want), and they take things literally. Even after I backed up quickly with assurances that
I wasn't serious, it took me a while to calm her down and
regain her *confiance*, which was imperative because I needed
her on my side. No matter how brilliant (or witty) I thought
my solution was, my photo-editing skills aren't even good
enough to figure out how to erase an errant crumb next to a
cookie on a photo for my blog, which I've spent hours trying
to do before giving up. There was no way I could digitally

make opaque windows transparent. It'd be faster to replace them.

Apparently, I wasn't the only one hoping to get a break that summer: the people at city hall were maybe just as anxious for their *vacances* as I was, because they responded promptly and said the conversion to *résidentiel* was approved without changing the windows. Paris will constantly remind you who's boss. But every once in a while, it throws you a bone. I grabbed mine—the approval letter—and filed it safely away in one of the many real estate folders that had started to pile up on my desk, so no one could snatch that victory away from me.

Now we could move forward and finalize the sale. We made the arrangements to sign the *acte de vente*, transferring the deed of the apartment to me and letting the bank know that we were finally ready to close. It was going to take Madame Bernachon a little more time to gather all the documents, incorporating the extra paperwork into what had grown into a stupendously thick dossier she had compiled for the apartment. It had been nearly ten months, and I was very ready for this to be finished, so I could get the keys to the apartment, do the renovations, then get cooking (and baking) again. I was excited to get going. It was finally time for the fun part to begin. I thought.

12

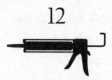

The kitchen was why I bought the place. Or I should say, the *potential* for a kitchen. It wasn't anywhere near what it could be, and I was constantly explaining to Romain how I intended to change it. Like Sicilians, who don't have a verb tense to describe the future, the French aren't so adept at imagining other possibilities. With soup plates that are only for soup and salad forks that can only be used for salads, the French get locked into how things *should* be, rather than seeing how they *could* be. That strategy is great for preserving the grandeur of the past, but hasn't been as successful for envisioning beyond the present.

The other difficulty was explaining that I wanted a kitchen with restaurant-style appliances. "But you're not opening a restaurant. Why would you want a restaurant-style kitchen?" baffled French friends asked when I told them what I was planning. It made about as much sense to them as a bodybuilder becoming the governor or an actor becoming president.

Once the walls come down, Romain will see it, I said to myself. I just had to wait a few more weeks until I got the keys.

In the meantime, I knew exactly where I wanted to start off: picking out the kitchen appliances. For years, I'd daydreamed over magazine spreads of French kitchens that were stone, barnlike spaces offering up sunbaked Provençal pottery bowls brimming with salty almonds and juicy green olives, platters of country ham and cheeses and a chilled bottle of pastis on the rustic stone counter, ready for *apéritif* hour. Time-worn gratin dishes and enameled casseroles lined the walls and rested on the shelf above the stove, ready to make a *daube* or *cassoulet*, and canisters held vintage whisks and wooden spoons, showing every bit of their age. The look was completed by an oversized farmhouse sink with salad greens and radishes resting in a colander alongside, still glistening from being rinsed under a spigot that ran *chaud* and *froid*.

On the other end were the very modern kitchens, well suited to the angularity of the sharp-edged design magazines, immaculate *cuisines* with fingerprint-free stainless-steel appliances and filtered light coming in through floor-to-ceiling windows that make everyone look like those effortlessly chic French people you read about, and aspire to be but probably won't. (Don't worry—a lot of them don't make it there, either.) On the wall is a lineup of sleek pots and pans with their lids in descending order next to them, and a concrete-slab bar, where you enjoy your morning shot of *café* from the machine seamlessly integrated into the wall of handle-less cabinets, sipping it while wearing a spa-white cotton terry bathrobe, accompanied by crumb-free—and nowadays, gluten-free—toast.

A country-style kitchen tugged at my cooking roots, having cooked at Chez Panisse, where legs of lamb roasted over an open fire and fruits were baked in actual Provençal pottery. The contemporary appealed to my OCD nature, wanting everything in a kitchen to be in precisely the right place, so the saucepan, scale, and stand mixer were exactly where I expected them to be when I needed them.

I decided that my new kitchen would combine the best of both, although I know from experience that there is no way to organize gadget drawers or pot lids, no matter how many online articles—accompanied by kitchen drawers with baskets for holding and organizing your garlic, onions, and shallots; racks for alphabetizing your spices; and a special shelf on hinges that lets you slide away your stand mixer to free up that valuable counter space—promise otherwise. (Or how much you remind your partner that if your measuring spoons aren't exactly in the place you expect them to be, that's grounds for divorce.)

I didn't want a designer kitchen with colorful jars of peppers packed in oil on the shelves, never meant to be opened, or racks of copper pots and pans that were too good to use. I wanted a kitchen to cook in, professionally equipped, but not over the top. I didn't require a wok burner or a wine refrigerator, but needed a kitchen counter that was more generous than one found in the standard Parisian kitchen, big enough to cook on while taking notes alongside, a gas stove, an oven that kept consistent heat for baking and recipe testing, and, most of all—a decidedly un-French touch—a large refrigerator.

The French don't rely on refrigeration as much as Americans do, and it's not uncommon for people to leave leftover roast chicken or *daube de bœuf* on the counter overnight—or in the kitchen cabinet, on the reasoning that it's somehow cooler. (Never mind that if it is, it's likely 1 or 2 degrees cooler, at most.) My in-laws kept the milk on the ledge outside the kitchen window overnight, even in the withering heat of summer, reasoning, "It's cooler out there."

"Yes," I tried to explain, "but do you know that it's even cooler in your refrigerator?" I decided not to bring up what could happen in your future if you drank milk, or ate food, that wasn't properly refrigerated, and took my coffee black when we visited.

In my current kitchen, the stove was so tightly wedged into the tiny space that the heat from the gas burners melted the plastic of the dishwasher on one side and charred the composite sink on the other, with black, alligator-like scales that resembled licorice Chiclets. Whenever I touched the metal on my electric stand mixer or blender, an electric buzz ran through my fingers and vibrated all the way up to my shoulder joint. I'd replaced the dishwasher, which shook my apartment so violently the first time I used it, I felt like I was still in the earthquake zone of San Francisco; I pulled the plug as glass mixing bowls and jars of jam and mustard traveled across the counters and shelves of the trembling kitchen, teetering to the edge just before I caught them.

My dinky oven was brand-new, but only because the handle on the previous one broke and there wasn't a brand name or serial number on the oven, or even in the instruction booklet either, which stumped me ... and every guy at each oven-parts supply store that I went to in Paris. So I ended up having to buy a whole new oven. Suffice it to say, I was looking forward to cooking and baking in a kitchen with decent appliances, ones that wouldn't shock, burn, bruise, or confuse.

You never feel more American than when you leave America. But I've learned that nothing makes you feel more American than being faced with a European appliance. Shopping for European appliances required learning not only a new vocabulary, but also changing your expectations of what a machine is capable of. My washing machine in America had a dial that you turned to choose the cycle and water temperature. A button next to it said "On/Off." And that was it—I thought it was sufficient.

Until I moved to France, I never knew so many washing options existed. With various dials and knobs that not only let you choose the water temperature, but pick a spin speed, add an extra rinse cycle, or even select the "easy iron" option, which I found out is necessary (the hard way) because Europeans do a lot of ironing, for a couple of reasons. One is to keep a neat personal appearance, but a reader who moved to Greece told me her doctor recommended she iron everything she wore, even her underwear. She didn't tell me why, and I didn't ask.

My washing machine offered a *prélavage* option, and I couldn't think of a reason why you'd want to prewash clothes before you wash them. There was also a "sport" cycle, which, for the *non sportif*, maybe gave their clothes a workout? The washing machine in my apartment also had an "emergency" button . . . I never figured out what it did. Good thing I never had a laundry emergency, but it was reassuring to know it was there if I needed it.

The dishwasher was even more mystifying. I needed to consult a dictionary to figure out all the puzzling dials and cycles just to run a load of dishes and glasses through it. Unfortunately, after the first, earthshaking time I used it, it ground to a halt the second time I turned it on. (In contrast to a laundry emergency, to a cookbook author/recipe tester, a broken dishwasher qualifies as an emergency.) Why it broke down was a mystery to me, until I saw that the insides of the machine and tubes were caked with the salty *calcaire* of Paris, the calcium deposits that not only permanently fog over your wineglasses with a hazy white mist, but also cause dishwashers—and radiators, washing machines, shower-heads, irons, and anything else that requires water—to seize up and die. I also learned that the mineral-rich water gives your clothing razor-sharp edges if you iron them. (They must not have a calcium problem in Greece. Otherwise—ouch!)

I eventually got the hang of my machines, but even European refrigerators can be tricky for some people. A couple I know who rent out their Paris apartment when they're out of town came home to find the refrigerator door ripped off the hinges. The renter left a note explaining that he couldn't figure out which side of the door to pull to open, so he must have just decided to go for the whole thing.

The hot water heater in my current rooftop apartment also had a *calcaire* problem, and the calcium-clogged pipes only eked out just enough tepid water for me to rinse myself rapidly, before the water went back to the temperature of melted snow. Eventually, a well-fed plumber came by to run some sort of acid through the pipes. Despite his girth, he was able to climb into my deep bathtub to check the dripping spigot, then climbed out to check the hot water heater while I stayed in the bathroom. While he was in the kitchen tinkering with the hot water heater, a blast of gray water suddenly came rushing from the spigot, and the thick, crusty, saucer-size hard water stain under the water spout (which had resisted my many attempts to remove it with a hammer and chisel) dislodged immediately into a pile of dust, and swirled away down the drain, leaving not even the slightest trace in its wake. I was pretty sure he wasn't running one of those "green" cleaning solutions through the pipes.

After the plumber finished off the dish of homemade ice cream I served him (which I later learned was the best way to assure that he'd return; I was his favorite customer, he later told me), he warned, "Don't drink any water from the faucet for three days." If you want to know why the French are the seventh largest consumers of bottled water in the world, that may be your answer. After seeing what whatever it was did to that stain, I didn't drink water from my tap for the next three years.

I was relieved that my rental apartment at least had a washing machine, albeit one that had too many qualifications for the job. Before I moved in, I scrutinized the pictures of the apartment the owner had sent me, but didn't see a dryer. I sent a message to him, and he responded by e-mail: "There is no dryer. People don't have dryers in Paris. They use drying racks."

That seemed quaint to me at the time. I thought, *Oh, how charming! I'll be living in Paris, like a Parisian, drying my clothes just like the old days . . . à l'ancienne*, imagining myself in my rooftop apartment, waving to *madame* across the way as we both hung out our clothes to dry in the breezy sunshine of Paris, with the Eiffel Tower in the background. Afterward, I'd head down to the local café for a *p'tit crème* and banter with the waiters while my blue-and-white-striped mariner shirts and stiff linen sheets flapped in the sunlight, drying on the roof.

After clipping my first load of laundry on the rack outside my apartment, I headed out for that coffee. A screeching voice from behind stopped me. It was the *gardienne*, scolding me for hanging clothes outside the building to dry, and I had to go back and pull them all down. According to the rules, I was told, it's forbidden to hang laundry outside. Everything needed to come back in.

————

When French friends heard I was getting a dryer, they had only two words for me: *très américain*. But I was tired of my apartment looking *très Naples* with laundry hanging from every window, railing, and doorknob, and I was spending hours a week washing and drying my clothes. I ironed what was necessary in what little space I had. Once, when I just didn't feel like dragging out the ironing board yet again, I took the iron to my shirt while I was wearing it . . . and spent the next week explaining to people how I got an upside-down V-shaped burn on my neck.

Appliance shopping is the fun part of renovating. Appliances fill you with hope. They're not just machines; a refrigerator isn't just a place to keep things cold. I am at one with my refrigerator, and live and breathe everything that's in it. As a chef and baker, I know exactly which dairy product is in there, and where, and how long it has got left to live (certainly longer than it would have if it were left out on the windowsill, no matter what anyone else says). I keep track of which eggs are from a local farm and best for poaching or using for mayonnaise, and which are from the grocery store, to be used more indiscriminately, as I crack through the few dozen per day testing cake and ice cream recipes.

I've got bags of citrus stored in the refrigerator drawers, telepathically aware of how much, and what kind, is in each; if I find rinds in the garbage, I know Romain has used one of the last lemons and mentally add them to my shopping list to get more tomorrow. The racks inside the doors hold repurposed wine bottles, filled to various degrees with all sorts of fruit syrups, elixirs, and homemade *apéritifs* infused with cherry leaves and bitter oranges; half-finished bottles of wine in there will either go to poaching fruit or, more likely, to accompany lunch.

Because many Parisian apartments don't have space for a full-size refrigerator and thrifty French people are happy with lower electricity bills, refrigerators in France are smaller than those in the States. It's not uncommon to see people (or even families) living with the kind of refrigerator you had in your college dorm: great for keeping a few six-packs of Pabst cold, but not much else.

We hadn't signed the final papers for the apartment, but I was already digging through websites, fantasizing over the gorgeous French ovens that were available, and a dryer, so my towels wouldn't make me feel like I was drying myself with a sheet of matzoh after a shower.

But when I clicked through pages of refrigerators, I saw something that made my heart skip so many beats that I worried my bank's worst fears were going to come true. After I saw it, I could not get it out of my mind and had to have it.

My potential new refrigerator was in a class by itself. It had huge double doors and a pull-out freezer underneath. If you live in the United States, you are probably flipping to the recipe at the end of this chapter right now, but in Paris, a large freezer is a Very Big Deal. Especially for me, who wrote an ice cream book with a freezer the size of a bread box.

What started out as just poking around to see what was out there (I mean, we hadn't even signed the closing papers yet) quickly became an obsession, as I scanned through pages and pages of European appliance catalogs and on-line stores. But there's nothing like seeing new appliances in person. It took quite a bit of sleuthing to find a place in Paris where I could actually see the refrigerator *de mes rêves,* which I finally found at Darty, an electronics store wedged in a passage between the Louvre and the Seine. Darty is popu-lar because of the rows and rows of electronics and appli-ances on display in their showrooms. But they're also known for their *service clients,* which means they actually show up when they say they are going to and will let you return something within fifteen days. (Which Americans may also be yawning at. But in France, that's also a Very Big Deal.) And I know they mean it: At the beginning of winter one year, I bought a space heater at Darty to take the chill off my glacial apartment. When it stopped working shortly after I bought it, I returned it to the store, and true to their word, they took it back and fixed it. It took a while, but by June, I was wheeling the repaired heater back to my apartment.

On the pretense of going to take more measurements or see if the refrigerator handles were really as perfectly molded to my hands as I had remembered them to be, I'd hop on the *métro* to visit the store, where I had mentally constructed a shrine around my refrigerator. I'd stand in front of it, with my hands on the two brushed-metal handles that curved down the front, which were good in case I ever decided to rent my place out: visitors could have their choice of opening either door, no removal necessary. Grasping the pair of smoothly polished metal tubes, I'd carefully pull the handles until I felt the gentle release of pressure as they lifted away from the rubber door gaskets with only the barest trace of resistance, like a sigh. Once I had the doors fully open, I'd inspect (and reinspect) the glass-front drawers, sliding them in and out, and running my hands over the pristine rimmed, glass shelves that didn't have so much as a dried raspberry seed or a stuck-on stain of red wine wedged between the metal strips that framed them in. If there was an appliance that said "clean slate," this was it. Every time I pulled open those doors, I felt like I was opening a new chapter of my life in Paris, which no one was going to close on me, or rip off.

BEEF STEW WITH OLIVES

(Daube camarguaise)

SERVES 8

On my first day of French class, shortly after I arrived in Paris, our teacher went around the room and asked all of us what we missed most about our home countries. Nearly all of the Americans in the room said the same thing: "customer service" (although a few mentioned "ice," which I later found out my new refrigerator would provide me with).

Life in France is charmingly quaint to outsiders, which is why the country is such a popular tourist destination. The customs and *politesse* add a veneer of gentility, which causes Americans to remark upon how much they wish the United States were more like France. I couldn't agree more, although I'm not sure how long they would put up with no ice or indifferent customer service.

Another difference between the two cultures is our approach to hygiene. I've been a dinner guest and seen the host wash raw chicken in their sink, with its juices splattering everywhere, then fill the same sink basin with water and wash the salad in it. Yet outside of the kitchen, men are required to wear the skimpiest of Speedos or they'll be refused use of a public pool for *raisons d'hygiène*. I don't know about you, but I'd rather swim past someone wearing surfer-style swim trunks than eat a salad bathed in raw chicken juices.

Living in France, I've learned not to feel too self-conscious in a slingshot-like swimsuit, and I've also learned more about the regions of France and their respective cuisines. The Camargue is a part of France that's known for being *un peu sauvage*, a bit wild, with large marshes and open fields, where horses run free and flocks of pink flamingos stand around on spindly legs.

Adding green olives to beef stew is a *camarguaise* variation of *bœuf bourguignon*. They add a bright, briny contrast to the meltingly tender morsels of beef. To peel the fresh pearl onions, trim off the root ends of the onions, then drop them in boiling water for two minutes. Drain and plunge the onions into ice water, then slip off the peels. If pearl onions are not available, substitute small shallots.

3 pounds (1.3kg) beef chuck, trimmed of excess fat and cut into 2-inch cubes

Salt and freshly ground black pepper

6 springs fresh thyme

6 sprigs fresh parsley

2 dried or fresh bay leaves

3 cups (.75l) fruity red wine, such as Gamay, Burgundy, Beaujolais, or merlot

7 ounces (200g) thick-cut bacon, cut into rectangles (about 1½ cups)

Olive oil

2 carrots, cut into ½-inch (2cm) pieces

4 garlic cloves, minced

3 (1-inch/3cm-wide) strips orange peel, peeled with a vegetable peeler

1 tablespoon tomato paste

10 ounces (285g) pearl onions, peeled (see headnote)

2 tablespoons butter

12 ounces (340g) button mushrooms, quartered

1 cup (120g) pitted green olives

Beurre manié

> 1 tablespoon all-purpose flour
> 1 tablespoon butter

1. Put the beef in a large zip-top freezer bag. (You can also marinate the cubes in a large glass or stainless-steel bowl.) Sprinkle with 1 teaspoon salt and a few generous turns of pepper. Tie the thyme and parsley together with a piece of kitchen twine and add that to the bag. Add the bay leaves and wine. Push the excess air out of the bag and seal it. Refrigerate overnight. (I usually put the bag in a large bowl to avoid "accidents.")

2. The next day, set a colander over a large bowl and drain the beef, reserving the wine in the bowl as well as the herbs. Pat the meat all over with paper towels to absorb excess moisture.

3. In a Dutch oven or large lidded casserole, cook the bacon until it's just cooked through, but not crisp. If the pan looks dry as the bacon cooks, add a tablespoon or so of olive oil. (Commercial bacon throws off a lot of fat; artisan bacon doesn't.) Remove the bacon with a slotted spoon and drain on a paper towel–lined plate.

4. Drain the excess fat from the pot. Add the carrots, season with salt, and cook over medium heat until almost tender, about 10 minutes. Add the garlic during the last few minutes of cooking. Transfer the carrots and garlic to a large bowl.

5. Increase the heat to medium-high. Working in batches, add enough beef to the pot so the pieces are in a single layer with space around them. Don't crowd them or they'll steam instead of browning. Cook the beef, turning the pieces only when one side is well browned, until

they are well browned on all sides. Add a tablespoon or two of olive oil to the pan, if necessary, as you go. Transfer the beef to the bowl with the carrots and cook the rest of the beef.

6. While you're browning the last batch of beef, preheat the oven to 300°F (150°C).

7. When the last of the beef has been removed from the pot, pour about one-quarter of the reserved wine into the pot and use a flat utensil to scrape up the browned bits from the bottom. Add the rest of the wine, the herb bundle, bay leaves, beef, bacon, and carrots. Pour enough water into the pot so the beef chunks are just barely submerged, about 2 cups (500ml). Add the orange peel and tomato paste.

8. Cover the pot and put it in the oven. Cook for 1½ hours.

9. While the beef is cooking, put the pearl onions in a medium saucepan and add water to cover, and a big pinch of salt. With the lid ajar, simmer the onions until tender, about 15 minutes. Drain.

10. In a large skillet, heat 1 tablespoon olive oil and the butter over medium-high heat. When the butter starts to sizzle, add the mushrooms, season with salt and pepper, and cook, stirring occasionally, until the mushrooms are browned and cooked through.

11. After the beef stew has been in the oven for 1½ hours, add the pearl onions, mushrooms, and olives to the pot and stir them in. Cover and return the meat to the oven. Cook until the meat is tender, 1 to 1½ hours more. (The total cooking time will be 2½ to 3 hours.)

12. Remove the stew from the oven and set the pot on the stovetop. Bring the stew to a low boil.

13. Make the beurre manié: In a small bowl, mash together the flour and butter. Carefully remove the lid from the

pot and add the beurre manié, about 1 teaspoon at a time, stirring it into the liquid. (Be careful while you're doing this: remind yourself that the pot handles are still quite hot.) Once the beurre manié had been added, reduce the heat to maintain a simmer and cook, uncovered, until the juices have thickened slightly. Before serving, remove and discard the herb bundle and bay leaves, and taste, seasoning with additional salt if necessary.

14. Serve with wide noodles or *purée de pommes de terre*, which is economically (and efficiently) referred to as *purée* in France.

13

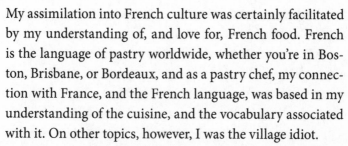

My assimilation into French culture was certainly facilitated by my understanding of, and love for, French food. French is the language of pastry worldwide, whether you're in Boston, Brisbane, or Bordeaux, and as a pastry chef, my connection with France, and the French language, was based in my understanding of the cuisine, and the vocabulary associated with it. On other topics, however, I was the village idiot.

When the discussion turned to politics or literature, I sat out conversations at dinner parties, nodding my head if someone happened to look in my direction, *faux*-fathoming that I was following along with the conversation. I understood maybe a sliver of what was being discussed, and usually my mind was wandering on to other topics, such as, what was going to be served for dessert?

But I was fluent in the history of croissants, baguettes, and *les macarons*. If the conversation was about the proper way to *enrober* chocolate or the technique of *fraisage*, incorporating the butter into pastry to make the flakiest *pâte brisée*, I would say to myself, with confidence, *Great. I've got this . . .* , and launch into a well-versed discussion on the topic. And in many instances, I knew even more about the varieties of fruits and vegetables at the markets than the French did, one of the bonuses of coming from San Francisco, where every peach, loaf of bread, bean of coffee, and stalk of kale had the variety and a producer's name attached to it. Food French came out of my mouth as easily as salted butter caramels and foie gras go into it.

Shortly after I started shopping for appliances, I realized that there was a unique vocabulary in French for each item I had to find for the apartment. Plumbing, electricity, lighting, cords, plugs, flooring, concrete, subflooring, paint, gas lines, drains, plaster, hand and power tools, as well as windows, doors, kitchen appliances and bathroom fixtures—each have their own very specific set of words. And they're not what you'd think they are.

Toilets aren't just *toilettes*. They're fixtures that *chassent d'eau*, although I'm not sure how they hunt (*chasser*) water (*eau*). Toilet seats are *lunettes*, which are also eyeglasses, although they are also called *abattants*, not to be confused with *abattoirs*, or slaughterhouses (which aren't exactly comfy places to sit).

A toothbrush is, naturally, a *brosse à dents*, a brush for your teeth. A brush for painting? That's not a *brosse à peinture*, but a *pinceau*, which has nothing to do with *pincer* (pinching). A *pince* is a pair of tongs, but could be pliers, which also pinch, like crabs, which also have *les pinces*. So be careful when someone offers to give you *pinces*; it might be a pair of tongs, or something you'll need to see your pharmacist to get rid of.

The *buanderie* is a utility room, not to be confused with a *bavererie*, which would be a place where people drool, a gaffe I made that left an architect wondering if Americans had rooms in their homes devoted to salivating.

For appliances, such as my beloved *réfrigérateur*, it's a fairly straightforward translation, although the French refer to it as *le frigo* or *le frigidaire*, even if it's made by Bosch,

Electrolux, or my favorite appliance brand, Candy (made by Hoover, an English word that describes what I sound like when I consume French chocolates, so at least there's some logic to it all). But confusingly, a double-door refrigerator in France is a *réfrigérateur américain*, whereas in America they're called French-door refrigerators. Like French-cut green beans, French kissing, French vanilla, French breakfast radishes, French's mustard, French's French-fried canned onions, French toast, and oddly orange French dressing, re-frigerator doors have been Frenchified to make them sound more alluring, even if, like the "French" foods I've just men-tioned, they don't exist in France. (The radishes do, but I've never met anyone in France who eats radishes for breakfast.)

A stove can be a *table de cuisson*, a *plaque à gaz*, a *cui-sinière*, a *piano*, or even a *châtelaine* ("lady of the house-hold"). Unlike a *frigidaire*, which produces frigid air, a *hotte* doesn't make things hotter—it's a hood fan that removes heat. So a *hotte* makes things cooler.

An oven is a *four*, even if it's just one. It can also be a *cui-sinière*, which is just like a stove, but different . . . somehow. And a *four* can morph into a *fourneau*, which isn't one of those goofy oven-dishwasher combos (*four* = "oven," *eau* = "water") with a dishwasher in the space underneath where the broiler would be. In my compact kitchen, I saw what hap-pens when a stove gets too close to a dishwasher and could only imagine what would happen if they were fused together as one.

A washing machine is a *lave-linge* (clothes washer), which makes sense, as does the *sèche-linge* (clothes dryer), but the dubious washer-dryer mash-up is the lengthy *lave-linge séchant*, also known as a *lavante-séchante*, for reasons that perplex me almost as much as why anyone would buy one, since I've never heard anything but complaints about them from visitors renting short-term apartments, who've almost missed their return flights waiting the several days it took for their clothes to dry.

A stand-alone dishwasher is a *lave-vaisselle*, and some are *encastrables*, or built-in. Others are *intégrables*, which are also—confusingly—built-in. When I first had a sales-woman ask me if I was looking for a *castrable* machine, as a man I winced at the idea, but relaxed when I learned it was a freestanding machine that washes dishes, not something that would raise my voice a few octaves.

I spent weeks hunkered down with dictionaries, study-ing in preparation for my visits to appliance and hardware stores. When friends asked if I wanted to meet for drinks, they didn't believe it when I told them I had to stay in and work on appliance and hardware terminology. But I didn't want to end up with a machine capable of doing a *castré* in my *cuisine*, and I knew the ultimate final exam was coming: remodeling. And I needed to bone up on my vocabulary.

———

To make things more challenging, always-busy Parisians have a propensity for clipping words into apocopes. You need to train your ear in France, since apocopes require carefully listening when conversing with Parisians, espe-cially challenging because spoken French already cuts off the last part of almost every word. Already-shortened words get further clipped: Breakfast goes from the more leisurely *petit déjeuner*, which rolls off the tongue like a soft brioche spread with Normandy butter, to the frantic *p'tit déj*. A pleas-ant afternoon, an *après-midi*, becomes a less-poetic *aprèm*, which means if you are enjoying a café crème in the Place d'Italie, you're having *unp'titcrèmecetaprèmdansleplaced'it*, when spoken at the speed of a local. Those apocopes can make you *apoplectique*—or *ap'tic*.

And then there's the metric system, always a contentious topic between the United States and . . . well, the rest of the world. Baking across two continents, I've gotten good at mentally toggling back and forth between the two systems with savantlike speed, converting sizes of cake pans, cups of flour, and the dreaded sticks of butter (which freak out Europeans when they come across them in a recipe) to their global counterparts. When the French ask me why Americans still hold on to an imprecise measurement system, I remind them of French recipes that call for "half a wineglass of milk" or a cake measurement that asks for a *cuillère à soupe* of baking powder. My measuring tablespoons are all the same size— but my spoons for *soupe* vary considerably, as do my glasses of wine, which range in volume depending on what kind of day I've had.

The one part of the French language that vexes even those who speak French fluently are numbers. But I don't feel so bad about those, because even the French get confused by them, too. When people leave messages in my voicemail with phone numbers, I ending up handing the phone to Romain to unravel the lengthy string of digits they've rattled off. He looks just as puzzled as I do, and I feel less like a dolt when he has to listen to the message four or five times (albeit versus my ten or twelve) to figure out the numbers.

Smaller numbers like eighteen, which is *dix-huit* (10 + 8), are easy. Even the more laborious ninety-seven, or *quatre-vingt-dix-sept* (4 × 20 + 10 + 7), has become close to second nature to me. And by necessity, I had to figure out a conclusive way of differentiating between *douze heures* and *deux heures*, as both are pronounced nearly the same way with the liaison: *doozeure* versus *dœzeure*. I was two hours late for my first lunch date with Romain, arriving at two P.M. rather than twelve P.M. Now when we're supposed to meet at noon, I say *midi*, and when it's two o'clock, I'll emphasize that by using my hands (Italian-style), holding two fingers up in front of the poor guy's face.

My greatest challenge with numbers was coming up: I soon found myself standing in the middle of the crowded aisles of a hardware or appliance store, trying to calculate how much grout I needed, or deciding between a dishwasher that is 84.5 × 60 × 60 centimeters, which comes out as *quatrevingtquatrevirgulecinqparsoixanteparsoixante*, or the one that the salesperson told me was 50 × 68 × 90 centimeters, or *cinquanteparsoixantehuitparquatrevingtdix*, which I had to go home to think about. Fortunately, I have plenty of wineglasses on hand, which, like appliances and fixtures in France, come in a variety of dimensions and sizes, although I have to admit, the largest ones seem to get the most use.

APPLE MAPLE TARTE TATIN

Tarte Tatin au sirop d'érable

SERVES 8

One of the most beloved of all French pastries is tarte Tatin, an upside-down caramelized apple tart that requires little expertise in baking but a measure of patience while the apples cook. I love when people bring me jugs of maple syrup, but the French are constantly wondering what to do with the bottles of *sirop d'érable* their American friends bring them. Since they don't eat pancakes or waffles, or douse "French" toast (page 75) with the stuff, they're not quite sure what to do with it when gifted a bottle.

Here I pair it with caramelized apples, a perfect Franco-American alliance that I first discovered at Des Gâteaux et du Pain, an elegant bakery presided over by pastry chef Claire Damon. My version hones closer to the original than the decidedly more upscale individual tartlets on display in her shop, which are so pretty, you'll want to take a picture. (But don't, as it's forbidden. Which I learned the hard way.)

Golden Delicious apples reliably hold their shape when cooked and don't exude too much juice, which results in a deeply caramelized round of apples on top of the buttery crust. If you prefer another apple that has similar qualities, feel free to use it. You might think all the apples called for won't fit in the pan, but trust me, they will. Or as the French would say, "*Pas de problème.*" But in this case, it's the truth.

Dough

> 1 cup (140g) all-purpose flour
>
> 1 tablespoon sugar
>
> ¼ teaspoon salt
>
> 4 tablespoons (4 ounces/60g) unsalted butter, cut into cubes and chilled
>
> 3 tablespoons (45ml) ice water

Fruit

> 2 tablespoons unsalted butter
>
> ⅓ cup (60g) packed light brown sugar (or half light brown and half dark brown sugar)

¼ cup (60ml) dark amber pure maple syrup
Pinch of salt
8 medium Golden Delicious apples (about 4 pounds/1.8kg)

Crème fraîche or vanilla ice cream, for serving

1. Make the dough: In the bowl of a stand mixer fitted with the paddle attachment, mix the flour, sugar, and salt together. Add the butter and mix until the butter pieces are the size of corn kernels. Add the ice water and mix until the dough comes together. Gather the dough with your hands and shape it into a disk. Wrap it in plastic wrap and chill for at least 1 hour.

2. In a 10-inch (25cm) cast-iron skillet, heat the butter, brown sugar, maple syrup, and salt. When the butter starts to bubble, cook, stirring gently, for 30 seconds. Remove from the heat and set aside.

3. Peel, quarter, and core the apples. Arrange them in the pan, rounded side down, in concentric circles. Pack them in tightly—*pas de problème*—they'll cook down considerably.

4. Place the pan on the stovetop and cook over medium heat for about 25 minutes, until the juices below the apples thicken.

5. Preheat the oven to 375°F (190°C).

6. On a lightly floured countertop, roll the dough into a 12-inch (30cm) circle. Trim the edges with a knife so they're neat and drape the dough over the apples in the pan. Tuck the edges of the dough between the edge of the skillet and the apples.

7. Bake the tart until the pastry has browned, about 40 minutes. Remove from the oven and invert a serving plate or baking sheet over the pan. Being very careful of

any hot juices that may spill out, quickly and surely flip the pan and the plate (or baking sheet) over together, making sure to tilt the pan away from you (so the juices don't land on you) to unmold the tart. If any apples have stuck to the pan, reunite them with the tart.

8. Serve warm or at room temperature with crème fraîche or vanilla ice cream. (If you want to increase the maple flavor, you can brush it with a little more maple syrup just before serving.)

14

Finally, after all that had unraveled between when I first signed the contract for the apartment and the final transferring of the deed over to me, it was time to close the deal. On one of the first bitterly cold days of winter, I found myself back in the *notaire*'s office with Monsieur Legrand, and his agent, to finish up. People I passed on the way to her office from the *métro* station were bundled up, rushing to appointments or huddling in doorways, pulling on their cigarettes as hard as possible so they could finish them and get back to the warmth inside. My fingers were already getting numb inside my gloves by the time I arrived.

We took our seats around the table in Madame Bernachon's warm office, with her in her usual position at the head of the table. An icy mist glazed over the windows of the conference room, giving the impression that we were sealed in with no way out. (Which was a good thing so maybe everyone would stay put for the final signing.) Monsieur Legrand, and his agent, wearing his perpetual grin, were seated right next to each other on the same side of the table, but were no longer on speaking terms. At last, there was finally something Monsieur Legrand and I had in common: I didn't want to talk to his agent, either.

Romain had joined us because he thought I could use the

support. We've only had a couple of fights in all our years together, although like most Frenchmen, he's capable of displaying a hot temper in situations that a timid American might casually let slide, to avoid conflict. I've seen the little fellow rip into someone—a bureaucrat or a customer service agent—with a ferocity that startled me. Well, it did the first few times. Now I sit back and watch in admiration. (I'm surprised he doesn't have a TV show in France. He'd be a nationwide sensation.)

Being pushy is something that took me a while to get used to, because it's not in my nature. With service in France sometimes at a *minimum*, though, if you're not getting the response or help you want, you've got to prod and push—sometimes hard—to get what you need. We also start off on a decidedly different foot: Americans go into situations expecting things to go well. When they don't, we have meltdowns. The French go into situations expecting things not to go in their favor, so they're prepared when they don't. That way, things can only get better. I had a lot to learn.

Even though I try to assume the best of people, I had been alarmed by the questionable counteroffer that had arrived and then abruptly vanished almost as soon as it appeared. And resentment over the extra work and expenses I'd incurred because the apartment had been incorrectly listed as a residential space had been stewing within me for the past few months. I was pretty upset about it, especially because neither Monsieur Legrand nor his agent had helped out at all. But most of all, I resented that neither of them had taken responsibility for the error. An apology would have been nice. A check to help pay for the architect would have been even nicer. But that would have assumed they were going to take responsibility. *"C'est pas ma faute."*

I came to the final signing armed with a stack of filled-out and signed checks to pay for everything I was responsible for. This included the *frais d'agence*, the agent's fee for the transaction, the largest check in the folder. Madame Bernachon glanced over her glasses at me in between reading through the paragraphs of the sales contract to us. Her eyes turned steely when she addressed those on the other side of the table, letting them know that any *cinéma*—as the French would say when someone creates drama—wouldn't be tolerated. Both sat there, the agent smiling and biding his time as if nothing out of the ordinary had happened, and the seller's gaze darting at various places around the room, trying to avoid eye contact with anyone else. I did my best to listen, and couldn't wait for it to be over. Once all the paperwork was signed, the apartment would finally be mine, nearly ten months after I first stepped inside of it. That had to be some sort of record.

The stony silence between the seller and his agent continued. I'd been simmering in my chair while Monsieur Legrand made sure the rest of us knew of his displeasure through a series of grimaces and studiously avoiding looking at any of us.

When Madame Bernachon got to the part in the contract with a list of payments and their amounts, I took out the checks for the taxes and *notaire* fees and handed them to her. The substantial check for the agent was the last one in the folder. It was time to give him his.

Pulling the check out of the folder, I looked at all the zeros—not the two on the other side of the table, but on the check—and I couldn't do it. Everything simmering inside me suddenly bubbled up and burst to the surface.

I refused to hand the check over. It didn't feel right rewarding someone who hadn't done his job well, especially someone I hadn't even hired in the first place. The agent's

smile cracked just the tiniest bit when I said I wasn't paying him. He looked at me, then over at Madame Bernachon.
Her job was to be impartial, so she couldn't really say anything, but I could tell that if it were up to her, he would have
been walking out of there empty-handed. And if she truly
had the power of France behind her, she would had brought
back the guillotine just for this one last time. I told him the
apartment had been misrepresented and it took a lot of work
and money to rectify this error. I didn't bring up the disappearing counteroffer because it seemed so outlandish, like a
prank a twelve-year-old would play. But he kept his cool, he
was a pro.

"*Malheureusement . . .*" he replied, trying to appear un-
ruffled, ". . . *mais, c'est pas possible.*"

I knew that I was obligated to pay him, but decided to
draw this out as long as I could to make *them* uncomfortable,
for a change. Monsieur Legrand became even further agi-
tated by the delay and had started working himself into such
a state that I thought he might need a medic. He was *ap'tic.*

As a Frenchman, Romain would have started off on a
completely different footing with them months ago; not only
would he have refused to pay for anything, but he would've
reprimanded them and made sure they knew that what they
had done wasn't just *pas correct*, but was wrong. I was at a
cultural disadvantage and didn't want to make a fuss, so I
had capitulated quickly, doing whatever I could to move the
sale forward, just so we could close and I'd get the apartment. I stood my ground, saying that he should at least take
less, to cover what I had spent.

"*C'est pas possible*, Monsieur Lebovitz. I cannot accept
less than what is my commission," the agent repeated.

"After all the problems you caused, and the money you

cost me? It's not right what you did. *C'est pas correct.*" I gathered up my courage to lobby back at him. *Pas correct* doesn't
quite mean the same thing in French as it does in English. It
literally means "not right," but at the same time, critiques a
person's values—even if they don't have any. Telling someone in France that they did something that was not *correct*
is an affront to their honor, almost as severe as being told
they're *mal élevé*, or "badly raised."

After some discussion, the agent agreed to call his boss
and ask him if they could lower the commission. He sat back
in his chair and dialed a number on his phone, then started
discussing it with his boss. He carefully explained the situation, and they went back and forth about whether it would
be possible to reduce it. While the conversation was going
on, Madame Bernachon looked at him, then at me. I looked
at him, too, then back at her. We both saw the same thing:
The screen on his phone wasn't lit up. He was carrying on a
conversation with himself.

When he hung up, or pretended to, he wrinkled his brow
in an attempt to express concern and gave me the bad news.
"*Désolé*, Monsieur Lebovitz, it's *pas possible* for us to reduce
the commission."

He didn't look very *désolé*, but the *notaire* looked like
she'd be delighted to make him feel sorry. She called me into
the next room and said that she was *choqué*, but that I didn't
really have a choice.

Taking a deep breath, I followed her back into the room,
sat down, opened my folder, and reluctantly handed over the
check—careful to avoid making eye contact, because I didn't
want to see him savoring his victory over me. He pocketed
the check with a grin so big, I could feel the fluorescent lights
reflecting off his teeth without even looking up. He quickly

said *au revoir* before grabbing his coat and hustling out the door and on to his next mark. I mean, his next client.

Once all the papers were signed, the worst was over. Now I would get going on renovating the apartment so I could move in and return to my sweet life in Paris. Except . . .

Before it was a done deal, Madame Bernachon told me Monsieur Legrand asked for a few extra days to move in to his new place, which wasn't yet ready. (I wondered, was it because he kept walking out of those meetings, too?) As a kind of insurance, she was going to be holding back a six-figure amount from the sale. Being easygoing, I thought I would be a nice guy and let him stay on without the seemingly excessive deposit.

"Oh—*non. Non, non, non* . . ." she told *l'Américain.* "If he decides not to leave, you'll have to go through the eviction process. It's December, and in France, you can't evict anyone during winter months, so you'd have to wait until June to begin that. And even then, it can take months to get someone out . . ." Seeing how the last ten months had gone, I agreed with her—*pas de question.*

CERVELLE DE CANUTS

SERVES 4 TO 6 AS AN APPETIZER

Parisians are bolder than they look, although they're timid when it comes to spicy or pungent foods. They tend to favor herbs rather than spices. This pugnacious spread is from

Lyon, a city that once had a thriving silk industry, and one story says that it was named "silk-worker's brain" by upper-class people in the nineteenth century, who turned their noses up at the garlicky-smelling spread that the lowly silk workers (*canuts*) enjoyed.

No matter where you are, or your social standing, if you like garlic and herbs, this spread is terrific smeared on rustic bread for a *tartine*—an open-faced sandwich, perhaps with thin-sliced radishes, avocado, sliced tomatoes, ham, or smoked fish on the top. It also make a nice dip for crudités. If you can't find chervil, which is less available elsewhere than it is in France, substitute an additional tablespoon of fresh tarragon in its place.

2 cups (500g) fromage blanc or plain Greek yogurt

3 tablespoons minced shallots or scallions

2 tablespoons finely chopped fresh flat-leaf parsley

2 tablespoons finely chopped fresh chives (or extra scallion greens)

1½ tablespoons finely chopped fresh tarragon

1 tablespoon finely chopped fresh chervil

1 large garlic clove, minced

2 teaspoons olive oil, plus more if needed

1 teaspoon red wine vinegar, plus more if needed

1 teaspoon kosher salt or sea salt, plus more if needed

½ teaspoon freshly ground black pepper

1. Line a mesh strainer with cheesecloth, set the strainer over a deep bowl, and scrape the fromage blanc into the strainer. Refrigerate for 4 hours.

2. Remove from the refrigerator and transfer the strained fromage blanc to a bowl. You should have about 1½ cups

(375g). (Discard any liquid that gathered under the strainer.)

3. Stir the shallots, parsley, chives, tarragon, chervil, garlic, olive oil, vinegar, salt, and pepper into the fromage blanc. Taste and adjust the flavors, adding more olive oil, vinegar, and/or salt, as desired.

15

With the keys almost in hand, I had already gotten a jump-start on the renovation. I'd already been scoping out appliances. Nothing could sway me from that French-door, American-style (or vice-versa) refrigerator, and I decided to keep the oven and stove that were already in the apartment, since they were a well-known French brand, but also get a larger one that would fit a standard, American-size baking sheet, which won't fit into most European ovens. Believe me, I've tried.

The jury was still out on the dryer. *Maybe I don't really need a dryer . . .* I pondered. I mean, most Parisians do without one. Part of me felt, if I was going to live in Paris (and I'd just paid a handsome price to do so), I should live like a real Parisian. People pay good money to live like a local for a week in Paris. And here I was, squandering a chance to do just that.

So I decided not to get a dryer for my new apartment.

"Are you insane?" said Laura, an American friend who's lived in Paris for over twenty years.

Maybe I was hanging on to the fantasy of being a true Parisian a little too much. I had already gotten used to European washing machines that have four-hour wash cycles, versus their American counterparts that will do a load in

thirty to forty minutes, something I was never able to figure out. Is it because Europeans like to relax and linger over
the finer things in life? I doubt washing your socks is one of
those finer things. But I reconsidered putting a dryer back on
my list of appliances, so I'd have more time to enjoy the finer
things in life, instead of spending it on drying clothes.

———

My new apartment was fairly large by Paris standards—
nearly 80 square meters, including the basement *cave*, about
850 square feet total. I'd downsized substantially before
moving to Paris years earlier, spending months getting rid
of almost everything I owned before I left, arriving with
just a few suitcases. I vowed not to amass so much stuff
ever again and not cram my small apartment with clothes,
kitchenware, and cookbooks, and would only have the es-
sentials in my new, simplified life. I wouldn't even have a
stand mixer.

I started off with one bookshelf where I kept a few guide-
books and two or three cookbooks. By the time I moved a
decade later, I had ten sagging shelves crammed with cookbooks. I not only had three stand mixers, but a blender, a
food processor, an espresso maker, and two ice cream machines in my apartment. (I had also cultivated a collection
of French cookware that rivaled that of any of the stores in
Les Halles.)

Now here I was, starting over again, again, and I didn't
know if I wanted to begin filling my new apartment with
extraneous stuff that I didn't really need, especially a clothes
dryer. I considered the hybrid *lave-linge-séchant*, the single
machine that washes your clothes, then dries them in the

same drum. I was still skeptical, but heard they'd gotten better over the years.

When I asked a French friend how she liked hers, one of the newer models, she told me she was overjoyed with it, exclaiming in superlative terms how well it worked. When she saw that I didn't look convinced, she insisted I come over to see for myself. I arrived a few days later, just as her machine was finishing up. She opened the door and pulled out a few items, handing them to me, "See, see . . . *Daveed*?" she said, as I felt the clothes. "Everything is *complètement* dry!"

I squeezed a shirt, which was so wet that water was already dripping onto the floor from it. When I questioned how completely *sec* the soggy clothes were, she answered, "Well . . . of course, you have to iron everything . . ."

I couldn't imagine myself ironing everything, Greek-style, but the deal sealer (or deal breaker, in my case) happened during one of my many trips to Darty to visit my refrigerator. I took a stroll down the aisles of washer-dryers and asked a saleswoman about the combination machines, telling her I'd heard that the newer generation of washer-dryer combos were much better than the old ones.

"*Mais oui, monsieur!*" she responded, with enthusiasm the French usually reserve for when it's close to mealtime. "*Bien sûr, ça marche très bien!*" ("Yes, of course, they work very well.")

As we chatted further, she suddenly stopped talking, tilted her head, and looked a little closer at me. "*Vous êtes . . . américain?*"

"*Oui, je suis américain,*" I answered.

"Oh, *non* . . ." she replied, backing up and wagging her index finger at me. ". . . *Non, non.* Do *not* get one of these machines. You definitely won't like it."

Based on her advice, I decided to get a separate dryer and

went home to continue packing cartons in preparation for my move; there were lots of files and plenty of books still to go. I was boxing up kitchen utensils I knew I wouldn't be needing through the winter, and folded up some of the clothes I'd hung to dry around my apartment, to put into boxes, too, hoping they were going to be some of the last loads that I'd be drying *à l'ancienne*—the old-fashioned way.

———

The DIY food movement that swept America, à la Brooklyn and Portland, never made it to Paris, because Parisians are content to leave making sausages, cheese, and beer; raising chickens; and even baking macarons to the pros. Traditionally in France, people who became bread bakers or worked in butcher shops started working in their trades when they were fifteen years old. In some cases, it was because they were expected to be part of the family business. In others, it was because they didn't have the aptitude for a more elite career. (Which is a polite way to say they didn't do well on the *bac*, the standardized test every high school student in France takes that determines their future employment possibilities.) Baking was considered manual labor, and few people aspired to wake up at 2 A.M. and stand on their feet for hours, kneading and shaping loaves of bread, while the rest of the village slept soundly. I tried it for one night at Acme Bread bakery in Berkeley and that was enough. (I never complained about the price of bread again.)

The idea of building a home kitchen that resembles a restaurant didn't have the same appeal in France as it does in America. Parisians didn't aspire to be chefs, setting up *fumoirs* (smokers) on their terraces or sheeting puff pastry for croissants. That is, until *MasterChef France* first aired in 2010, and a several-year surge of interest followed, with over-wrought appetizers served in Asian soup spoons and diners forced to cut steaks on slabs of scratchy slate. My guess is that the attraction wore off when people found out that real chefs worked more than thirty-five hours a week.

I was no longer a working chef, but my line of work as a cookbook author involves having a reliable home oven that will fit various sizes of baking sheets and cake pans without having to worry about fluctuating oven temperatures (or the door handle falling off). A full-size refrigerator was neces-sary: I had to keep lots of butter, milk, and cream in stock, and I kept a lot of things I made in there, including a freez-erful of ice cream, just in case I needed to get priority treat-ment from the plumber again.

It's common for major appliance companies to work with chefs and other professionals and offer reduced "VIP" prices. Since I had a Wolf range in America and liked it a lot, I in-quired with their distributor in France. They firmly replied that they don't do discounts. Their prices aren't listed on their French website, but I saw them on a British one and prices went up to 17,000 pounds, or $25,000. Perhaps the shipping had something to do with the eye-popping prices. Ameri-cans who live in Europe joke that the extra-baggage fees we pay to lug back corn tortillas, thick bath towels, pecans, and Reynolds Wrap are an "expat tax." But the only way I'd get a Wolf range over to Europe is if I took it over in pieces, over multiple trips.

I decided to try another well-known U.S. appliance com-pany that had opened a flashy showroom in Paris. Using a different tactic, I wrote to their representative in America, since they might be familiar with me. Yes! They were abso-lutely delighted to get my message! For weeks, e-mails flew back and forth between us, with me trying get prices nailed down and them trying to get me to confirm the number of tweets I would post about the oven. (Tweets and followers may be the new currency, but I was more comfortable just paying for the stove.) They came back with what they said was an extra-special price, which they would honor only for me—because I was so special. I felt very privileged when I got that e-mail, until I scrolled down and found out that my special VIP price for the hood to go over the stove was only $4,038. They added that the special price didn't include shipping or TVA (19.6% tax, or about $800), nor did it include the fan that goes in the hood, which was an additional $4,724, and also didn't include shipping or tax. I was learning why restaurant-style kitchens never took off in France.

I ended up getting all my appliances from an American appliance company that I like, which has a presence in France and promised me a 90cm (36-inch) professional-size oven (that would easily fit an American-size baking sheet) in exchange for doing a demonstration for them at a culinary show in Paris. They're considered *haute gamme* (at *haute* prices) in France, and were kind enough to offer me a generous discount on a dishwasher, too, and—yes!—my dream refrigerator, which they manufactured. They didn't ask me to do any social media cheerleading, and the deal sounded good to me. Nothing smelled fishy, yet.

16

Monsieur Legrand's additional three days in the apartment had passed. I thought it was rather gracious of me to let him have the extra time, especially after he flew into a rage just before we finished signing the final papers over a 43-euro electrical bill that he wanted me to pay because the closing date fell before he was actually leaving. It had been a few years since I last stayed at a hotel in Paris, and I suspected the same was true for Monsieur Legrand; if I hadn't been so accommodating, he would have found out that 43 euros was a pretty good deal for a three-night stay, which he was getting for free. But for some reason, I took out my checkbook and gave him the 43 euros . . . and said *au revoir* to him once and for all.

The grueling purchase period was finally over. It had been excruciating, and when I picked up the ring of keys at Madame Bernachon's office, it was a relief to finally feel the scratchy metal against my fingers. I headed straight to the apartment, where I worked one of the ancient keys into the front door lock, which jiggled like a baby tooth that if you fiddle with one too many times, will easily drop loose. I heaved the wooden door open and found myself standing in the middle of the apartment. It had been completely cleared of almost everything and I was able to take in the space without all the distractions, especially the human ones.

The heat had been cut off, and there was no temperature difference between the icy air outside and the chill within. It was as if the door and walls didn't exist. (The cracked and broken windows didn't help.) I pushed my bundled-up scarf higher around my neck as I looked around. The only hint of color in the place was the faded blue ceiling. My guess was that since they couldn't see the sky through the clouded-over windows, they came up with the idea of simulating one inside. Like many of the old cafés and bistros, the walls had likely once been painted white, but were stained with that familiar yellowy patina from smoke over the years. Bare wires stuck out of the walls in spidery bunches, and most of the outlets had been pulled from the walls by electrical cords no doubt being unceremoniously yanked out of them in the previous owner's haste to leave.

The carpet, which I hadn't paid much attention to, was matted and thin. I tried pulling up a corner but it was fused to the subfloor. All that was left in the bathroom was a roll of toilet tissue sitting on the counter with the last of a few wayward sheets of paper trailing off the side, which had not been worth the previous owner's effort to pack. (Although I'm sure it was a tough decision to leave it behind.) Lining the walls of the soon-to-go bathroom, as well as both walls leading down to the *cave*, were hundreds—no, thousands—of random postage-stamp-size pictures clipped from magazines and newspapers over the years, held firmly in place by staples that had rusted to the walls.

In spite of the grim condition of the apartment, it was the first time that I could get a really good look at it. After realizing the place was finally mine, my next instinct was to take a sledgehammer and knock everything down, starting with the walls to the bathroom that squeezed the kitchen into the corner. Next I'd have a go at the wall sealing off the dank *cave*, allowing fresh air and natural light to flow in. And I couldn't wait to see the beautiful stone arch freed from the brown paper covering, and restored to its original grandeur.

I walked down the concrete stairs and saw that somehow the grand piano had been removed from the basement. Everything else was gone, except for more frazzled bunches of crumbling wires coming out of walls, which made me happy that the electricity had been turned off. I went back upstairs and took in the space of the cold apartment again, imagining how in a few months, it would be completely transformed and include a real kitchen where I'd soon be baking and cooking away, while light streamed in through new windows. I'd be warmly welcoming friends, who'd sit around the counter sipping glasses of citrusy Lillet and chatting while I tended to a *coq au vin* simmering on the stove, or nibbling on various types of French hams I like to lay out, or maybe a few slabs of pâté, a crock of cornichons, and Lucques olives, with dinner followed by a wooden board of carefully selected French cheeses along with a big green salad tossed in mustard dressing, everything gathered at my new market. I was eager to get going.

Contractors are a hard-to-find commodity, globally, and because things sometimes move at a more leisurely pace in France than what I was used to, I figured it'd be a wise idea to start looking around for a good contractor a couple of months before we signed the final papers, so we'd be ready to go as soon as I got the keys. Romain was still scratching his head as to why I'd bought the apartment in the first place, but remained supportive, which was odd because Frenchmen (especially Romain) have strong opinions and aren't shy about voicing them. But in this instance, he knew how much I loved the apartment and wanted me to be happy. Perhaps some of my American optimism had worn off on him, and from here on out, all was going to be okay.

––––––––

Everything is negotiable in France, which means everything has value. But in France, the currency that has the most value is information. Getting it is a delicate skill, because it's not always easy to obtain.

Coming from a country where the customer is always right, I've found that actions and transactions in France can be a bit of a game, to see who has the upper hand. Some of this goes back to when France was a monarchy and society was stratified and feudal. That changed during the French Revolution, when the people took the power from the higher-ups and *égalité* become one-third of the motto of France. So since everyone is ostensibly now equal, why should anyone be "at the service" of anyone else?

There's a story of someone who was getting bad customer service and remarked to the salesperson that the customer was supposed to be king. Without missing a beat, the clerk replied, *"Monsieur, le roi est mort"*—"Sir, the king is dead."

That means a big part of living in France is "investing" in relationships. Shopping the same vendors at the market, going to the same butcher, even getting in line for the same checker in the supermarket means you'll get a more sympathetic response if you need someone to grind the exact 455 grams of beef you need for an American recipe that calls for one pound. Or if you are stuck with one of those dreaded 50-euro bills that always elicit a grumble when you try to pay for anything with it. I've gone without bread for days because I couldn't find anyone to break even a twenty so I could buy a 1-euro baguette. Knowing the women at the bakery from being a regular customer, you'll have a lot more success than if you're trying to break it "cold."

Neighbors present another challenge. The lawyer friend in Paris who helped me navigate through the thorny issues that came up when I was purchasing the apartment made sure I understood that after I closed, "the worst thing you can do is let your neighbors know they have any power over you. Once they do, it's all over." Many Parisians are just a generation or two away from being *paysans*, and the feudal mentality is sometimes felt behind the massive doors of those grand apartment buildings that line the streets and boulevards.

Nos chers voisins is a hit television series in France. It chronicles fictional battles between neighbors in Paris, bickering over petty issues, spying through keyholes, and doing their share to keep La Poste in business with dreaded *lettres recommandées* (registered letters) flying back and forth. (A clerk at my local post office told me that only one out of every one hundred registered letters gets picked up by the recipient, because they invariably contain bad news.) In the show, a dash of romance may happen whenever the neighbors aren't at odds over who slashed the tires on someone else's baby carriage or who'd suffered through yet another sleepless night due to the noise coming from constant parties down the hall. In other words, it takes place in what would be a typical Paris apartment building.

I'd lived in my previous building in Paris for close to a decade and never had a conversation that lasted more than ten seconds with any of the neighbors. I'd say *"Bonjour, madame"* or *"Bonjour, monsieur,"* receive a *"Bonjour, monsieur"* back, then we'd scurry into our apartments, closing the doors, with the sound of multiple locks on both sides bolting into place as quickly as possible.

To prod Parisians into being more convivial with their neighbors, once a year is the Fête des Voisins, an evening where you're encouraged to have a party with others in your building. At one I attended, the husband of one of my neighbors in the building had started "partying" well before the party. Fueled up, he made a few derogatory comments about gay people (which was odd, considering that he once made a pass at me); afterward, I sat there for a bit with two of the other people from our building of over fifty apartments, eating Pringles and sipping Oasis (a soda similar to Orange Crush), before I politely excused myself and called it a night.

I'm admittedly biased, but you could not ask for a better neighbor than David Lebovitz. I remove my shoes as soon as I enter my front door. (Fortunately for my neighbors, I was never able to master walking in heels.) I speak softly, I don't blast music, and I'm happy to engage in a friendly chat with others in stairwells and on elevators—but am also happy to *not* engage in small talk, should you choose to keep your distance. I have a party once every other decade, and gave up slashing the tires on baby carriages years ago. Best of all, I have an endless supply of cookies and cakes coming out of my oven and am more than delighted to share with neighbors, who always get first dibs.

I wanted to start off on the right foot with my neighbors in my new apartment building. The French are not only adept with paperwork, but also with formalities. Combine the two, and you've got the formal French letter; whole books and websites are devoted to how to properly write one. If you're doing construction or having a party—even if it's just every other decade—it's *correct* to post a note to your neighbors in the entryway of your building to apologize for any *dérangements d'avance*. Foreigners sometimes think they're open invitations to everyone in the building, and show up at the party with a bottle of wine. But the notes are a courtesy to the others that there's an upcoming event, and a tip-off that you might want to find another place to sleep that night.

Since I would be causing a certain amount of *dérangements* and *nuisances occasionnées*, I wanted to be a good *voisin* and drop everyone in the building a friendly note to let them know how happy I was to be a part of their community. I asked them to *excuser par avance les perturbations*, ending my highly structured letter with a mention that I looked forward to meeting my *chères voisines* and *chers voisins* and the closing line that ends nearly every formal French correspondence: "*Je vous prie d'agréer l'expression de mes salutations distinguées*" . . . "I pray that you accept my distinguished regards."

My friend Matthieu corrected it, because like one-third of the people in France, he works for the French government, which makes him an expert at paperwork. Once it was perfect, I made a copy for everyone, then signed and sealed each letter in a nice envelope and placed one in everyone's mailbox in the building, then went back to my apartment to work on the outline of the cookbook I was starting and continue packing.

———

The next day, I went back to the building and checked to see if there was anything in the mailbox. Turning the key, I opened the metal door to find it empty except for one of my letters, crumpled up into a ball. Well, that wasn't quite the welcome I'd been expecting. Perhaps I needed to pray harder.

17

If you want to see a Parisian go ballistic, don't ask them about politics, *service clients* (customer service), or hard-partying neighbors: ask them what they think of their bank. They'll erupt with stories, furious about how their own money was held up for some unspecified reason, how a major mistake was made in their account, or how a banker refused them a loan. I always thought it was odd to distrust banks with money, until on more than one occasion, I arrived at my bank to find a handwritten note posted on the door that they had decided to close up for the rest of the day, with no reason given.

A class of workers that makes Parisians go even more bonkers, though, are *entrepreneurs*. Ask someone how a renovation went, and you'll be able to add a lexicon of new curse words to your French vocabulary. Everyone has a story, each one worse than the one before, involving faulty work, dishonesty, overcharging, and underperforming, sometimes ending with the contractor disappearing before the work is completed.

There are problems with every renovation, but I was particularly scarred by a renovation-gone-bad in San Francisco. I'd hired a group of Irish brothers, a jovial troupe of lads. After a few weeks of work, I was living in a full-on construction zone, with no bathroom, shower, or kitchen. My *cuisine* was an upended cardboard box next to my bed, and my *batterie de cuisine* was a toaster oven, which I used to rewarm the San Francisco burritos that I lived on every day for nearly a year.

As the project progressed, I learned why they were called the "fightin' Irish": the brothers would show up on Monday morning, after a rough weekend, with black eyes. Progress on my renovations slowed to a crawl, until the crew stopped showing up altogether. Not having a kitchen was inconvenient, but the worst part was that they had demolished the bathroom, leaving me with a Porta-Potty on the sidewalk. The company stopped servicing it when the contractor disappeared, and while my neighbors were more welcoming than some of their Parisian counterparts, even they had their limits; they greeted me as a group one morning, timing their intervention to when I was exiting the blue plastic pod, to ask me when it was going to be removed from the sidewalk. Most people eventually get through their renovations, but I never got over my neighbors having intimate knowledge of my bathroom habits. After that experience, I said: Never again.

Alors, here I was in Paris, about to embark on a renovation. Again. But this time I vowed to do it right.

An acquaintance invited me over to visit his apartment, a duplex he had renovated near the Place de la Madeleine. As he was an architect, his place was spectacular, although my first impression was learning that his street was notorious for its high-end prostitutes. I passed through a gauntlet of upper-middle-aged women wearing Chanel suits, vying for my business. I didn't realize how much of a fuss could be made over a middle-aged man walking alone down a side street, and in any other situation I would have been flattered. Once I left the ladies behind and was safely inside the front door of my friend's everyday-looking building, my jaw dropped. Rather than the classic Paris apartment with ornate molding and separate rooms dedicated to each activity, nearly a third of his top-floor apartment was a two-story terrace enclosed in glass, with a jungle of living plants climbing up the wall. I walked across the frosted glass floor he had installed to let more light in, and marveled at his laundry room, a luxury that I'll admit made me tear up a little. I asked him if he would oversee the construction of my place, but he told me that he only takes on larger, complex projects, not a simple apartment renovation, which mine was supposed to be. (If only he/we knew.)

Next I tried my pals Karine and Benoît, who lived near my new apartment and were finishing up a renovation. They were satisfied with their team, so I made an appointment at a café to talk to their architect, who, like me, lived in an *atypique* space. She came off a little cold when we met, but since she was recommended—and had experience with *ateliers*—I laid out the plans for my apartment. After we parted, my phone calls and e-mails to her went unanswered, which Romain told me was known as *faire le mort* (to play dead), so I took that as a "Non." Aurélie, the architect who had given me the prepurchase assessment, had just given birth, so she couldn't help me herself, but recommended a young man who was just starting out. I went to see him and he was interested, but his only experience was designing a movie theater in a small village in the south of France. And while my place was relatively spacious, my concerns were kitchen cabinets and spaces for appliances, not rows of seats, acoustics, and popcorn stands.

Over coffee, I mentioned to an American acquaintance that I was buying a place and getting ready to renovate it. She's a sharp, earnest woman who once worked for a Paris apartment rental company and who had the name of a contractor the company had used for over a dozen years. He was so good, she even hired him to work on her own apartment, as well as remodeling projects for private clients—including one at the moment that was moving along very well. They'd become such close friends that she and her husband had dinner with him and his wife at their home.

I made arrangements with Claude, the contractor, to meet me at the apartment and walk through it, before the sale had been finalized. I had started a list of everything that needed to be done. Bakers are obsessive about details and are the masters of the prep list. We make lists in our sleep. I don't know a baker or pastry chef who hasn't woken up in the middle of the night to start a prep list or add to one that was already in progress. No frosting, cookie dough, cake batter, fruit compote, sauce, or batch of streusel topping is forgotten. The list can make or break your day and we live, breathe, and sleep (or try to) with the terror of forgetting to put something on it. I started my list practically the minute I got home after my first visit to the apartment. I was prepared.

———

A nice-looking man showed up at the apartment wearing a jaunty cap and a thick navy overcoat, exuding a reassuring smile. It was my first face-to-face meeting with Claude, and we shook hands. I instantly liked him. He was joined by an architect—a younger fellow who lived in the 10th, a sketchy neighborhood that was gentrifying, due to more welcoming rents in that *quartier* than the high-priced Left Bank or the Marais.

I took them through the apartment, pointing out what

I wanted to have done so Claude could prepare a bid, making sure I was as thorough as possible. He didn't seem fazed by any of the work—taking down the wall and making the kitchen larger, replacing the floors, repairing the electricity, moving the bathroom, and rehabilitating the walls of the *cave*—everything was *pas de problème*. Once we parted, I became excited that it might work out and went home to finalize my detailed list, which he said to send him before our next meeting, when he'd give me the full price to do everything.

He arrived for the meeting the following week in my soon-to-be-old rooftop apartment precisely on time (an event that I should have videotaped for posterity), carrying a folio of paperwork.

He was nicely dressed, again, and accompanied by another warm smile. It wasn't the toothy grin of the real estate agent, but a gentle French *sourire* that exuded a quiet, professional confidence. We sat at my folding kitchen table, along with Romain, the three of us wedged close together under the sloped ceiling (the one I wasn't going to be whacking my head on for much longer every time I stood up). Remarkably, Claude had responded to every part of the job with a price attached for each task: replacing the floors, knocking down the bathroom walls and rebuilding the bathroom downstairs, installing kitchen cabinets and building a kitchen island, rewiring the electricity, repairing and painting the walls, and updating the plumbing. When I mentioned that other things might come up, things I hadn't thought of at the time, he deflected my concerns with a smile— "*Pas de problème, Daveed*, we'll just add anything else if we need to. Don't worry."

It was hard not to like him. He was adorable, and I was happy to have found someone so easygoing, who would be easy to work with, especially after all the problems I'd had buying the place. His price was within my budget, with leeway for any additional work as it came up. Romain, who is a lot more skeptical than I am, didn't have any objections, either; I took that as another good sign.

His bid was actually less than I had anticipated, something I should have thought about more carefully. Since he had such a good reference, even though it was only one, I agreed to hire him and we signed the contracts. When I asked about using the architect he had brought along to our first meeting, he said, "Oh, *c'est pas nécessaire.* You don't need an architect. I can do what he does. And you'll save some money." Later, an architect told me, "Never, *ever* do anything in Paris without an architect."

———

A major expense in the renovation was going to be replacing the windows. I already had a bid from a highly regarded window company in Paris. If you are willing to pay for it, the service and quality in France is second to none. Go to Hermès and buy a 23,000-euro handbag, or to l'Ambroisie in the Place des Vosges for a 600-euro lunch, and you'll see why the French are second to none in service. Closer to (my) reality, if I spend a bit more on a pastry from an artisan *pâtissier,* I'll get a nicely bronzed croissant with flaky, buttery layers that shatter into a blizzard of irregular crumbs when I take that first bite, rather than the pallid, spongy ones sold at the chain bakeries. And the chocolates at Jean-Charles Rochoux, Patrick Roger, and Fouquet may not go *en promotion*, but there is nothing I'd rather do than experience that unmistakable sensation of letting one of their smooth chocolates dissolve in my mouth, bathing it in a velvety layer of bittersweet chocolate that makes me crave (and reach for) another one, then another one, then . . .

The woman who'd recommended Claude said he'd ordered replacement windows from an outfit outside of France for one of their other projects, which had saved her client a ton of money. The bid I had from the window company in Paris was high—around 50 percent of the cost of the entire renovation. I'd never bought windows in Paris, but the cost seemed steep in proportion to the rest of the work.

It's not unusual to buy things from other European countries—friends who live in Gascony and the Basque region drive to Spain for plumbing fixtures, others go to Portugal to get tiles, and Hungary seems to be doing a brisk dental business, attracting patients from overseas with websites I've seen in multiple languages, including French. Dental work isn't something I want to economize on, and a friend who I sent to my dentist in Paris called me afterward to tell me he was "the best-looking man in France." So you definitely won't find me booking any trips to Budapest or Szigetszentmiklós.

Claude reassured me that the windows he could get in eastern Europe would absolutely be of the same fine quality as the ones I had priced in France. I was relieved to be able to save a chunk of money . . . and the replacement-window company was recommended by the same woman who'd recommended Claude, after all. Since I was writing him a check, the first of the three payments for the work—one at the start, the second check midway through, and the third payment when he was finished—I told him I'd just write him another check for the windows.

"Oh . . ." He suddenly paused. "*Non, Daveed, c'est pas pos-*

sible. They need to be paid in cash. They can't do it if you pay by check, only cash." Since the windows were being made in another country, I didn't think that was all that unusual, so I handed over a wad of cash in an envelope. If Claude was thinking he'd hit the jackpot when he received that sizable pile of cash, he had the perfect poker face. I had placed a bet on him and hoped it would pay off.

———

Now that I had the keys and the apartment was mine, Claude met up with me again, at the apartment, to make a plan for how the work would proceed. He was accompanied by an older man with frazzled gray hair and a leery gaze, with a faint look of displeasure, who I wasn't expecting to join us.

The three of us walked to a local café that was *un peu triste*—a little sad, as the French would say. We sat by the window alongside pots of plastic flowers speckled with black soot, and a display case that offered up limp *pains au chocolat* and chocolate éclairs, their icing cracked with age, each with a blob of cream oozing out the side that had developed a cracked, dry crust.

As Claude and I talked, I picked out bits of chocolate from the middle of my *pain au chocolat,* wincing as I sipped the murky *café express* (understanding why the French call the coffee *eau de chaussettes,* or "dirty sock water"), and cast glances at the man Claude had brought along. His eyebrows and steely hair gave him the ferocity of a rudely awakened eagle, and I still wasn't clear what he was doing there.

As Claude and I went through the list of what was going to be done, after each point the gray-haired man shifted forward in his seat, looking more and more displeased, but not saying anything . . . until he all of a sudden leaned forward to dispense an opinion on a point that was being proposed. It wasn't a question or comment, but more of a directive. I wasn't sure what his role was, but as the meeting went on, every subsequent task we discussed prompted him to offer up a one-sided pronouncement about how it should be done, making it clear that it wasn't up for discussion.

He knew what kind of cabinetry I should get (and what color they should be), what shade of white would suit the walls, what finish should go on the wood floors, how high the bathroom tiles should go up the wall, the type of grout that should be used, the height of the toilet paper holders . . . I was expecting to be told which side of the bed I should sleep on. He also had ideas about where the electrical outlets and light switches should go, which I later learned was an area where his opinions were merited. He was the electrician.

I didn't pipe in as much during this meeting as I should have, but I listened. And listened and listened and listened, nodding through most of it, wondering how I was going to get through the renovation with someone who objected to every point of discussion and had to have not just the last word, but every single word between the first and the last ones.

With the floor plans spread out on the table, I was supposed to mark down where I wanted the electrical outlets, the lights, and their switches. It was hard, looking at an empty rectangle, to know where I wanted them to go. Once the space was opened up and I knew where the counters would be, as well as bathroom fixtures and the layout of my office, I'd have a better idea of what would go where. That wouldn't be a problem, Claude said, because the plans could be modified later. They just needed to know, *en général*, where to run the wiring.

Since they were rewiring the whole apartment, I wanted to have a few American outlets installed. Several friends who had them in France said they were easy to install if the electricity was being redone, and the idea didn't seem to bother the argumentative electrician, either, especially when I said I could have someone bring a couple over from the States. I wanted to avoid a kitchenful of rubbery black smoke, like the time I plugged in an American ice cream cone press when testing recipes for an ice cream book. I'd tried to find a cone-maker in France, but had learned that in addition to not wanting to make charcuterie or macarons at home, Parisians were happy to let their local *glacier* supply them with ice cream cones as well. After a few days had passed, and my kitchen no longer smelled like burning rubber tires, I couldn't say I blamed them.

So I made sure to mark two American outlets on the electrical plans. I also wanted USB ports, those little rectangular godsends for all the electronic devices we're always frantically charging. I anticipated tossing the binful of annoying plugs and adaptors that I'd amassed during my years in France to get all my devices to work. Since the U in USB stands for "universal," anyone who is an electrician nowadays would surely know how to install them. I didn't think they would be an issue, and neither did Claude, who said when I asked about adding those, too, "*Pas de problème, Daveed. Pas de problème . . .* Just mark where you want them." Reassured, I added them to the plans. Sébastien, the electrician, didn't say anything . . . he only furrowed his brow more deeply when he was handed the plans.

18

A French friend (who isn't a department store clerk) once told me, "We had a revolution, but we didn't kill the king." And even today, French society remains highly structured and layered. A common person doesn't rise through the ranks to become prime minister or *président*. Those positions are filled by those who are carefully groomed at special schools for the elite to become professional politicians, and you don't hear politicians talking about their humble beginnings, working as a dishwasher in a restaurant after school or delivering newspapers on their bikes. The stratification becomes clearer when workers march in the streets for their rights, and after each side has shown its respective force, political leaders eventually make concessions to get them back to work, and little gets changed. This is reflected in their homes, too—with the kitchen (i.e., the workers) segregated from the rest of the house.

When Romain's father came to see my new apartment, the first thing he suggested was that I move the kitchen into the windowless basement *cave*. I never minded working for other people, or serving others, but I couldn't imagine baking in the scullery, as suggested. As with most of the suggestions from the electrician, I simply nodded my head, acknowledging his *spéciale* idea.

Like the doors of French kitchens that separated *les do-mestiques* from the well-heeled, the *politesse* inherent in the French language also keeps others at a distance. Unlike English, French has a familiar and a formal verb tense. If you are friendly or close to someone, you *tutoyer* them. When speaking to someone you don't know, or someone whom it's prudent to keep a polite distance from, you *vouvoyer* them.

I started off *vouvoyer*-ing Claude, as one does *correcte-ment* in France. I have a hard time using the *vous* verb tenses, partially because they don't flow easily when being spoken. And that's not only because they include extra syllables that complicate things by needing to be conjugated differently, but also because I wasn't used to speaking to certain people using different words than I do with others. I learned much of my French speaking to Romain, and we use *tu*. So I instinctively *tutoyer*—asking someone if they would like something by saying "*tu veux*," instead of "*vous voulez*"—then quickly backtrack and apologize to the chafed bank teller or bureaucrat for crossing a line, overstepping an unbending rule for keeping the proper social distance between us.

Thankfully, the French are forgiving of foreigners who mangle their beautiful language, because they know it's a challenge, even for them. I doubt many conversations at dinner parties in other countries turn to discussing grammar, as they do in France. Most online comments on U.S. newspaper websites discuss the content. The French debate if the verb tenses used by the author, and other commenters, are the right ones.

Romain, whose bedside reading is Karl Marx and Che Guevara (in contrast to mine, copies of *In Touch Weekly* and *People*, airplane reading left behind by visiting friends), nevertheless warned me not to *tutoyer* the contractor and all of the workers. "*Ne sois pas trop gentil, Daveed*," he warned me.

"Don't be too nice. Remember: You are in charge." I took his advice, for two days. By then, I was *tutoyer*-ing not only the contractor, but everyone in the crew.

———

The hard, grueling work of demolition had started. I walked in on the very first day to find a guy with arms as big as *deux jambons* ripping down the walls with his bare hands. Equally impressive was to see him wearing just a T-shirt on such a bitter winter day. It was so frosty inside the apartment that we looked like a bunch of smokers when we talked. (For better or worse, I'm not *that* French yet.) His forehead and shirt were soaked with sweat, and even from a few feet away, I could feel the heat coming off his body.

He handled the task with the ease of someone grabbing things off a store shelf and tossing them in a shopping sack. He was filling an overstuffed canvas bag full of rubble (some of the chunks of concrete were larger than a head of cabbage), which he slung over his shoulder and hauled out to the sidewalk. There was a pile of bags outside already, proof of the considerable work done. The old bathroom sink and bathtub had been separated from the wall and were lying on the ground next to their previous places. He wasn't French, so didn't speak the language very well, but proudly gestured to me that he had ripped them out of the wall with his bare hands, pulling them away from the tiles using brute force. That was impressive, but when I saw him strap the refrigerator to his back a few minutes later and carry it down the steps and out the door to the street, I figured it best to keep a wide berth around the electrician. I had to remain on this guy's good side.

With the power (and heat) turned off, the other workers worked at prying pipes and electric wires from the walls; shards of crumbling plaster fell to the floor as they yanked and pulled. Sometimes crowbars would be used to remove a particularly stubborn pipe, which would bring down entire sections of the wall with it. It was more than I was expecting, seeing massive chunks of plaster being ripped away from the walls as water pooled on the floor, spilling out of corroded pipes that were tossed onto the concrete floor with loud clanging noises. The ratty carpet had been scraped off, stuffed into garbage bags and carried out to the sidewalk with the rest of the rubble, where everything waited to be hauled away. I hadn't been prepared for the extent of the demolition, but the apartment was opening up, which tempered my fear. It was exciting.

―――――

The job of a baker is to bring people together and to feed them. The French word *copain* came about because your friends (*copains,* from *compagnons*) are the people with whom you break bread, or share *pain*. I'm admittedly biased, but I think that people who bake are the nicest people in the world, because no one bakes a cake or a batch of cookies just for themselves (unless it was a particularly rough day). We do it to share with others.

As a cookbook writer, I end up with lots of extra treats from testing recipes. Many days, there is a constant supply of cakes and cookies coming out of my oven, so you'll find me doling out packages of treats to vendors at the market, or handing off ice cream to the people at my pharmacy after I found out about that large freezer in the back.

I'm sure the crew thought they hit the jackpot when I started bringing them cakes, madeleines, and *financiers* while they were working. I was finishing up my cookbook proposal, getting recipe ideas together and testing them. (Although it didn't end up in my book, they were particularly smitten with the chocolate fudge I made with a jar of gooey marshmallow creme from the States that I found in my cabinet when I was packing up my stuff.) I felt bad for them, working in the freezing cold without heat, and by day three, I was packing up a box of chocolate brownies that I'd made for them. "Why are you bringing them that?" Romain asked, with a look as if I were covering myself with raw meat before stepping into a lion's cage.

"No, no, it's fine. They're working really hard, and it's December," I assured him. "The apartment is really cold and damp. The crew's working very hard and will appreciate a little something sweet," I replied, as I tied one final loop of satin ribbon to close the box. It couldn't hurt to butter up the crew with a little extra *beurre*, could it?

They were so appreciative that I started bringing them snacks and treats regularly, which made them happy to see me and made me feel better, knowing we were getting off on the right foot. We joked around and happily chatted about the progress whenever I'd stop by with a tin of cookies or a glazed pound cake. Often I'd hit the café at the end of the street, too, and bring them warming shots of *café express* in plastic cups. I didn't think any further about Romain's admonition not to get too friendly. That was part of the uptight French culture, I thought, and I wanted the workers to like me, and to think of me less as the boss and more as a friend whose kitchen they were creating.

Every few days, I met with my pal Claude at nearby cafés,

away from the noise and rubble, where he'd update me on the progress and discuss the next steps. Sometimes he'd take me out for lunch, and we'd eat croque monsieurs or the *plat du jour*, along with a glass of wine. He always picked up the check, which I thought was very kind of him. What I didn't realize is that I had broken down another important social convention: workers and employers don't fraternize or dine together. The relationship between the proprietor or *chef*—which means "boss" in French—and the workers is rarely close. If you're the boss, you surely got whatever you've gained off the back of the workers. Even if you spent your life standing in the back of a restaurant kitchen chopping nuts and pitting cherries, once you've become the boss, you're an authority figure.

The conflict manifests, in its most extreme circumstances, as "boss-knapping," which takes place at factories during worker protests. One Air France executive had his clothes ripped off as he tried to escape from workers by climbing over a fence. Americans were shocked to see the pictures in the news, not only because an angry mob was chasing their boss, but because the middle-aged executives were in remarkable shape underneath their starched white shirts, in marked contrast to some U.S. bosses.

They're not barbarians, though: boss-knappers at 3M served mussels and French fries to their kidnapped superior while he was being held. I would have been terrified of boss-knapping Alice Waters when I worked at Chez Panisse, making sure any mussels were sustainably harvested and the heirloom potatoes locally grown. But for the moment, I should have been focusing on not losing my own shirt.

MARSHMALLOW CREME FUDGE
Fudge à la pâte à tartiner guimauve

MAKES ONE 8-INCH (20CM) PAN

During construction on the apartment, I did my best to keep my food blog going, which was tough when I didn't have a kitchen. Finding a jar of marshmallow creme that I smuggled back from the States inspired me to make this recipe while I was packing up my old kitchen, as did my reasoning that if I fed the crew well, they'd work more diligently.

It also gave me a chance to offer up my own take on this popular classic, otherwise known as Fantasy Fudge. I added unsweetened chocolate, which not only ramps up the chocolate flavor, but I figured the extra stimulants in the dark chocolate might get the crew to work faster. If you ever remodel in France, I recommend shipping over a case of marshmallow creme to keep the crew motivated and moving.

⅔ cup (160ml) evaporated milk

12 tablespoons (6 ounces, 170g) salted butter, cut into cubes

3 cups (600g) sugar

8 ounces (225g) bittersweet or semisweet chocolate, chopped

4 ounces (115g) unsweetened chocolate, chopped

7 ounces (200g) marshmallow creme

1 cup (120g) almonds, walnuts, peanuts, or pecans, toasted and coarsely chopped

1. Line an 8-inch (20cm) square pan with aluminum foil, leaving an overhang on at least two sides. Smooth out any wrinkles or creases.
2. Put the evaporated milk in a 4-quart (4l) saucepan and fix a candy thermometer to the side.
3. Add the butter and sugar to the pan, and heat over medium-high heat, stirring frequently, until the temperature reaches 234°F (112°C).
4. Remove the pan from the heat and stir in the bittersweet chocolate, unsweetened chocolate, and marshmallow creme.
5. Stir in the nuts, then scrape the mixture into the prepared pan and smooth the top. Let cool at room temperature for at least 4 hours.
6. Once cool, lift the fudge from the pan and cut it into squares, whatever size you like.

19

The demolition continued. Down came the walls of the bathroom, liberating a good one-third of the living space. I didn't have a live-in *domestique*—in fact, for most of my life, I *was* the *domestique*—so I didn't need separate facilities for myself and considered just having one full bathroom (downstairs), using the newly freed-up space to expand the kitchen. When I discussed that with Claude, he repeated a now familiar refrain: *Pas de problème*, assuring me that the change wouldn't be an issue and not to worry about it. I was happy that I had a contractor who was so flexible.

I'd finalized the electrical markings on the plans, noting where every light, electrical outlet, and USB port should go, and handed it off to the electrician. I was looking forward to no longer worrying about electrocuting myself when whipping up a meringue, or getting flash-fried hopping out of the shower by my bathroom heater with its exposed heating elements—*à l'ancienne*—which burned orangey-hot and hissed with anger when steam from the shower got close to them. (Which made me wonder if it was possible to be electrocuted through steam.) But the bathroom was so cold in the winter that it was die of either frostbite or electrocution, and I was looking forward to no longer having to choose between the two.

The wall and door that barricaded the *cave* from the rest of the apartment fell, and it felt as if the arched stone walls of the underground space were just as relieved as I was to be inhaling the fresh air that had finally found its way into the newly opened space. The French like to hide things, which is why so many houses and buildings in Paris are behind nondescript front doors, especially the more sumptuous ones. Some wanted to hide the number of windows they had, in an effort to escape taxation; your rate was based on how many rooms you had (which could be assessed from the outside, based on the number of windows). Reblochon cheese got its name because the farmers and producers held back some of the *lait* from the first milking of the cows so they wouldn't be taxed on it. Once the milk was accounted for, they remilked (*reblocher* in Savoyard French) the cows to get additional (non-taxed) milk, to finish the cheese.

I couldn't wait to see what the *cave* would look like once the ancient stones hidden under the glued-on paper were sandblasted and cleaned. The *misère* of the recently papered past would soon be gone. As the crew continued to pull, chop, saw, rip, cut, and sweat, I was surprised at how deep the demolition continued to go. My initial plan was to remove a couple of walls to expand the kitchen and reconfigure the bathroom, and do some cosmetic work, nothing structural. The apartment was now almost completely gutted, with debris everywhere: splintered wood beams, ladders, thick shards of concrete, power tools with tangled cords, chunks of plaster, metal pipes lying in muddy puddles of water, and garbage all over the place.

The apartment was an obstacle course of plastic trash bags half filled with wreckage and radiators that had been torn off the walls and left lying on their sides where they'd fallen. Plumbing fixtures were smashed to bits, but the porcelain pieces remained in big chunks wherever they happened to fall. The bathtub, like the refrigerator, was carried out of the apartment on the *déstructeur*'s back. All that was left in the plumbing department was one toilet in the corner of the apartment, which had once been surrounded by walls and a door. Soon the toilet was ripped out, too, and my bathroom was a metal tube, as wide as a can of tennis balls, poking out of the ground. It had even less privacy than my San Francisco Porta-Potty and required better aim.

The apartment was a mess, and it was impossible to take more than one or two steps without tripping over something. A well-heeled friend in Miami was renovating her kitchen at the same time and was in a tizzy, insisting that her place was a "complete mess," too. Her e-mail was accompanied by a picture of a kitchen stripped bare of absolutely everything— not a speck of dust, dirt, or debris in sight. The second picture was of the "complete mess"—a lone paint can sitting on her balcony, overlooking a sandy beach and the ocean. For the first time in my life, I was jealous of a paint can. I replied with a photo of my kitchen, which looked like an earthquake had violently shaken everything to the ground. Almost immediately I got a reply: "Okay, you win."

I didn't feel like I was winning. A couple of days later, the crew finished what they had started by pulling down the ceiling, too.

There was junk everywhere, but the largest pieces of debris were removed; all that remained from the original apartment were the windows, the small stainless-steel countertop with the severe German black sink, and the stove and oven built into it. That was it. (Oh, and the tube sticking out of the ground in the corner that was our bathroom.)

Claude had told me that the project would take two

months—three, tops—with a wave of his hand suggesting that he had it handled, while we sipped our cups of over-roasted coffee during one of our café meetings. Because of my tendency to be excessively organized, I pulled out my calendar to make a timeline for when I should order everything for the apartment, considering how long everything might take to arrive.

The order for the windows had been placed right from the start. Claude told me another company, located just outside of Paris, would supply the new front door, as it was only a matter of time before the ancient door that was there would collapse from its hinges. The new door would be installed with the windows. They always had the doors in stock, he promised, so there was nothing to worry about. But I paid for mine up front anyway, since two months wasn't that far away and it seemed better just to get it out of the way. One less thing to think about later. Why not?

Appliances would take a few weeks, and plumbing fixtures would take about two weeks, too, but Claude said not to order them until the middle of the second month, after the workers put the new floors down. Wood flooring is usually warehoused, and when it was time to get it, we could load the planks into Claude's truck; it was a relief to know that we could pick that up the same day, so I didn't have to worry about availability. Or so I thought.

I dutifully marked all the dates in my calendar so everything would arrive and be ready right when they needed it, so there wouldn't be any delays. I also had to let my landlord know I was moving, but since Claude said it might take three months before the apartment was move-in ready, I decided it was best to wait and see how the job progressed before I gave my notice, just in case.

The work had started in mid-December, and Claude assured me that by early March, I'd be cooking in the apartment. No matter how comfortably ahead you think you are when you're writing a book, as the due date for the manuscript looms closer and closer, a full-on panic attack is inevitable as you scramble to the finish. I wanted to get a jump start and decided to start writing and working on recipes for my cookbook in my soon-to-be-old kitchen, where I'd written several other books. The good thing about baking and testing recipes in a less-than-ideal environment is that you're cooking in the kind of kitchen many readers have to cope with, where people don't have counter space for an army of bowls or a set of professional ovens with multiple racks. (I'm sorry if I've ever published one, but is there anything more frustrating than a three-layer cake recipe aimed at home cooks that calls for baking all three layers for the cake in three different cake pans, in the same oven at the same time?)

I also thought the renovation would be fun for readers of my blog to follow along with. *What could be more exciting than witnessing a full-on apartment and kitchen renovation in Paris?* I thought. (Without the dust . . . and the bills, of course.) It was fun to start writing about the renovation and building my dream kitchen in Paris, sharing my hunt for fixtures and appliances, chronicling how I found my vintage French factory lamp that was going to hang over the kitchen island, the search for just the right sink, and talk about why I was choosing the countertops I did. Starting with the demolition, readers followed avidly along, leaving comments and encouraging me to share more. And more and more, as the job progressed.

Overseeing a renovation (in a non-native language), packing up my old apartment, picking out all the elements for the new one, keeping my blog (and visa) updated, and starting a cookbook meant I had a lot on my plate. But I only had to hold out for a couple of months.

————

I wanted a kitchen that wasn't cluttered and didn't have any unnecessary decoration. To me, functionality is the best design and I'd let the elements, and their purpose, speak for themselves. The *cuisine* would be a combination of wood, stainless steel, and white cabinets and tile, in keeping with the feel of the loftlike space of a former metal shop. I decided to get my cabinets at Ikea because they carry plain white ones and the price is right. Ikea usually has all the parts of their cabinets in stock—except, of course, the one or two that you really need, which was the case in San Francisco when they neglected to include one lone kitchen cabinet in my order. After the Irish brothers had assembled the cabinets and installed them in the kitchen, there was a gap right in the middle of the row of other cabinets where one was missing because Ikea forgot to include it in the order. But the cabinets were out of stock because the country where they were made had dissolved into civil war, and Ikea didn't know when they'd be getting them back in, if ever. I prayed for peace, then said "Never again" to buying cabinets at Ikea.

Yet time, and budget, have a way of clouding (or obscuring) one's judgment, and I was—once again—seduced by the Ikea catalog that had landed in my mailbox. I was happy that Claude had extensive experience with Ikea cabinets. "They are like Lego to me, *Daveed*. No problem installing them!"

he promised, adding that we'd go to the store together to get everything and bring them home in his truck.

I was still charmed by the French oven and stovetop that had come with the apartment, embedded in the stainless-steel countertop. (The black sink, though, was definitely going.) The enameled oven door was crimson with a wide brass handle across the top that was capped off with royalist finials on both ends. The handle might have been tough to consider parting with—especially because I could have said, "Let them eat cake!" when pulling one out of the oven—but I knew the regal-looking brass bar would look out of place in contrast with the clean white cabinetry and tiles and stainless steel. I figured I could replace it with a plain steel one without too much trouble, because unlike my other oven, this brand I knew.

———

Fortunately, there is a dedicated company store for that particular brand of oven in Paris, which I found on a website, accompanied by twenty-nine 1- and 1½-star reviews.

Customer service, admittedly, isn't the strong point of many businesses in France, and I don't expect people to vault over the store counter to help me like they do in the States. But I have learned, from shopping in the restaurant supply shops around Les Halles, that stores that cater to professionals or those that carry higher-end items make an effort to help their customers.

I tried to visit the showroom of the oven manufacturer half a dozen times but kept arriving to find a handwritten sign on the door, *Fermeture exceptionnelle*, letting me know that the store was closed for an "exceptional" reason. *Ruptures* occur just as frequently, which means an item is out of stock. During my time in France, I've seen more *ruptures* and closures than a trauma surgeon.

But as I was strolling through the neighborhood one day, I walked by the oven store and was taken completely by surprise to find the lights on and no sign on the door. I pulled it open and walked into the showroom, feeling a little like the plane crash survivors in *Lost Horizon* who, after trudging through the rugged mountains in a brutal snowstorm, walk through a magical portal and enter a sunny, lushly colorful paradise, known as Shangri-La.

I was in my own Shangri-La, surrounded on both sides by a lineup of shiny, enameled French ovens and stoves in a variety of colors and styles. I marveled at the gorgeous *fours* that came in colors like sun-drenched Provençal yellow and a royal *bleu France*, which wouldn't have looked out of place in a *château*, and professional *pianos*, with extra-generous burners for stockpots and drawers underneath to keep plates warm during service. I didn't need any of that, though. I just needed a handle.

A lone woman sat behind a desk in the back corner of the store, chatting on the phone. She was clearly not pleased that I was there to interrupt what didn't seem to be a business call. After a few minutes of waiting, she stopped talking and stopped smiling, putting the receiver against her shoulder to ask what I wanted. I told her that I had one of their ovens and was it possible to get a new handle for it, in chrome or stainless steel, to match a kitchen I was renovating?

"*Non, monsieur, c'est pas possible* ... If you want a new handle, you'll have to buy a whole new oven," she said with no facial expression, but her eyes letting me know that I had used up my one question. The second one would be at my own risk. Next time, I was bringing Romain. Or a screwdriver. (And would faux-stumble on the way out, taking a handle with me.)

Fortunately, I had a generous contractor. Claude said he would buy the oven from me, paying me later, and I'd use the money to get a small oven to fit in that space. I never gave him a *devis*, *bon de commande*, or *facture* for the oven, which I should have, because I never got paid for it. I had much to learn.

20

Like replacing an oven handle, paying a bill in France is more complicated than one might think. In the United States, someone hands you a bill and you pay it with a check or credit card. The canceled check or credit card statement can be your receipt. French banks don't offer copies of canceled checks. And if you paid by *carte bleue*, the payment appears on your online credit card statement, but doesn't always say who was paid, or what the payment was for. It often just gives the amount.

I'd heard a rumor that the bank can give you a copy of a canceled check, which my bank in Paris said would take three months when I needed proof of payment for something. I decided it'd be easier (and faster) just to pay that particular bill twice. Which ended up being a good idea, since I never got a copy of the canceled check I'd requested. (And I didn't want to spend another three months debating a 29-euro payment. Since banks in France charge 34 centimes a minute to call them, I calculated that I'd come out ahead if I just forgot about it.)

But for me, the main problem with *les chèques* is that things go in different places on French checks than they do on American ones, and if I had *cinq centimes* for every check I've bungled while filling it out, I'd have more money in my check-ing account than the lamentable amount I spend on calling the bank. I instinctively write the amount of euros where the payee should go, because they're in the opposite place from where they are on an American check. Europeans also write dates differently than we do in America: November 10, 2010 is 11/10/10 in the United States, but 10/11/10 in Europe. (Un-fortunately, unlike checks, you can't just shred airline tickets and rewrite another one. I found that out the hard way when I planned a trip home for Thanksgiving but ended up with a ticket that would get me there in time for Halloween.)

I've also never figured out why there's a space on French checks where you're required to fill in what city you're writing the check in. Why it matters if you're in Paris, Lille, or Dijon when writing a check, I'll never know. I've often wanted to try writing "Mumbai" in that space to see if they cash it.

Either way, you do need to be careful how you fill out checks, because banks carefully ration them. When you've run out, you need to go to the bank and request another checkbook, then come back and pick it up in person. And people ask me what I do all day . . .

———

The time had come for me to start writing more checks for things, which, like anything else in France, involves paper-work. After the demolition was finished, the bills started coming in for the construction materials.

Before you even reach for your checkbook, the first in-kling that you'll have to pay for something in France comes in the form of a *devis*, a piece of paper that tells you how much you have to pay for materials and labor. This differs from an *estimation*, which isn't so precise. (I later found out not all *devis* were all that precise, either.)

In theory, this is how it goes: Once you agree to pay a *devis* and sign it, you will be issued a *bon de commande*, a piece of paper that serves as a voucher if you paid in advance for goods or services. Once you get the goods, or the services are provided, you'll receive a *facture*, an itemized summary of how much you paid, that usually gets signed. Then it gets an official stamp that business owners are required to have that provides a proof of payment. If something was sent or delivered, you'll also get a *bon de livraison* as proof of delivery. (As retina scans become more common, they'll probably add those, too.)

Once all these forms are received, signed, paid, stamped, scanned, initialed, and photocopied, everything goes into one of the many binders that are filed and archived, then saved for eternity. When Mitt Romney made a statement about having "binders of women" during his run for president, Americans chuckled. But since he was a missionary in France for several years, it seemed perfectly normal to me.

In addition to frequent tutorials from Romain on how to receive and pay bills, which I'd always considered a relatively simple process, I continued trying to learn and absorb the French vocabulary for the hardware and fixtures I was shopping for. Lighting and plumbing, cabinetry, flooring, painting, hand tools, electrical outlets and switches, hex nuts, pliers, towel bars, knobs, window locks, door locks—showerheads, showerhead hoses, showerhead brackets, clips that hold the showerhead bracket to the wall, and the hex nut that fixes the showerhead bracket to the showerhead holder, which holds the showerhead—I had to learn them all, and my French dictionary, which boasts having four hundred thousand translations in it, wasn't of much use here.

The first plumbing term I learned definitely wasn't in there. Everyone knows that Europeans are more enlightened than everyone else in the world, and after a few decades in San Francisco, I thought I'd seen everything. Still, I think that some things are better left discussed in the privacy of one's home—or doctor's office. I was lunching at a *tabac*, one of those "locals only" corner joints where people line up to buy cigarettes and workers in the neighborhood hack through 7-euro plates of *steak frites* on their lunch break, while others sip beers and banter at the zinc counter, their rosy noses giving away that they've been parked there for most of the morning.

The television mounted over the bar was tuned to a French news channel featuring a story about colorectal cancer, accompanied by demonstrations of the procedures used to diagnose it on an actual patient. The other diners (and drinkers) watched, fixated on the screen, while I found I was losing my appetite as I tried to spoon up a thick, gravylike *bœuf bourguignon* and down my glass of golden-yellow wine. Check, please!

Americans are perplexed when they check in to a European hotel and find there are no shower curtains to keep water from the *douchette*, the handheld shower, from spraying all over the floor. On the other hand, Europeans wonder how Americans shower with fixed showerheads, and complain you can't wash, uh . . . *thoroughly* without a handheld hose. I couldn't find in my *dictionnaire* the word for the specific kind of hose my European partner was used to, but Claude knew the right term because, as he told me, he had several Italian clients: a *douchette anale*. That wasn't something I was particularly comfortable going into a plumbing store and asking for, but I wrote it down on my list of things

I needed to order at the plumbing store. And thus, my classes in French construction materials had begun, at the bottom.

Back at the top, I learned that a *pommeau à douche* is a showerhead. The *tuyau à douche* is the shower hose that's attached with a *crochet* (holder) to the *mur en faïence* (a tile wall, not to be confused with a *mûre en faïence*, which would be a ceramic blackberry) using *les vis cruciformes* (screws). It's a lot to remember when leafing through catalogs of French plumbing fixtures, but harder when you're in a hardware store and the perplexed salesperson doesn't understand why you'd want to attach a showerhead to a ceramic berry.

We'd decided to move the main bathroom downstairs, but keep a half-bath upstairs with a sink, a toilet, a *douchette*, and a floor drain, which meant there was potential for a future full bath or shower. That ended up being one of the smartest decisions I made during the renovation.

Knowing that things can take longer than expected in Paris, I got moving on picking out my fixtures. The Boulevard Richard Lenoir is famous for its outdoor market that starts at the Bastille and radiates from there, encompassing several city blocks. On Sundays, it attracts a staggering variety of vendors. Shoppers clog the aisles scrutinizing fresh seafood and shellfish; follow their noses toward the spit-roasted chickens turning slowly over a bed of potatoes, which are marinated by the sizzling drippings; pick up lettuce, green beans, and heady-sweet French strawberries; then, faced with a display of the most impressive cheeses in the world, make the tough decision of which to bring home.

But the street is also known for its many hardware, cabinetry, plumbing, and flooring stores; I started spending more time in the shops that lined both sides of the boulevard than the market that ran down the center of it. I became a regular at Cedeo, a plumbing-supply store. When you go in, there are always a few people waiting to talk to the clerks, who each sit at their own particular desk with a wall of plumbing catalogs behind them. If something is available in France—from toilets to tubs, *lunettes* to *douchettes*—they can get it for you. I pulled out my list and the shop assistant walked over to the shelves, pulled down four or five heavy catalogs, and stacked them next to her.

I was glad she was French, because she didn't flinch when she saw my list and our conversation turned to intimate matters. Although turning through the catalog pages, she did tell me she wondered why urinals were available with or without a *mouche*, a fly embossed in the bottom.

"So men have something to aim at," I helpfully told her. She had to stop and think about that for a moment, before saying, "Oh . . . yes, of course," then going back to flipping through the catalogs to find my *douche* heads and *douchette* hoses.

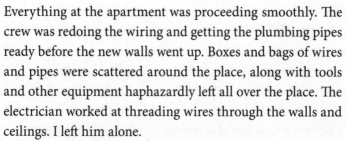

21

Everything at the apartment was proceeding smoothly. The crew was redoing the wiring and getting the plumbing pipes ready before the new walls went up. Boxes and bags of wires and pipes were scattered around the place, along with tools and other equipment haphazardly left all over the place. The electrician worked at threading wires through the walls and ceilings. I left him alone.

My search for light fixtures, tiles, and cabinet pulls continued, so they'd also be ready when the crew needed them, to avoid delays. The electric radiators had been tossed out with the other debris, and Claude had suggested installing radiant heat under the floors. In San Francisco, I'd lived in a mid-century modern home with radiant heat. The gentle warmth that rose through the floor came from coils embedded in the concrete subfloor, through which hot water passed. My first winter in that house, I learned not to store 10-pound blocks of baking chocolate anywhere near the floor. On the upside, I discovered a great technique for melting a lot of chocolate at once.

I also learned that it wasn't an economical way to heat a house. The system was installed in the 1960s when energy was cheap. It worked well, but in the 1990s, my heating bills went through the (uninsulated) roof. I wasn't anxious to see what they would be in France, where electricity is notoriously expensive. "Non, non, *Daveed*," Claude reassured me with a broad grin, when I expressed concerns about steep *factures* (or would that be *devis* . . . ?) from Électricité de France. "A lot has changed since then, and the radiant heat systems are very efficient now. The heat is wonderful. In fact, I installed it in my apartment and it's great. *Pas de problème . . .*"

Like the water filtration system that he'd talked me into installing, the same one he'd installed in his own apartment, which would rid my life of calcium, and clogged hot water heaters and dishwashers, radiant heat seemed like a good idea. I didn't think to ask why someone who was renting an apartment would rip up the floors to install a brand-new heating system at their own expense. But since my floors were already down to the concrete, it didn't seem like it would be all that difficult to lay the rolls of electrical coils down and install the new hardwood flooring over them. I was about to start the search for flooring, which I would buy prefinished, so it'd be ready to go after the heating coils were laid. I continued to take great pride at my efficiency in getting everything ready and organized, incorporating the thoughtful advice that I was getting from the contractor.

All I needed to do, Claude instructed, was to get hardwood flooring that was 9mm (about ⅓ inch) thick. Any thicker, and the heat would not pass through the wood. That was absolutely crucial, he insisted. I couldn't use anything else.

With that in mind, Romain and I set out on a quest to find 9mm wood flooring at the hardwood flooring stores just outside Paris. There are a number of stores within the city, but the warehouse-size showrooms in the suburbs have a lot more finishes to choose from. Plus, you can physically see what's available in the warehouse, to avoid the dreaded *rup-ture de stock.*

We didn't have any trouble finding plenty of hardwood flooring options. *Parquet* is very popular in Paris—although less so with people who live below (or even above) women who wear high heels—and there were an impressive number of styles and finishes. Everything from *brut* (untreated) to *naturel* (plain) to *sombre* (I can't image another culture that would use "melancholy" as a selling point for flooring) to *fumé vitrifié* (smoked and lacquered), which I passed on as I'd constantly be thinking about barbecue. Yet we couldn't find any wood flooring that fit Claude's specifications—everything was 15mm, about ¼ inch thicker. Dismayed, we went from store to store. When I asked for wood to use with radiant heating and cited the exact measurements, the salesmen looked confused and explained, "*Désolé, monsieur,* we don't have any 9mm-thick flooring." And that was it, which seemed strange since that's what I was told I must have for the apartment.

It was especially odd because radiant heat was popular in Europe, despite dire warnings that the heat would take a toll on your legs. I didn't know that warm legs could be the cause of a host of maladies (though no one who warned me about them could name any when pressed). When I moved to France, I also learned that adding ice to your drink would cause all sorts of stomach ailments, including causing your stomach to freeze, which, if true, the hospitals in the States would have to have separate wings to handle the ongoing epidemic of ice-related frozen-stomach emergencies.

———

After driving around all day, shivering from rifling through stacks of hardwood planks in unheated warehouses, Romain and I headed back to Paris, frustrated at not being able to find the right flooring. I have a knack for being able to find anything in Paris, a talent so admired that someone at the U.S. Embassy in Paris told me that when anyone inquires about where to find something in Paris, they refer them to me.

I remained determined to find 9mm-thick *parquet* flooring and trudged through the cold, wintery drizzle of Paris, criss-crossing the city from *métro* to *métro*, checking out all the stores: Monsieur Parquet, E-Parquet, Parquet Français, Concept Parquet, Parquet-Carrelage, Star Parquet, La Maison du Parquet, La Parqueterie, and the right-to-the-point Point P. There was *rien* in 9mm. *How can it be*, I wondered, between stops, *that no one has the right flooring to use with radiant heating in all of Paris?* But I wasn't giving up. After all, I've found corn syrup (at the Korean market), dried cranberries (at G. Detou), and even *renforcé* aluminum foil (American-style, heavy-duty foil) in Paris. If I could find those, I could find the right size wood flooring.

When I saw Claude between floor-scouting expeditions, I told him of the difficulty I was having finding 9mm-thick flooring and asked if he was *absolument certain* that's what I needed, because it seemed to *ne pas exister*. He confirmed that—*oui*—that's what I had to get; otherwise, the heating wouldn't come through the floor. So I kept searching and searching, and searching and searching, but couldn't find any flooring in that thickness in stores, or even online, in all of France, nor in any neighboring countries in Europe. Yet I remained optimistic that I'd find it somewhere, because Claude said so. I just didn't know where. And, oddly, neither did he.

I continued to tiptoe around the unpredictable electrician, who could be perfectly calm and reasonable one minute, then explode in a tirade that could be heard down the block in the next sentence. I walked on pins and needles—actually, screws and nails—in the apartment to avoid his wrath. I noticed the other workers steered clear of him, too.

Every question I had about the electricity was like tapping a hornet's nest; it was hard to tell what might release the swarm. His tendency to go on rants was evident when I tentatively asked about the USB ports when I didn't see anything that looked like them in his boxes of outlets. With his coarse eyebrows lowered in my direction, after a brief pause he launched into a tirade about how they were a specialty item, only available in one place in all of Paris.

I volunteered to go get them so he could stay and work, but he didn't know the name of the shop, so he gruffly ripped a flap of cardboard off a nearby box, grabbed a pen, and made a map for me. I watched for fifteen minutes as he drew series of lines and arrows, depicting streets and *métro* stations that he didn't know the names of. As he scribbled away, drawing circles and scratches to depict streets, he kept asking me if I was sure I understood what he meant. I stared at the piece of cardboard with a spaghetti-like knot of black marks on it and just kept saying "*Oui . . . oui . . .*," because admitting that I didn't have a clue would make him start explaining it again all over again.

After twenty minutes, he said he was done and handed me the "map" before walking away. Suddenly he turned, walked back, and grabbed the map out of my hands, tearing it to pieces and saying to forget about it, that he'd go. I didn't protest.

Outbursts aside, he was doing a good job with the electricity. I let him know that the U.S. outlets were stashed in a safe place, away from what was now a full-on construction zone so they wouldn't get lost in the *désordre,* and to let me know when he needed them. He nodded okay, and because he didn't mention them after that, I brought them up again (delicately, very delicately) a few times during the next few weeks. He kept the electrical diagram on which I had marked where I wanted everything to be nailed to the wall while he worked. I didn't think to make a copy of it— and was later surprised that I didn't, considering how living in France had made me an expert archivist. But on the other hand, some things are better left forgotten, or at least left in the past.

MOJITO SORBET

MAKES 1 QUART (1L); SERVES 6 TO 8

Many visitors come to France, especially in the summer, and are surprised that they have to beg to get ice in their drinks. The only time you get lots of ice is if you order a cocktail. (Ice being cheaper than booze.) But it's a widely held belief that icy drinks are bad for your health. I felt sorry for a friend who attended a mojito party at which the host didn't have ice for the cocktails; everyone sipped on warm, minty drinks all night.

While ice is shunned, ice cream and sorbet are not, which is especially obvious if you witness the lengthy lines in front of Berthillon on the Île Saint-Louis and at the many other ice cream shops that have opened in Paris during the last few years. I've always dreamed about opening an ice cream shop here, but after the *douche froide* I got renovating my apartment, I couldn't imagine taking on the task of opening a business. So I'll continue to churn up ice cream at home.

This frosty sorbet is a nod to the mojitos served in the trendy cafés around Paris, with lots of fresh mint and a dose of rum. The rum keeps it scoopable after it's frozen and icy-cold, which—in my opinion—is the best way to enjoy it.

2¼ cups (560ml) water

⅔ cup (130g) sugar

1 cup (40g) loosely packed fresh mint leaves, plus 5 leaves

Zest of 2 limes

½ cup (125ml) fresh lime juice (from about 5 limes)

5 tablespoons (75ml) dark rum

1. In a medium saucepan, heat the water and sugar over medium-hight heat, stirring occasionally, until the sugar is dissolved. Remove from the heat and add the 1 cup mint leaves. Cover and let stand for about 15 minutes, then remove the lid and let the mixture cool to room temperature.

2. Remove the mint leaves with a slotted spoon and stir in the lime zest, lime juice, and rum. Refrigerate until thoroughly chilled, then freeze in an ice cream maker according to the manufacturer's instructions. Finely chop the 5 remaining mint leaves and add them to the sorbet during the last few minutes of churning.

<h1 style="text-align:center">22</h1>

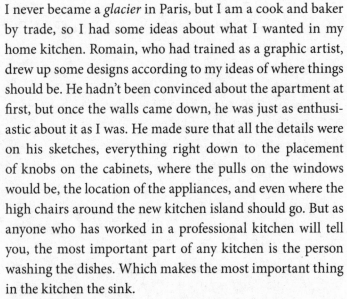

I never became a *glacier* in Paris, but I am a cook and baker by trade, so I had some ideas about what I wanted in my home kitchen. Romain, who had trained as a graphic artist, drew up some designs according to my ideas of where things should be. He hadn't been convinced about the apartment at first, but once the walls came down, he was just as enthusiastic about it as I was. He made sure that all the details were on his sketches, everything right down to the placement of knobs on the cabinets, where the pulls on the windows would be, the location of the appliances, and even where the high chairs around the new kitchen island should go. But as anyone who has worked in a professional kitchen will tell you, the most important part of any kitchen is the person washing the dishes. Which makes the most important thing in the kitchen the sink.

Like many Americans, I dreamed of a kitchen with a French farmhouse sink. An expansive white porcelain model with thick sides and a deep rectangular basin big enough to swish around bundles of spinach or leafy Swiss chard, to make sure I got rid of any traces of grit hiding in the wrinkles of the leaves, or to wash baskets of colorful wild plums I might forage from trees on the grounds of a deserted estate, like the ones I chanced upon on a trip a few years ago through the countryside, not far from Paris. (They produced the best jam I've ever made. Unfortunately, when we returned the next summer, we found someone had fixed up the place and chopped down the wild plum trees, probably vexed by the colorful stains they leave everywhere when the fruit falls.) I wanted a sink wide enough to soak a baking sheet crusted with baked-on frangipane from a batch of *croissants aux amandes*, sturdy enough to withstand the weight of the largest cast-iron Staub roasting pot, which I bought before realizing that it wouldn't fit on top of my stove, nor inside my little oven, and big enough to stack all the pots and cake pans I go through when recipe testing. For those who say, "Clean up as you go!"—if I did that, it'd take me a week to finish a single recipe.

I also wanted a hose sprayer like we had when I worked in restaurants, which have become popular with home cooks in the States. They make it easy to fill pots with water but are also great for power-washing dirt from vegetables. (An added bonus is that the hoses also make good weapons in kitchen fights. I once had a dishwasher take aim and soak me in the middle of my shift at Chez Panisse: proof that you don't mess with the person who washes dishes, and a reminder of who is actually in charge in the kitchen.)

There's just one problem with French farmhouse sinks: They don't exist in France. At least, not anymore. Most are either already in old farmhouses, or reproductions from America. How do I know that, you're probably asking, because you've seen them in all the home design magazines and on websites? Because I searched for one with a fervor that was only matched by my obsessive pursuit of 9mm floorboards.

I flipped through every single catalog at plumbing stores across Paris in hopes of finding a French farmhouse sink for my kitchen, and came up with nothing: there were no white porcelain sinks with a single large basin. Most of the sinks were either too small, too decorative, or too colorful. While shopping, Romain and I had seen many kitchen cabinets and fixtures in a variety of hues and colors, but *aubergine* (a shiny eggplant-purple) was especially popular, and it became a running joke between us when discussing everything from kitchen stools to cabinet colors. The answer was always "*aubergine*." The color has become such a fixture in France that it's just a matter of time before the French rugby team, known as *les Bleus*, becomes *les Aubergines*.

I did my rounds of the plumbing stores, showing clerks pictures culled from the Internet. "*Ça n'existe plus, monsieur*," they would say, shaking their heads—"They don't exist anymore." Looking for a reason, one salesman offered up, "Who cooks anymore? We get our food at Picard," a frozen-food chain that's wildly popular in France. But I wasn't convinced there weren't any farmhouse sinks in all of France.

After making the rounds in Paris, and online, I finally came across a farmhouse sink as part of a kitchen showroom display. I was tempted to call the bruiser who had pulled the sink out of the wall in my apartment to do a grab-and-run-for-it, but thought it would be more polite if I asked if I could order one. "*Désolé, monsieur. Malheureusement, ça n'existe plus*." I offered to buy that one right on the spot and drag it home, but he said it was the centerpiece of the kitchen and didn't want to let it go. I can't say I blamed him.

Hitting the Internet again, I decided to check with our neighbors across the Channel. I found plenty of English farmhouse sinks, in England, but unfortunately, they were only available there: no one delivered to France. But like their French counterparts, curiously, they were available in

America. But not in France. I researched what the luggage allowance was on the Eurostar, scheming how to get a 160-pound sink to the train station in London, then somehow haul it onto the train, then take it in a taxi from the Gare du Nord in Paris to my apartment.

Everybody knows the perfect time and place to hatch rational ideas is online at 2:45 A.M., which was when I decided to calculate how long it would take to drive to the coast of France in Romain's station wagon, take the ferry across the Channel, then make our way to the closest village in England. I'd arrange to have the sink delivered to the bed-and-breakfast where we'd be staying. The next morning, we'd head back to the Channel, cross it again on the ferry, then drive to Paris with my sink in the trunk.

Surely there was an easier (and cheaper) way to buy a simple white kitchen sink. But if there was, the Internet wasn't revealing how.

I asked Claude if he knew where I could get one, since that's the kind of information one assumes general contractors are supposed to know. But if he knew, he kept his sources to himself, just as he couldn't give me the address of any store that had the elusive 9mm hardwood flooring. I attributed both mysteries to how close the French hold information to their chest, which they're not eager to give away.

———

Sink-searching meant I had to expand my French vocabulary yet again. There aren't just sinks in France: there are *éviers*, *lave-mains*, *bacs à lave*, *bassins*, *vasques*, and *lavabos*.

Each type of sink has its own *raison d'être*. You might

use one sink to wash your hands, but if its primary use is laundry, it's called a *bassin*. If it's in the bathroom, it's a *lave-mains*, a hand-washing sink. (I'm pretty sure you could use it for brushing your teeth, too. Unless there's a *lave-dents*, a sink specifically for brushing your teeth.) *Éviers* are only for kitchens; *lavabos* only go in the bathroom. I think.

The vocabulary lessons don't end there. For a faucet, you need to decide between a *robinet* or *mitigeur*, *robinet mélangeur*, or *robinet à eau* . . . once you figure out what the differences are. I also never figured out why some sinks were advertised as having a *bandeau*. I thought it might mean "dish rack," but when I searched for *bandeau* online, thousands of pictures of women in halter tops (*bandeaux*) came up. The only connection I could see between the two was that they both had racks. Romain was puzzled, too, but in a different way: he was surprised to catch me looking at pictures of busty French women in halter tops on my computer.

It was tiring spending hours online, but I kept going, adding the words "*commercial*" and "*industriel*" to my searches, remembering an "aha!" moment I'd had when remodeling in San Francisco. I was having trouble finding standard-issue bathroom fixtures. A plumbing supply shop clerk pulled out a plumbing catalog for toilets and sinks for public schools and prisons. Bingo!—that's where they all were. I opted out of the prison-grade stainless-steel urinal (which didn't offer the option of a *mouche*)—and the toilets, which weren't available with seats because, the salesman told me, they could be used as weapons in the event of a prison riot. Thankfully, most French protests are nonviolent so I felt comfortable having toilets with seats.

We were having dinner with a friend of Romain's one night, and I told her how frustrated I was trying to find a big white sink—"like the kind they use in schools," was how I described it. The idea of putting a sink intended for a school (or—*mon dieu*—a prison) in your apartment was unthinkable to most French, who tend to have fixed ideas about things. Romain's father was so surprised to see me eating a mid-morning bowl of fresh fruit and yogurt that he had to stop what he was doing, come over, and look at what was in the bowl. "*C'est formidable!*" he remarked as I spooned fruit into my mouth, astonished to discover that someone would eat something outside of the prescribed mealtimes.

She listened to me describe the kind of sink I was looking for. "What you want to do is search for a sink along with the word *collectivité*." And thus, I added another new French word to my vocabulary. But I was still in France and, *malheureusement*, every sink link that I clicked on gave me a message that there was a *rupture de stock*, with no dates given for when they'd be available again, usually a sign in France not to hold your breath.

I decided to print out the pages of the two models of sinks for a *collectivité* that were (allegedly) available: One had a larger basin than normal, but was very shallow. The other was exactly what I was looking for: large and deep. It was almost perfect, except it had a divider, which I'm not fond of because they often get in the way. But each side of the sink was larger, and deeper, and plainer, and less eggplanty, than any of the other sinks I had seen. And I imagined that when the apartment was finished, one half the sink could be filled with ice and bottles of Champagne at the party I was already planning to celebrate my finished kitchen. That was my sink.

I did the rounds of the plumbing supply shops again, this time with printouts of the sink. "Ah, yes, *monsieur*. They're right here, in these catalogs . . . ," pulling different catalogs off the shelves. I did ask one of the clerks who remembered me why he hadn't shown me that catalog before, even though he knew the sink was in there. "You said you wanted a large white sink for a home kitchen. These are for commercial kitchens." A rationale I was starting to understand. Sort of.

At every shop (and at this point I knew every shop in Paris—and they knew me), the salesmen all looked at the pictures and serial numbers but no one had it in stock. Checking their computers, they gave me the bad news that even their distributors were *épuisés* (exhausted—or kaput). I was beginning to sense a conspiracy by Picard to deprive people of large sinks so they'd buy more of their prepared foods. (Otherwise, I can't imagine any other reason why someone would buy a frozen *jambon-beurre* baguette sandwich when there is a bakery on every corner selling fresh ones.)

Not willing to give up, I started each day perched in front of my computer with my morning bowl of *café au lait*. I entered the lengthy serial number of the sink into the search engine field to see if anything had turned up overnight. Most days, I was greeted with the usual sites that tormented me with pictures of my sink, along with the usual message that the sinks were exhausted. (Which I understood—so was I.) But one morning, after I sleepily tapped in the serial number, I was suddenly wide awake.

At the top of the page on my screen was a listing accompanied by a picture of the exact sink that I was looking for, on LeBonCoin.fr, a French website dedicated to people selling everything from vintage Le Creuset gratin dishes that their grandmother owned (many of which are now mine) to rusted-out old Renaults stripped for spare parts. At any given time, there are nearly 26 million items for sale on the site. LeBonCoin.fr is less polished than eBay. Sellers have no problem putting their phone numbers on the site because of the French preference for the process over the result. Why send an e-mail, which takes eight seconds, when you can have a leisurely thirty-minute phone chat with a stranger about a busted garden gnome they're selling?

We called immediately, before anyone else in France who was desperate for a French farmhouse sink spotted the listing. Romain asked the seller if it was still available . . . then where the sink was located, how long the seller had lived in his town, why he bought the sink in the first place (he had a flower shop), and if his parents were in the flower business, too?

After a discussion of what region his parents came from and the material the cathedral in the town square of their village was made of—stone or granite?—I was starting to hyperventilate and made the universal index finger across my throat to cut the conversation short so we could close the deal. After Romain told the guy on the other end of the phone that I was silently signaling for him to hang up, the seller agreed to hold it for me, and we arrived in Lille the next morning to find the sink in his garage with the original factory sticker still on it: it had never been used. But I was even more stunned to actually see that, yes, the sink actually existed. The proof was lying on the ground right in front of me. And to top it off, it was 75 percent off the list price—the first break I got during the renovation. Finally, something was going my way—even if it ended up being the last thing.

I wanted to get it in my possession as quickly as possible, so after a tour of the seller's workshop, his house, and his garden, then meeting his family, including the kids, and discussing what they were studying in school, and where they spent their last family vacation, we loaded the sink into the car.

It had taken us two and a half hours to get to Lille, but our return was slower, as I made Romain drive extra carefully because I was so worried about the sink in his trunk.

Eight hours later, we arrived at the apartment and unloaded the sink, putting it where the kitchen was supposed to go, *en principe*, although there was a long way to go before I would be chilling anything bubbly in it. Fortunately, in France, Champagne is easier to track down than a sink, so at least I wouldn't have any trouble finding that when the time came to pop the cork and celebrate my new kitchen.

SANDWICH JAMBON-BEURRE

SERVES 2

Unless I'm missing something, there's no reason to buy a frozen sandwich in Paris, especially a *jambon-beurre*, which any bakery in Paris can provide you with. But even if you don't live near a bakery that makes them, don't despair: it's easy to make one at home.

Jambon de Paris is the catchall name in France for boiled ham, but only one true jambon de Paris, the majestically named Le Prince de Paris, is actually made in Paris. Once you taste it, you'll realize why it's worthy of its elevated status. The real deal will always be branded on the outside with a likeness of the Eiffel Tower. (You can find it at better-quality charcuteries, La Grande Épicerie, and at the Terroirs d'Avenir butcher shop on the Rue du Nil.)

When I first moved to France, I asked for some mustard to go with a ham-and-charcuterie plate I'd ordered at Le Baron Rouge, a wine bar near the Marché d'Aligre, a place where it's not unusual to find people sipping wine and chatting at ten A.M., taking a break from shopping at the market. The servers can be gruff, but that's part of their charm. My request for mustard didn't go over well. "Our charcuterie is too good for mustard!" the waiter bellowed when I asked for a pot. The French love mustard as a condiment with steaks and sausages, but it doesn't get paired with cured meats. It's butter you'll find smeared on a *jambon-beurre*.

It used to be forbidden to eat on the streets of Paris. But times have changed. With the reduction in hours that workers are allotted to eat lunch, it's no longer the infraction it once was to eat while walking. (It still is frowned upon to eat while riding public transport, though.) While it's a little unseemly navigating the sidewalk and chomping down on a baguette sandwich, if you want to be truly Parisian, grab your sandwich, walk to the nearest river, and enjoy your freshly made sandwich in any slip of sunshine you can find.

1 baguette
Butter, at room temperature
6 to 8 slices boiled ham

1. Starting from one side, use a bread knife to split open the baguette lengthwise, cutting almost all the way through but leaving a hinge to open the bread so you can fill it. If the baguette is very thick and bready inside, rip out some of the excess *mie* (crumb) inside the baguette.
2. Generously smear butter all over both cut sides of the bread. Do not be *radin* (stingy). Drape ham inside the sandwich, then press the top closed.
3. If you'd like, add a few slices of Emmenthal or Swiss cheese and/or sliced cornichons to the sandwich.

23

The crew had been working for several weeks, and the sink was the only thing in the apartment that gave any clue that it would someday be a place to live. The kitchen was nothing but a few pipes sticking out of the walls and floor, the bathroom was still a lone vertical tube, and my future bedroom was a storage room with piles of boxes filled with electrical cords, dirt-crusted tools, and broken plumbing fixtures. It didn't look like somewhere I would be moving in to anytime soon, even though Claude insisted I'd be in the apartment by the end of the following month.

A phrase you hear a lot in France is *en principe*, or "in principle." The *fromagerie* or bank is open on Thursdays, *en principe* . . . There's a nationwide train strike, but they'll be running one train for every three that usually run, *en principe* . . . The new chocolate shop on the other side of Paris that you've been dying to visit and are taking three *métros* to get to is open Saturday, *en principe* . . . *mais* . . . Too many times I've arrived, or planned my day around something, only to find myself facing a closed and locked door, with a note on it.

I was supposed to move out of my apartment at the end of the following month, *en principe*, and most of my things were packed up and ready to go, including the recipe testing notes I was keeping in a separate box so they didn't get lost among all my other stuff. In between scouring Europe for a sink and nonexistent hardwood flooring, any chance I got, I took a break and worked on recipes for my cookbook, which was a nice respite from standing around a chaotic construction zone, wondering when my apartment would start to come together.

I write recipes the old-fashioned way, with pen and paper, to avoid buttery buttons and cake batter on my keyboard. I keep the recipes I'm working on in separate folders, filed by chapter; for stories that accompany the recipes, I make notes on a separate piece of paper and clip them to the corresponding recipe page to keep them handy. Writing a cookbook is not just typing out a recipe. You want to introduce and entice the reader to make the recipe, then be sure you give them enough information to successfully do it, but not *too* much (like the three-page recipe for brownies that I once saw in a pastry chef's cookbook), because you don't want to overwhelm people. I had a deadline, but wanted to get a good head start, until I could get into my new kitchen to finish.

———

A month into the project, the apartment was a disaster, a word that comes from the French *des astres,* or "from the stars." I was still starry-eyed and believed that they'd be done when they said they would be. *Quelle déception.* True, the walls had come down and the crew seemed to have gotten the basic wiring and plumbing in place. But everything else was in shambles. Work clothes were left piled up on the floor, shoved in corners, and lying on dusty boxes. Sand-wich wrappers, soda cans, and plastic yogurt pots from past lunches were strewn about. I don't know how they worked with tools and boxes of nails and screws dumped out every-where. It was hard to tell what was trash, with wood scraps, electrical supplies, and coils of wire piled up next to pieces of broken glass and garbage. It sure didn't look like a place that would be livable by the end of next month, or even the one after that.

Claude and I continued to meet every few days for cof-fee or lunch. I gently prodded him about the progress as the place was obviously nowhere near being close to finished. I had gotten the all-important sink for the kitchen, which was shoved in the corner; now I just needed his okay to start ordering the appliances, cabinets, and bathroom fixtures, so they'd be there when the crew was ready to install them, which he kept saying would be soon, very soon. I also brought up, again, that I was having trouble finding the flooring. Was he sure I couldn't use 15mm floorboards? Because that's all the stores in and around Paris, as well as in the rest of Eu-rope, carried. He assured me he'd let me know when every-thing should arrive at the apartment, and when they were ready to finish the kitchen, we could go to Ikea together and pick up all the cabinets. He shook his head, though, about the wooden flooring, reiterating that if I didn't get 9mm-thick floorboards, the radiant heating system he was install-ing wouldn't work. So I kept looking.

The move-out date for my apartment was coming and I was getting anxious that progress didn't seem to be going as fast as he had promised, but told Claude that if he could make at least one room livable and the kitchen usable, I could move in and they could continue to work on the rest of the apart-ment while I slept on a mattress and worked in one corner of the kitchen. He said, "*Bien sûr, Daveed*," assuring me that they could do that, "*pas de problème.*"

I was skeptical, but remained optimistic. After all, when someone says something to me, I assume they mean it. But in case they don't, I know that when things are written in someone's own handwriting, they're more likely to stick to it. (Well, I didn't know that for a fact. But guessed it might work.) So I had him write the completion dates for the various projects to complete in the apartment—installing the heating, the floors and windows, cleaning the *cave*, installing the bathroom fixtures, and, finally, assembling the kitchen, adding the final move-in date to my calendar, written in his own words, to avoid any future *désastres*.

———

One thing that was blocking the project, that neither one of us had control over, was that we needed to connect the pipes for the new bathroom downstairs to the water main for the building. For that, I needed permission from the *copropriété*, shortened, or apocopated, to *co-pro*, at the next *assemblée générale des copropriétaires*, or the "AG" to Parisians, who are too busy to say all those lengthy terms in French, let alone go to meetings. Unfortunately, the annual AG for the owners in the building wasn't yet scheduled, and I needed permission via a majority vote at the meeting, which I was told would likely take place in late spring or early summer.

After hearing some harrowing stories about these meetings among neighbors, I was concerned if the vote would go in my favor, especially since I hadn't met any of the neighbors yet (though a few had tried to take a Parisian-style disinterested glance inside the apartment, without being noticed).

Romain assured me that having running water was *un droit humain*, a human right, and that *collectivité*-minded French people wouldn't deny me that privilege. (Except I know there was one paper-crumpling person in the group whom I shouldn't count on for a vote in my favor.) "Of course they'll vote to let you do it," he said, adding, "as long as you don't say anything during the meeting."

Optimistic about my chances, I sent an e-mail to the woman at the *syndic*, the one who had sent me a three-page registered letter reprimanding me for making a repair where water was leaking into the building and causing green mold to grow in the walls of the facade and on the interior walls of the *cave*, which I surmised was why Monsieur Legrand had kept the heat on in the spring and summer. I wasn't that excited to reinitiate contact with her, but needed to ask about calling a special meeting to vote on whether or not I could have water for my bathroom. As someone who can hold a grudge like no one's business (when I found out Barbra Streisand had eaten at Chez Panisse on my night off and no one had called to tell me, I didn't speak to anyone in the restaurant for two weeks afterward), I admire that the French can be explosive one minute, then perfectly charming the next, as if nothing had ever happened. And in typical French fashion, she responded as if she was an entirely different person, but she did let me know that if I wanted to call a special meeting of the other owners in the building, I could.

In order to do so, I'd have to photocopy my request, as well as the several pages of additional paperwork to officially announce, certify, notarize, and attest to my request. Then I would need to send a copy of all the certified paperwork to each of the owners of the forty apartments, with me covering the costs of photocopying the packet for everyone, and the costs of the pricey registered mail with a return signature for everyone required. I was looking at hundreds of euros right there, not to mention a week of paperwork. Once that was done, I would have to find, and rent at my own expense, a dedicated space to hold the meeting. "You can't just hold it in your apartment," the woman from the *syndic* firmly added. "It needs to be in an *espace neutre*"—a neutral space. (Which effectively killed my plan to sway the vote by serving home-made ice cream and cookies.) But I was relieved that at least I wasn't required to charter a plane to Switzerland and hold the meeting there.

I would also need to pony up her one-night salary, as well as pay her social charges, a percentage of her salary that covers her health insurance and retirement, approximately an additional 50 percent of her salaried rate. If a quorum failed to show up—and the usually contentious AG meetings are not exactly popular events—I couldn't call for a vote. So after going through all that, I'd most likely have to wait until the next regular meeting. Which I decided to do instead.

In anticipation of a yea vote, the plumber went ahead and laid the pipes for the bathroom and I ordered the bathroom fixtures and the tiles. If necessary, I could shower in the half-bathroom, using the *douchette* for something other than its intended purpose (which I kept to myself, because I didn't want to scandalize anyone by using something not for its intended purpose), until permission was granted to hook everything up. After the meeting took place a few months later and I got the okay from the neighbors, Claude would return to the apartment and hook it up, "... *pas de problème*," he told me, "*pas de problème, Daveed ...*"

Things were coming together, somewhat. A brand-new fuse box had been attached to the wall with shiny new white switches with a tangle of wires bunched up like smooth gray spaghetti behind them. Before we could turn it on, I'd need to tell Électricité de France how much electricity I intended to use. I couldn't figure out why they don't simply charge you for what you use, which I assumed was the purpose of an electric meter, but I went ahead and selected the maximum because I had an electric oven, a large refrigerator, a dryer, and worked a lot on my computer, often running other electrical devices as well. I later learned the benefits of a usage cap.

The painters were finishing the plaster walls, carefully shaping the corners into sharp right angles with trowels and scrapers. The ceiling was being rebuilt to include spaces for lots of light fixtures. (I like to see what I'm cooking.) While it was pretty clear that I wasn't moving in as soon as I had anticipated, I was starting to envision the space that was going to be my kitchen. I could wait a little longer, I supposed.

———

There's a reason the French word for "to ask" is *demander*. And there's no better proof of that than to contrast Romain and me. During the renovation, when Romain would stop by, he'd walk around the apartment scrutinizing the work and asking tough questions about what the workers were doing and why they were doing things a certain way. He'd follow up even before they finished their sentence if he wasn't getting an answer he thought was good enough. Being confrontational is part of the French character. (Americans think we are, but for all our bravado, we're not in the same league as the French.) I squirmed as he poked around the place, pointing out what wasn't done to his satisfaction, but no one got upset. I'm too sensitive and don't want to hurt other people's feelings, which perhaps explains why I kept getting passed over for a long-term *carte de résidence*. I probably should have been more demanding.

Going into situations with a *soupçon* of cynicism is the key to living in France. It manifests itself by being *exigeant* (demanding). If you take what's first offered, there's a good possibility that you're getting duped. If the vendors at the market don't know you, you won't be offered the freshest radishes, and if you're not watching, the ones with the wilted leaves might be quickly bagged up for you. Ask for a crois-sant at the bakery, and they won't reach around the others to grab the perfectly baked one that has its two crispy ends still intact. When going to a restaurant, I'll take the first table offered and head toward it, because there's nothing worse in America than to be tagged as "a difficult customer" or "a complainer," and I don't want to be that person. But Romain will survey the room before taking a single step forward to see if there is a better table, which he knows there is. And being *exigeant*, he'll get it.

Whatever objections my *exigeant* Frenchman brought up with the contractors, in terms of how the work was progress-ing, or how promptly I paid any bill that was handed to me, I downplayed. I thought he was being fussy. My lunch buddy Claude had that nice smile, and I kept imagining myself in my new kitchen, baking up recipes not just for my book, but for the whole crew in gratitude. I dreamed of having a big party and inviting everyone who had worked on the apart-ment to come celebrate when it was all over. I didn't want to be difficult and alienate them. We'd keep in touch, and if I had any more work in the future, I knew I'd have a diligent team of workers that I could count on. Everything would turn out fine.

————

As with any renovation, once you see things falling into place, other possibilities and ideas emerge. I had originally planned to put the dishwasher underneath the dishware cabinets, a few paces away from the sink. Thinking about it later, I decided it'd be better right next to the sink, where I could stand in one place and load the machine up with dishes. Being obsessive about things (like large white sinks, for example), I spent days walking myself through different scenarios, repeating the act of loading and unloading the dishwasher over and over in my head while waiting for the *métro*, standing in line at the cheese shop, or during one of my many sleepless nights, making sure the dishwasher was going to be in exactly the right place once it was finally installed.

So after careful (to put it mildly) consideration, I swapped the positions of the dishwasher and a base cabinet in the plans. The kitchen was still nonexistent and the space was still just a big rectangle; we hadn't even measured the kitchen for cabinets or ordered them, so I didn't imagine it being a problem. With space always at a premium in Paris, I also decided that a sliding door on my office would be better than a swinging door, which takes up valuable real estate when you take into account the room it needs to open and close. And after one of the plaster walls came down, I saw a brick wall behind it and wanted to keep the original brick exposed rather than patch it back over.

I didn't think the changes were major and didn't haggle, paying the workers promptly when they gave me the bill to refinish the bricks and for cutting the space in the wall to accommodate a sliding door. Anxious to move in, I prodded them to get going on sandblasting the stone vault arching over what was going to be my bedroom. Once they did that, I could sleep there as they worked on the rest of the apartment.

The crew would see me living down there, camped out on the floor, I reasoned to myself, and understand how much I was looking forward to moving in. My scheme was based on a still-unproven theory of mine, which hadn't worked as well as I thought it would in San Francisco, but thought it somehow might in Paris.

———

I had scheduled the movers for the end of the month, and the time was approaching for me to finally leave my old apartment. I was all packed and ready to go. But where to, I wasn't sure.

When pressed as to when they would start on the *cave*, Claude said that he'd been looking for a sandblaster to rent for the past few weeks. Astonishingly, he told me, with a shrug of his shoulders, there wasn't a single sandblaster available to rent in Paris or in the surrounding region. Every *sableuse* had either been rented out or reserved for the next few months. There were none available now—or even later.

I couldn't believe it. (Yet somehow, I did.) True, I'd never tried to rent a sandblaster in Paris, but do know that finding things in this city can be like trying to catch a feather: the more desperately you search for something, the more elusive it becomes. Having apparently exhausted all his options, Claude set two fellows of the crew to cleaning and resurfacing the 37-square-meter *cave,* each wielding a vibrating drill fitted with a corrugated square the size of a postage stamp. Watching them tackle 57,350 inches of stonework with the dinky little metal scrapers was like watching a couple of bakers roll out six hundred croissants with toothpicks.

Nevertheless, they bravely kept at it, and by the end of the first day, my future bedroom resembled a Dark Ages dungeon, with a thick haze of dust clogging the air, making it impossible to see. When the workers emerged for air, a fine, mud-colored powder caked their clothes, hair, cheeks, ears, and eyelashes. I suggested they wear masks and goggles, but they just shook their heads. Perhaps there was a shortage of those in Paris, too.

BACON, GREEN PEA, AND TARRAGON QUICHE
Quiche aux petits pois, lard fumé et estragon

SERVES 8

I worked in a vegetarian restaurant back in the 1980s and, being the '80s, quiche was a fixture on the menu. It was a French dish that enjoyed wide popularity in America at the time, so ubiquitous that it became a cliché. Before we moved on to *mesclun* (baby lettuce), chèvre, and Chablis that didn't come in a glass jug, *Real Men Don't Eat Quiche* was published, a satirical book that made it clear that if you were a real man, you didn't eat foofy French food.

In *la France*, quiche is anything but girly, or stuffy: It's sold by the wedge in French bakeries and served in working-class cafés. Because it's French, some Americans have difficulty pronouncing it. At the restaurant where I worked, we had a customer order the "quickie," which, of course, became a running joke among ourselves.

Most French cooks have a secret little "quickie" of their own, which is not what you think. They buy premade dough, which is sold in grocery stores packaged like a roll of aluminum foil. It's not bad, but I still prefer the buttery taste of homemade tart dough, so I'm not afraid to admit that I make my own.

1 cup (150g) cubed thick-cut bacon

1 medium shallot or 3 scallions, minced

1 cup (140g) fresh or frozen peas

Salt and freshly ground black pepper

1 prebaked French tart dough shell (recipe follows)

1 cup (250ml) half-and-half or heavy cream

1 large egg

2 large egg yolks

2 teaspoons Dijon mustard

Generous pinch of cayenne pepper

1½ tablespoons chopped (but not too finely chopped) fresh
  tarragon

¼ cup (25g) grated Parmesan cheese

1. Preheat the oven to 375°F (190°C). Line a baking sheet with aluminum foil or parchment paper.
2. In a medium skillet, cook the bacon over medium-high

heat, stirring frequently, until cooked through but not crisp. Transfer the cooked bacon to a paper towel–lined plate to drain. Wipe the excess fat from the pan and add the shallot. Cook over medium-hight heat, stirring, for 1 to 2 minutes, until translucent. Add the peas, season with salt and black pepper, and cook for another minute or two. Remove from heat.

3. Scatter the bacon pieces over the bottom of the baked tart shell. Spread the peas and shallot over the bacon. Place the filled tart shell on the prepared baking sheet.

4. In a medium bowl, whisk together the half-and-half, egg, egg yolks, mustard, cayenne, tarragon, and ¼ teaspoon salt.

5. Pour the egg mixture over the bacon and vegetables in the tart shell, filling it to the rim of the dough. Sprinkle the Parmesan evenly over the top and bake the quiche until it no longer jiggles when you shake the pan and the top is beginning to brown, about 25 minutes. Remove from the oven and let cool slightly before serving warm or at room temperature.

VARIATIONS: The tarragon can be replaced by the same quantity of chopped fresh chervil, dill, or chives. If you'd like to add some extra cheese, sprinkle ½ cup (40g) coarsely grated Swiss-style cheese, like Emmenthal, Gruyère, Comté, or Jarlsberg, over the bacon and peas before adding the egg mixture.

To make mushroom quiche, replace the peas with 6 ounces (170g) sliced mushrooms, sautéed in butter with the shallot or scallions until cooked through and browned on the edges, about 5 minutes.

FRENCH TART DOUGH

My good friend Paule Caillat showed me how to make this dough, which quickly became my go-to tart dough. (She was also kind enough to give me a demonstration of her combination washer/dryer. Which I took a pass on.) It's easy to make and doesn't need to be rolled out; instead, it's pressed into the tart pan. If you have a scale, use that to measure the ingredients, especially the flour.

> 6 tablespoons (3 ounces/85g) unsalted butter, cut into cubes
> 1 tablespoon vegetable oil (I use canola)
> 3 tablespoons water
> 1 tablespoon sugar
> ⅛ teaspoon salt
> 160g (5.5oz/1 rounded cup) all-purpose flour

1. Preheat the oven to 410°F (210°C).
2. In a medium ovenproof bowl, such as a Pyrex bowl, combine the butter, oil, water, sugar, and salt. Put the bowl in the oven for 15 minutes, until the mixture is bubbling and starts to brown around the edges.
3. Wearing oven mitts, carefully remove the bowl from the oven. Dump the flour into the bowl and stir it in quickly, until the mixture comes together and forms a ball that pulls away from the sides of the bowl. (Be careful while you're stirring—the bowl is hot!)
4. Transfer the dough to a 9-inch (23cm) tart mold with a removable bottom and spread it a bit with a spatula to help it cool down.
5. Once the dough is cool enough to handle, pat it into the mold with the heel of your hand and use your fingers to press it up the sides of the mold. Reserve a small piece

of dough for patching any cracks. (For extra security, you can take a fork and press the dough gently against the sides of the tart mold, as Paule does.)

6. Prick the dough all over with the tines of a fork, about ten times, then bake the tart shell for 15 minutes, or until it's golden brown.

7. Remove the tart shell from the oven; if there are any sizable cracks, use bits of the reserved dough to fill them in, using your pinky to smooth and patch them.

24

As the next few weeks passed, progress slowed even further. My BFFF (Best French Friend Forever) lunches with Claude tapered off around the same time he (and the crew) started showing up less and less often. At first, a couple of days would go by and I'd give them a call to see where they were. If the call didn't go right to voicemail, Claude would tell me they had an emergency on another project and they'd be back "*sûrement mercredi, Daveed,* for sure on Wednesday." Promising to show up on a particular day and then failing to do so meant I was left standing in the apartment for hours, waiting for no one to show up, with nothing to do but stare at the mess they'd left the place in.

Two months had passed, and the apartment wasn't anywhere near being finished, let alone close to looking like a place someone could ever live in. The heating coils had been laid, but I still hadn't been able to find the right wood flooring to put over them. The walls of the *cave* were finally done. They weren't quite as polished as I was hoping, and when I looked closely, hundreds of rusty iron nail heads stuck out from the stones. I spent a few days yanking those out myself with pliers, to keep myself busy while I waited for the crew to return and apply sealer to the stones.

The weather in Paris was still very chilly, and whenever I

went over to check if there had been any progress, I'd open the door to find the stone-cold apartment eerily silent. I would sit alone in the drafty apartment for hours, wrapped up in my winter coat and scarf, because I didn't want to miss them if they showed up, even though *mercredi* (and *jeudi* and *vendredi)* had come and gone. Time had become something intangible and I started losing track of days.

Looking around, I tried to remain optimistic as I stood in the middle of the mess of tools and jumble of construction materials, which were all in the same places they'd been yesterday, and the day before that, and the day before that, an obvious sign that no one had been there for a while, except me. My chance of moving in started to seem very remote.

I had no choice but to move out of my apartment and into Romain's studio, an artist's atelier. Some of my furniture had to be put into storage, but all my other belongings—suitcases of clothes, cases of cookbooks, bins of paperwork, boxes of kitchenware, and cartons holding my cookbook recipes and notes—were dumped in one mountainlike heap in the middle of the unfinished apartment. Because there was so much dust everywhere, Romain helped me drape a patchwork of plastic tarps over the whole mound. It was a crazy quilt of plastic, held together with haphazardly placed sticky tape that wasn't quite effective at keeping the tarps from sliding off. The ten-foot-high hillock of my stuff was hemmed in by a disarray of power tools, dirty plastic bags of miscellaneous electrical parts, ripped-apart boxes, half-empty buckets of plaster, with most of it caked and dried out from being left open, and lots and lots of trash.

I didn't look much better than my apartment. After the stressful closing period that went on for nearly a year, any sane person would have either taken a vacation or called it a day and gotten on the next plane home. I persevered and soldiered on. I was determined to make it work. The entire apartment had been demolished, which was quite different from my original intention of just moving a wall and extending the kitchen counter, and the work had slowed to a crawl (or more like a halt). Instead of getting up in the morning, grabbing my basket, and shopping at the market, or visiting a bakery and nibbling on éclairs and *flans*, I was spending my days stepping over tarps and bundles of wet metal pipes, occasionally tripping over coiled stacks of electrical wires or broken plastic light sockets, wondering how (or if) I would ever get out of this mess.

I'm an upbeat guy, but one morning when I went to shave, I looked at myself in the mirror, and saw that my cheeks were sunken and there were worrisome creases around my eyes that hadn't been there before. I felt grimy all the time, spending my days going back and forth between apartments in clothes caked with plaster dust, wearing dilapidated sneakers because I didn't want to ruin my good shoes walking in the filth. I'd lost a considerable amount of weight during the past year and had one of those enviable waistlines French men seem to have. And like them, I needed a cigarette.

I was reassured when I found Claude and some of the crew working in the apartment a few days later, although Romain remained skeptical. And he was right; it was time for a payment. The joy of finding them working in the apartment was short-lived when Claude took me aside to talk money. True, I had made some changes and added a few things—I had decided I wanted a better lock for the front door, for example. And changing where the dishwasher was going to be installed required moving a pipe, etc. Nothing drastic.

Romain watched as I was handed another bill, then signed and tore another check out of my checkbook. We'd been together for a while by this point, and he was used to my American ways. But this time, he pulled me aside. "You know, *Daveed*, you shouldn't pay them anything, anymore. If you pay them, they'll stop coming again, and only come back when they need money." That didn't make sense to me. "You need to withhold payment as long as possible. No one in France would ever pay a bill until the last possible moment. Make them *soif* [thirsty] for it."

I brushed away Romain's advice, saying that I didn't want to be that kind of person. When someone hands me a bill, I pay them. It seems like the right thing to do. I didn't want to cause conflict with the contractor, either, because I didn't want to ruin our *sympathique* (friendly) relationship. So I continued to pay bills when they were presented to me, and continued to be the kind of person without a place to live.

―――――

I had already made the second of three payments, which Romain wasn't thrilled about, either. Yet more things, and some of the changes (e.g., stuffing soundproofing material in the ceiling, moving the dishwasher, removing the old metal roll-down door, and building a bathroom vanity) had me handing over additional checks, and I started growing concerned about the budget. Living in France, it's easy to get overwhelmed by *l'administration*, which, if you don't keep up with it daily, quickly backs up like a clogged drain, and gets more difficult to wade through the deeper it gets.

I'm not a numbers guy, except when it comes to quantities of cups and tablespoons in recipes, and I'd been jotting down an informal list of expenses in a notebook. It became one of many notebooks I carried around with me in a gray messenger bag, which had ballooned in width to include plumbing and Ikea catalogs, drawings Romain had done envisioning the kitchen, folders of receipts, and a separate series of notebooks dedicated to phone numbers and resources, another to the various dimensions of appliances, another to vocabulary, and still another for expenditures. Someday, I presume, they will be unearthed in Paris and archived, used as a reference (or a warning?) for *les Américains* who rebuilt parts of the city. (Or one who almost took down a whole neighborhood when remodeling his apartment.)

We had agreed from the start that I would pay for the project in three equal payments, and any additional work would be added on as necessary. Yet I was still caught off-guard when I was handed an envelope by my *sympathique* friend, accompanied with a coy smile. I ran my finger under the flap of the envelope and slid out two pages that were stapled together. I read through the first page, a recapitulation of things they had done that weren't specified in the original bid, some that seemed like they should have been part of the job, like attaching the stair railing to the wall or putting a doorknob on a door they installed, and others that I was expecting to be added. "*Pas de problème, Daveed*—let's talk about it later," he had said when he was attaching or installing something, and I didn't bother to bring up the issue of how much they were going to cost.

I turned to the second page and scanned down to the bottom, where the total was. My heart stopped for a moment while I focused my eyes on the number. French numbers are hard to understand when they're spoken because of their length and complexity. When printed out, though, there's no mistaking them. The number on the bill took my breath away: It was an amount equivalent to three-quarters of the cost of the entire renovation.

I felt tears moving toward the front of my eyes. Had I

been alone, I would have let them flow. (On the plus side, at least he handed the bill to me, rather than slipping it into my mailbox. That would have traumatized me, making it impossible for me to ever open my mailbox again.) Crying would have felt good and it would have let some of the stress that had built up inside me pour out. But I didn't, and found myself getting a *douche froide*, even though I didn't have a *douche* to shower in. After all those complimentary lunches, I now realized there is no such thing as a free lunch, even in Paris.

I tried to negotiate, but was no match for the obstinate French. Romain tried, too, and he's a pro. But it was no use. The work had been done, and I hadn't agreed on a price beforehand, so I was stuck. Taking a deep breath, I wrote a check. But I didn't write the check then and there. I waited until I got home, then took out my *chéquier* to write one, then had a good cry afterward.

————

Construction surprises and shocking bills are almost as hard to take as people repeating clichés to you about renovation when you're in the thick of things. Having people say, with a chuckle, "You know, David, when remodeling, it always costs twice as much as you think . . . and takes twice as long!" doesn't make you feel any better. Which I know, because I had reached the "twice as much" mark, and they weren't even close to being done. And later, I would have considered myself lucky if the work had only taken twice as long.

The upside of paying that eye-watering bill was that I used it as leverage to urge them to get moving on the kitchen.

As they started framing out the space to prepare it for the kitchen cabinets, I thought it would be a good idea to install waterproof electrical outlets next to the kitchen sink, rather than the regular outlets the electrician was installing. "Isn't it dangerous to have open electrical outlets right next to the kitchen sink, with all that water splashing around?" I tentatively asked Sébastien, who was fiddling around with nearby wires. "Shouldn't they have circuit breakers, or be waterproof outlets with covers . . . for safety?" Tiptoeing around him had become another source of stress, because it was hard to know what could cause an explosion. I had found a toiletry kit stashed away in the apartment, with a paper bag of clothes nearby, and made a general inquiry to the crew as to who they might belong to. He came over to me, snatched them out of my hand, and yelled that I didn't have any right to be touching his things. I didn't bring up that his things were actually in my apartment, but I did wonder why someone was keeping an overnight bag there. (Especially because there was nowhere to sleep yet.)

When asked about the potentially dangerous outlets, he stopped what he was doing and straightened up. Then he turned, furrowed his eyebrows, leaned toward me, and bellowed, "*NON! C'est PAS NÉCESSAIRE* . . . You can't get water into *these outlets*. They're TOO FAR from the sink!"

My job involves washing a lot of dishes, and I know that water from the sink can and does go wherever it wants. It seemed prudent to have waterproof outlets in the splash zone from a sink, which I later learned was part of the building code in France. (So I wasn't the only one who considered them dangerous.) He then started haranguing me for changing my mind (actually, I hadn't changed my mind) about the outlets, while Claude watched the whole thing in amusement. I was starting to get blamed by them for any problem that arose, which they said was because I changed my mind about something, even if the problem had nothing to do with whether I had actually changed my mind about it, hence my vigilance while they worked.

I didn't realize what a big deal it was to install an electrical outlet with a cover, which I'd seen in every hardware store I'd been in. So while he continued to grumble about the additional work he would have to do because I was changing my mind, I offered to run to the hardware store and get one.

An hour later, I returned with a waterproof outlet and handed it to him. "This?! THIS is what you want? Okay . . . *OKAY*! Here you go, then!" he said, snatching the outlet out of my hand and reaching for an iron mallet nearby, which he used to start pounding away at the electrical outlets he'd already installed there, smashing them to bits, as well as a wide swath around the freshly smoothed-over plaster wall surrounding them.

"Here . . . here . . . now we'll put it *HERE*!" he barked while he continued pounding. Claude was amused by the scenario, although I didn't see what was so funny. I thought it'd be easier to just unscrew the outlet that was there and replace it with the new one, which was the same size and made by the same company. But he had other ideas, as he continued to pound away, creating a wider area around the outlets, then pried the old outlets loose and replaced them with the one I'd bought. When finished, he stood back and yelled, "Now are you happy!?" and stomped off in a huff. Well, if I wasn't before, I certainly wasn't now. But at least I didn't have to worry about being electrocuted in the future. Or did I?

———

My relationship with the crew had been sliding downhill. I didn't know why, because I hadn't done anything differently, except spend an inordinate amount of time waiting for them to show up, and paying them what seemed like an inordinate amount of money. I believed their excuses for the delays, but after that alarming bill, I told them not to do anything that was going to cost extra without running it by me first, which seemed like a reasonable request. Claude responded as if I had grossly affronted him, telling me that if that's the way I wanted to be, then *fine*—from now on, they were going to charge me for every little thing, no matter how insignificant or minuscule.

When Romain stopped by later, he was less happy than I was. Sébastien told him that he was going to start doing *service minimum*, since that's what I was paying for. Romain wasn't having any of that, telling them that they were getting paid a lot of money and were taking advantage of the situation. Furthermore, working at *service minimum* wasn't something that he personally knew how to do. They should be doing the best job they could. He was outraged, and no matter what they said or how much they tried to talk around him, they were no match for a true Parisian. Standing defiantly in front of them, using his index finger to punctuate his points, he cut them off midsentence as they tried to offer excuses, telling them repeatedly that they were *pas corrects* and how ridiculous it was that the place wasn't anywhere near done. He was my *héro*.

———

My naïveté had turned me into an anxious mess. I was ridiculously behind on my own work, and spending too much time stuck in the apartment waiting for them to show up, which they didn't, more often than not. But I needed to be there because if I wasn't and they did something wrong, I would get blamed.

The fixtures had been installed in the small half-bathroom, and it had been tiled, so there was finally a working toilet. But as soon as it was finished, the floor and walls got covered over with tarps to protect the tile from dirty footprints and muck. As for the rest of the apartment, the three-month mark came, and nothing else was anywhere close to being finished. I was now in the *merde*.

I'd reached a dead end with my search for 9mm wood flooring that would be compatible with the *sol chauffant*. Desperate, I went back to one of the first shops I'd visited, which had the flooring I wanted—a natural oak with a bit of an aged patina to it—and had enough of it in stock, so it was available immediately. The salesman remembered me and was confused as to why I'd returned, surprised that I was still searching for flooring so many months later. He told me that he sold a lot of wood floors to people with radiant heat and 15mm thickness was the standard. There was no question— *"Je jure,"* he swore to me, holding up his palm, swearing that it would work.

When I told Claude what the salesman had said, he shook his head and said, *non, non*, it wouldn't work. Since he had the same heat in his apartment, he must've known what he was talking about. But I was fed up with being in the middle of a he-said, he-said scenario, so I decided to get both him and the store clerk in the same room because I didn't want to get the wrong flooring and get blamed by Claude when it didn't work. We drove over to the store together in Claude's van (which was hard to find a place to sit in; it was a bigger mess than my apartment), hopped out, and went in to speak with the clerk. The salesman and I had already priced out the amount of flooring I needed, and it could be delivered tomorrow. Which meant the crew would have no reason not to lay the floors and get going on the kitchen. Claude shook his head when he saw the 15mm-thick flooring. *"Non, Daveed, ça marche pas"*—it won't work.

The salesman disagreed: *"Excusez-moi, monsieur,* but I've worked in this shop for eleven years and I sell a lot of flooring to be used with radiant heat. This will definitely work."

Claude looked baffled, and I could see he was thinking about something. Sometimes the French will create a scenario or story that will evolve to be the truth, at least according to them. Ice in drinks will cause your stomach to freeze, radiation from Chernobyl was stopped from coming into France at the Italian border by the Alps, etc. And they'll staunchly defend it, no matter what. In this instance, Claude was face-to-face with an expert on wood floors, yet he still wouldn't admit that the floorboards the salesman was recommending would be okay. Other salesmen in the store came over to say the same thing, backing up their coworker (another time *collectivité* helped me out), so Claude didn't have much of a choice. He was rubbing his chin, trying to figure out how to respond. He looked at me and said sharply, "Okay, if you want it, we will install it. But if it doesn't work, it's your fault, *Daveed*." I felt validated but, at the same time, was anxious about the blame that was being put on me if the floors caused problems, because Claude was so convinced they would. In the end, those planks worked just fine at transferring heat. In fact, they worked a little too well.

25

The hardest part of any construction project isn't the surprise bills, the delays, waiting around for contractors, or having to listen to people repeatedly tell you that you should expect the work to take twice as long and cost twice as much. No, the most challenging part is The Trip to Ikea. And "Trip" usually becomes plural, because it's not possible to make just one.

When I told Claude at the onset of the renovation that I wanted to use Ikea cabinets, he said they were a snap for him to assemble. "Just like Lego for us, *Daveed—pas de problème!*" he happily replied. I've spent many an afternoon just trying to figure out how to unfold one of their folded-up canvas storage boxes, let alone assemble furniture: I once put together a nightstand, and when I stood back to admire it, realized I had put the doors on backward, with the unfinished side facing outward. Years later, Romain still looks at it, then at me, and laughs. So I was glad to be working with someone better than I at assembling and installing Ikea cabinetry.

Travelers think that Charles de Gaulle Airport is the most confusing place in Paris, but I give that honor to Ikea. Romain and I went one evening to get in-person help selecting the kitchen cabinets.

Romain had done drawings of the kitchen, but he's not an architect or contractor so they didn't include precise measurements. But it didn't matter: we were at Ikea just to see what was available and get a rough idea from one of the kitchen planners for which cabinets I'd need and what they'd cost. Their online planning tool hadn't been updated in years and seemed to be only compatible with Netscape, which is nostalgically remembered by how it was accompanied by the boingy ricocheting noise of your computer connecting through a dial-up line.

My kitchen space butted up against a very large, long window. The ceiling was 10 feet high, and I envisioned two rows of cabinets mounted on the fixed wall that was adjacent to the window, with my kitchen island in the middle of it all. The rest of the room, now that the wall had been demolished, opened out onto the living area, which was going to be an extension of the grand kitchen.

Information may be the unofficial currency in Paris, but space is priceless. Every square inch or centimeter is so precious that apartments aren't sold by number of rooms, but by square meter, or *mètre carré*. The measurement is called the *loi Carrez*, the precise dimensions, which are scrutinized down to the centimeter.

According to law number 96-1107 (technically, it's Loi n° 96-1107 du 18 décembre 1996, because France requires that the date it was decreed be added to the title of any law, which seems to me to be as important as what city you are in when you write a check), if the *loi Carrez* measurements are found to be incorrect before the purchase, the buyer can nullify the sale. If it's after the sale, the seller can be forced to give a refund. By now, my year was unfortunately up. But it would have been a *loi* worth invoking just to see the look on the agent's face if Madame Bernachon summoned him back to her office to get some of my money, and his commission, back.

A second measurement for apartments in France is the *superficie Carrez*, or the actual usable area. Here, things get a little looser—but only slightly. This is still France, after all. Anywhere you can't stand or sit, such as where there are pipes, stairs, low ceilings (which included 75 percent of my previous apartment and I have a few permanent dents in my head to prove it), and even the area where doors swing open and closed, are not considered "livable" areas.

No matter how you measure it, every bit of space in a Paris apartment has a price, whether it's up, down, side to side, or wall to wall. Like the leftover croissants that are stuffed with almond paste and baked again and sold the next day, nothing is wasted in France.

The stainless-steel countertop and stovetop that were already there would remain against the low wall that butted up against the windows. At the other end of the counter would be the pièce de résistance—my hard-won *évier*, or *robinet*, or *bassin*, or sink—or whatever you call it. Around the corner from the sink, there would be another kitchen counter with a row of base cabinets, next to a long cupboard for the hot water heater and fuse box.

The *réfrigérateur américain* with *portes françaises* would be at the end of that counter, next to the hot water heater and fuse box cabinet. In the far corner of the room was the *chiottes*, a word that the French use colloquially to describe a small bathroom. Trying to act more French, I was casually throwing that term around, including in conversations with the women at the plumbing showrooms—until I learned it translated to "shithouse." I learned the power of keeping one's mouth shut, and stopped using it.

The kitchen island would be 8 by 5 feet, which was even larger than the pastry counter at Chez Panisse that three of us worked around while we made desserts for hundreds of people a day. But it was also going to be our dining table, as well as a satellite of my home office. Underneath the kitchen island would be storage drawers and a space for my wide 90cm (36-inch) baking oven, as well as a washer and dryer—separately, with high chairs placed around the counter. The size of the counter was unbelievable to some—actually, to every French person who saw it. A few passersby asked if I was opening a restaurant. Being a witty sort of fellow, I joked that I was opening a bakery, until a few threatened to call the authorities and turn me in for unauthorized use of the space. (If they knew what I had gone through to get authorization just to live in it, they'd definitely realize I was kidding.) But to me, the large open area with tons of counter space would be the perfect place to cook and bake. In a noncommercial capacity, for the record.

Since there was plenty of room above the counter that was lined up against the high wall, I planned to have two rows of cabinets, one on top of the other, for all the wine-glasses, vintage crockery, sets of apéritif glasses, well-used French jam jars, café au lait bowls, and miscellaneous French cookware I'd been maniacally amassing ever since I came across my first *vide grenier*, the French version of a clean-your-attic rummage sale. I hadn't realized how much I had, though, until I started packing boxes for the move and grew concerned that I might have to start looking for a second apartment to hold everything. Or realize my neighbor's worst fears and open a shop.

For the time being, though, I had my hands, as well as my future cupboards, full. Walking down the aisles of kitchen cabinets at Ikea, Romain thought I should have one single row of double-high cabinets, rather than my planned two rows of separate cabinets, one on top of the other. I, on the other hand, thought it would be ridiculous to have to open a coffin-size cabinet door any time I wanted a water glass or soup bowl (or soup plate).

We never fight. Even during the renovation, often cited as a cause of many divorces, we didn't have a single one of those near breakups that couples have over something as insignificant as the finish on the inside of a cabinet or whether a screw should be brass or stainless. Luckily, Romain's taste aligns with mine, and you really have to cherish someone who would go through a remodel with you. Going to Ikea is definitely above and beyond the call of relationship duty. (Don't tell, but I would have had to think long and hard about it, if the situation had been reversed.)

But there he was, accompanying me to *EEy-Kay-a*, as they say, my little Frenchman with his melting brown eyes and bushy moustache extending down the sides of his upper lip to a salt-and-pepper patch of hair framing his sweet smile. Standing at around five feet tall, like most French people he packs a lot of personality into his compact size. I was glad he was with me, for the time being.

We'd made the obligatory rounds through the store, stocking up on tea candles, a cutlery tray (which I optimistically put in my cart on the assumption I'd be unpacking my knives and forks shortly), and an extra-large box of their exceptionally crisp oatmeal cookies dipped in dark chocolate, which give French pastries a run for their money. We finally reached the area in the store where the kitchen designers are, and joined a lengthy line of already-weary Parisians roped in tightly on each side, like livestock being corralled, a technique used in France to prevent line-jumping. (The BHV/Marais department store has the best I've seen: an elaborate series of metal rails at the bottom and top landings of their escalators to curb the practice.) Off in the distance were desks with kitchen designers behind their computers, the kind you imagine were once attached to dot-matrix printers, waiting to help me envision my kitchen.

Being winter, everyone was bundled up in several lay-ers of clothes, Parisian-style; they manage to keep their cool even in wool overcoats and sweaters, with long scarves snak-ing around their necks in macramé-worthy knots. We were packed in closely, roasting together like the meatballs in the steam table we passed at the Ikea cafeteria. While we waited, Romain continued his one-sided crusade for a single row of long cabinets. You have to love the strong-willed French, who seem to live for *la manif* (short for *manifestation*, which is used to refer to a protest, but also means to "express your-self"), and Romain continued to *manifester* his idea.

The lips and fingers of the people around us were now starting to twitch because they had gone too long without having a smoke; a few dangled unlit cigarettes from their mouths, and some looked to be in the early stages of with-drawal—I grew concerned that if the line didn't move any faster, someone would need to scan the aisles to see where the nicotine patches were, and what they were called. (Nösmøke? Wythdråwl? Göttahavit?)

It was dinnertime and I was hungry. Actually, I was starving—as well as hot, and getting hotter. The line hadn't moved in nearly an hour, and I'd already peeled off a few layers of clothing; my coat and sweater became scratchy as I perspired. My breathing became labored in the heavy air, but somehow the Parisians were able to stand there, unfazed by the heat and lack of ventilation, or space, pushing their scarves up higher around their necks to ward off any possible drafts (even in the summer, Parisians defiantly wear scarves to protect themselves against any possible *courant d'air*). But I would have killed for a few gulps of *air frais* as the pile of my clothes in our shopping cart grew and grew as I shucked them off, pondering whether I'd be removing my trousers next.

While I wondered if Ikea sold oxygen machines, too, Romain brought up the long cabinets again. I said *non*, again, and that I didn't want to talk about it anymore. I was desperate to see a designer so we could get out of the stifling kitchen department. We'd made it that far, though, so even if my respiratory system was on the verge of shutting down, I thought I could wait it out. But I was hot, hungry, and getting grouchier by the minute, warning signs that were leading to one conclusion: I was close to a meltdown.

Romain should've known better than to ignore those signs, which he'd seen before. (At that point, "hangry" hadn't made it into the *franglais* lexicon, perhaps because the "h" isn't pronounced in French, and angry is a natural state in France.) Regardless, he brought up the tall cabinets *again*. I said *non, again*. I'd made up my mind and that was the end of it, I firmly told him. Knowing that of course he'd bring it up again, I added that if he mentioned it two more times—I emphasized this by holding up two fingers so he wouldn't confuse *deux* with *douze*, and think he had twelve more times remaining to mention it—I was going to leave.

Being French, he brought it up again. Being American, I held up a finger to signal that if he brought it up *one more time*, I was outta there.

Then he brought it up again.

That was it. My forehead was so hot I felt like it would blow off. I was damp, itchy, worn out, and famished from standing there for so long.

"*C'est fini, Romain. JE PARS!*" I screamed. "That's it. I'M LEAVING!" People turned and looked at me. A few jaws would have dropped had they not been clamped around unlit cigarettes. We'd been in the store for nearly three hours, and had waited and waited and waited in that mob of *misère*. Romain looked at me, having never seen me completely lose it like that, as I pushed past the Parisians, squeezed under the rope barrier, and headed toward the *sortie*. I'd grabbed my discarded clothes, but left the rest of the items behind. I walked past the formidable checkout lines, passing desperate people hunched over their overloaded shopping carts, looking just as anxious to get out of there as I was.

Once outside, as soon as the cool air hit me, I inhaled quickly, gulping in as much air as I could. I had a flashback to when I was six years old and almost drowned: my mother sprinted through the sand toward the ocean in her oversized Oleg Cassini sunglasses and white PF Flyers, as the waves brutally dragged me out to sea. I gasped for air when she pulled me back to the sandy beach. As the oxygen flowed back into my brain by the Ikea parking lot, I began to feel a little more normal. I wanted my mommy.

The cold felt good for the first few moments, but was soon giving me chills. I stood in the parking lot, illuminated by the blue and yellow lights of the Ikea sign that hovered overhead, until Romain arrived with what had been in our shopping cart (thankfully, this included the two boxes of Swedish oatmeal cookies), lugging our purchases in crinkly blue Ikea bags and loading them into the car. I was relieved to be out of there, but still angry. (Tearing into the cookies, though, took care of my "hanger.") We tried to find the exit, avoiding the pandemonium of drivers enveloped in a haze of cigarette smoke clouding up their windshields, with flat-packed cardboard boxes sticking out the back or weighing down their roofs, madly speeding around as they tried to find their way out of the confusing parking lot. (Actually, it wasn't all that confusing. It's just that Parisian drivers aren't known for heeding signs.) Most were so desperate to get out of there that they would have run over anything in their path, including us. Which also was not unusual for Parisian drivers, in Ikea parking lots or elsewhere.

As Romain drove, he tried to talk, but I didn't respond, and he looked a little scared of me. All that was on my mind was that I would never go back to that place ever again. We drove home in silence, with the sound of the Ikea bags rustling around in the backseat, which seemed to be quaking in fear of me as well.

SWEDISH CHOCOLATE-OATMEAL COOKIES
(Galettes suédoises à l'avoine)

MAKES 25 SANDWICH COOKIES

The one thing that might get me to go back to Ikea—someday—are the *Havreflarn*: crisp oatmeal cookies with dark chocolate sandwiched in between them. But to avoid going back any more than I have to, I wanted to make them at home. I searched around for a recipe and found one at *Cuisine de Bernard*, the blog of French cookbook author Bernard Laurence, who said he had tested the recipe dozens of times. His conclusion was that margarine worked better than butter. So, like remodeling an apartment in Paris, I experienced another first: I bought margarine.

The French are known for their love of butter, so it surprises some to hear that margarine was invented in France. Napoléon directed a chemist to come up with a substitute so that soldiers, and people who couldn't afford butter, would be able to have something similar. I did some side-by-side tests, and I'll keep my battles to Swedish department stores, because there's no contest here: butter is the clear winner.

The original recipe also made a lot of cookies, and I spent almost as much time baking them all off as I did waiting for my turn at Ikea, which, admittedly, was much more fun. But still . . . I made some adjustments and adaptations, and cut the recipe in half, hence the slightly awkward ½ egg measurement, which you get by beating an egg in a measuring cup and using half. Or you can double the recipe and refrigerate half the batter if you don't want to bake all the cookies at once. (It'll keep for about 10 days in the refrigerator.)

6 tablespoons (3 ounces, 85g) unsalted butter or stick margarine (see Note)

1 cup (95g) old-fashioned rolled oats (not instant)

½ large egg (see Headnote)

⅔ cup (130g) sugar

¼ cup (35g) all-purpose flour

¼ teaspoon baking powder, preferably aluminum-free

½ teaspoon pure vanilla extract

Big pinch of salt

6 ounces (170g) bittersweet or semisweet chocolate, coarsely chopped

1. Melt the butter in a medium saucepan. Remove from the heat and set aside.

2. In a mini food processor, pulse the oats six or seven times until they are broken up into powdery bits with some visible pieces of oat flakes.

3. Stir the oats into the melted butter, then mix in the egg, sugar, flour, baking powder, vanilla, and salt. Scrape the mixture into a small bowl or plastic container, cover, and chill for 1 hour.

4. Preheat the oven to 375°F (190°C) with a rack in the center position. Line a baking sheet with parchment paper or a silicone baking mat. (This recipe bakes three sheets of cookies. You can use the same sheet, letting it cool completely between each batch, or use separate baking sheets.)

5. Remove the batter from the refrigerator. Use a small, spring-loaded ice cream scoop that holds 1 teaspoon of batter (1 inch/3cm across) or a 1-teaspoon measuring spoon to scoop up slightly rounded spoonfuls of the batter, and place them 2½ inches (6cm) apart on the baking sheet. (If using a measuring spoon, you'll want to roll each portion of dough into a ball with your hands, so they bake evenly.) With a damp hand, very gently press the tops of the dough balls down just until the tops are flat, similar-looking to gumdrops.

6. Bake just until they turn light golden brown in the center, 7 to 9 minutes. Near the end of baking, the centers will brown quickly, so it's best to keep an eye on them and pull them out before they get too dark. Remove from the oven and let cool. When cool, transfer the cookies to a wire rack. Bake the remaining cookie batter, letting the pan cool completely between batches.

7. Set a small heatproof bowl over a small saucepan of barely simmering water. Put the chocolate in the bowl to melt, making sure not a drop of water or steam gets into the chocolate. (That will cause it to seize.) Stir gently until the chocolate is mostly melted, then remove from the heat and stir until the chocolate is smooth.

8. Working one at a time, drop one cookie, bottom-side down, on top of the chocolate. Push it down slightly, then slide a fork underneath it to lift it out.

Choose another cookie that's about the same size, turn it upside down so the bottom is facing up, and slide the chocolate-dipped cookie on top of it to sandwich them together. Place the sandwiched cookie on a platter or baking sheet. Dip and sandwich the rest of the cookies with chocolate the same way, then refrigerate the cookies until the chocolate is firm. Remove from the refrigerator and let them come to room temperature before serving. The cookies can be stored in an airtight container at room temperature for up to 5 days.

NOTE: If using margarine, buy a good-quality brand at a natural foods store. Don't use margarine sold in tubs—only the kind sold in sticks.

26

Even though, after that night, I swore I'd never return to Ikea, somehow I found myself back there a week later.

But this wasn't just any Ikea. It was a special Ikea, called Ikea Cuisines—a store in Vélizy entirely dedicated to kitchens. Romain and I had made up after my meltdown, and I decided to give it another all-American try, going in with the positive attitude that we're known for. We wouldn't be sidetracked by rugs, folding tables, and boxes of Swedish cookies: we'd get in, get a list of what cabinets I needed, and get out.

But when I looked up the address, the online reviews in the search engine sidebar said otherwise. And you don't have to speak French to understand them:

The wait was "*interminable.*"

"*J'ai détesté!*"

The personnel was "*non qualifié.*"

A "*catastrophe.*"

Getting there was "*un labyrinthe.*"

And these reviews were from people who already have low expectations for customer service. I figured they were just being overly *exigeant*. This store was a whole new concept, and a great-sounding one at that. It's a store full of kitchens. How bad could it be?

Getting there, as it turned out, was indeed like driving

through a labyrinth. We had to pass through the Duplix A86, a 10-kilometer (6.2-mile) tunnel, the longest in France, which required a 9-euro toll. (The tunnel is so imposing that it actually has its own website.) Before we even got to Vélizy, I was already 27 euros poorer, as we had to cross back through the tunnel two more times because the labyrinth-like highway routing was so bewildering. We were relieved when we finally saw the familiar blue-and-yellow Ikea sign after driving eighteen miles through a tunnel, next to the highway, but couldn't figure out how to actually get to the store. We drove back and forth past it multiple times; none of the markers on the highway pointed to the right direction or which exit to take. The *catastrophe* was beginning.

Things were looking up when we did it the French way: We asked somebody how to get there. (French people love giving directions; it gives them a chance to tell someone else what to do.) We finally pulled in to a parking space and went inside. At this store, they work on the take-a-number system so you can avoid the roped-in crush of people in line. *How civilized*, I thought, as I sauntered over to pull off the paper ticket with my number hanging from the machine. That is, until I looked at the number at the bottom of the ticket that noted the approximate wait time: 4½ hours. I read that and chuckled to the young clerk whose job it was to stand next to the machine and make sure customers knew how to pull the ticket from it.

"This can't be true," I said incredulously. "A four-and-a-half-hour wait?" Another customer leaning against a wall for support brushed the cobwebs off his shoulder, stood up, and weakly chimed in, "*C'est vrai, monsieur,* I've been here since . . ." His voice trailed off and his broken eyes went back to staring into the white and gray nothingness of the waiting area. Using his last bit of energy, he extracted a wispy paper ticket from his pocket, confirming the time he had arrived at the store to prove his point.

The 45-minute ride had taken us nearly 2 hours, so we decided to wait. Surely Ikea doesn't make people wait 4½ *interminable* hours to help them purchase thousands of euros' worth of merchandise. It was a pretty small store. Surely we'd be able to see someone shortly.

To pass the time, we looked around the showroom, strolling through the model kitchens on display, checking out the knobs, pulling out drawers, and opening cabinets. When we were done, we checked out the kitchens again, pulling on knobs, opening drawers, and checking out the cabinets. Then we went back to the kitchen design center to see how much time was left before we could see someone.

The waiting time on the board said we had another 3 hours and 55 minutes to go, so we went back and checked out the kitchens—and the knobs, and the drawers, and the cabinets—again. By now, we were very familiar with every style, cabinet, knob, and drawer, so we resigned ourselves to sitting and waiting, taking our place in two of the white plastic chairs whose overused legs bent and splayed outward when we sat on them, until it was our turn. According to the board, it was now only 3 hours and 10 minutes away.

———

Lunchtime had come, a pastime still sacred in France, which was a relief because at least we'd have something to do other than continue to try to make ourselves comfortable on the rickety folding chairs.

One good thing about Ikea is that you can count on getting a decent plate of hot food there. Much has been made about the French paradox: a culture that drinks a lot of red wine and eats plenty of fat, yet has a low rate of heart disease. I learned there's also a Swedish paradox: it's that all Ikea stores have kitchens to prepare food . . . except their one store exclusively devoted to kitchens.

In place of the usual Ikea cafeteria there was a walk-up stand with a prickly-faced young man who looked like he'd just woken up and taken a slug of strong coffee and a pull on the rest of last night's *clope* (cig) for breakfast before slipping on his blue-and-yellow apron to start his shift. His job was to scoop rewarmed meatballs into paper cups. We joined the line of other people to wait for our cups. If we'd all been wearing jumpsuits, the scene could have been easily mistaken for a prison cafeteria.

Being winter, it was *la grippe* season. During those months, I do whatever I can to avoid touching handrails and grabbing bars on the *métro*, since the idea of sneezing into your elbow hasn't made it across the Atlantic yet. As a professional cook, that's something I just do instinctively. (I once had a supermarket cashier in the Marais sneeze into the handful of change that she was handing back to me. I told her, "*Gardez la monnaie*," or "Keep the change.") The server wasn't as careful as I am, as he inhaled and sniffled deeply as he continued to portion meatballs into cups. I was losing my appetite, and my mind wasn't far behind. Just as it was my turn, he realized that he was losing the battle against what was coming out of his nose and used his hand to wipe it away. If I wasn't so eager to have something to do to pass the time, I would have done something unheard of in France: given up my place in line. (Or skipped a meal.) But instead, I took my chances. Desperate times . . .

A few hours later, our number was called to meet with a kitchen planner. We were led to a high gray desk outfitted with a computer in a gray cubicle in the midst of rows of other gray cubicles with gray-faced customers stationed in each one of them. Next to us, a woman glumly slumped in her folding high chair, looking like her hair would fall out if she frantically ran her hand through it one more time. She was looking around desperately for someone to help her. Rolling on the linoleum floor next to her were two small children, rocking back and forth and bawling their eyes out. I looked at them and understood. I was ready to join them.

But I can't entirely fault Ikea: they had kept their word about the 4½-hour wait. Finally, a young clerk came rushing over to us, introduced herself, and I gave up my seat in front of the computer so she could get started. She opened the kitchen planner with a click of the mouse, and said, "Here is the program." She showed us how moving the mouse around moved the cursor over the screen, then said, "*Voilà!*" . . . jumped off the seat, and left us as fast as she had arrived.

I'd waited 4½ hours for someone to show me how to use a mouse? *J'ai détesté.*

This time it was Romain who had an Ikea meltdown. He jumped out of his seat and raced after her, down the aisle, saying louder and louder as he closed the distance between them, "*Excusez-nous, excusez-nous, mademoiselle . . . mademoiselle, s'il vous plaît! . . .*" while she did her best to ignore him and get away as fast as possible. But it was no use. He finally caught up with her, and she didn't have a choice. "*C'est pas correct . . . C'est pas correct,*" he repeated, as she reluctantly sauntered back to the computer with him.

Romain may have been furious, but he is always *correct*, and let the woman with the children have a moment with the clerk first. After helping her figure out how to do whatever she needed, the kitchen planner came over to help us again, showing how the mouse can be used to click on icons and other things, finishing up with "... *et voilà*" before she began to run away again, making her way toward an Employees Only door.

Again, Romain chased her, brought her back, and stared not at the computer screen, but at her, until my kitchen was laid out on the screen. We printed the pages out and took them home.

When we left, it was getting dark out. That three-minute consultation had taken up the entire day, but unlike our disastrous last visit, at least I had an idea of what cabinets I'd need. As we drove back toward the darkening sky of Paris, my throat began to feel scratchy and my nose started to run: Unfortunately, I was bringing something else home from our visit.

SWEDISH MEATBALLS

Boulettes suédoises

SERVES 6 TO 8

Ever since they were scooped onto a plate from steam tables in my elementary school cafeteria, I've had a thing for Swedish meatballs: bouncy nuggets of ground meat under a blanket of thick, wrinkly gravy. I still love them. In spite of how challenging Ikea can be, one of my guilty pleasures of going there—in addition to the chocolate-filled oatmeal cookies—is sliding a warm plate of meatballs from the stainless-steel counter, warmed by heat lamps, onto my tray, then taking a seat and eating them. (I heard their kitchen-only store finally opened an actual café, but when I tried to find the information online, their website kept coming up with error messages, maybe because I hadn't updated my Netscape browser?)

Swedish meatballs are easy to make at home, and while the rumor used to be that Ikea used reindeer meat in them, I use a combination of pork and beef, because my butcher in Paris never seems to have ground reindeer in stock.

If you don't have a stand mixer, you can prepare the meatball mixture in a food processor or a large bowl, using a bit of moxie. The aggressive beating of the ground meat gives the meatballs their sticky, springy texture. I use a large non-stick skillet to fry the meatballs and wipe it clean between batches. Since they are fried in batches, you can make the sauce as you cook the meatballs and add them to the sauce-pot as you go.

Meatballs

⅔ cup (160ml) whole milk

⅔ cup (75g) bread crumbs

1 tablespoon vegetable oil, plus more for frying the meatballs

1 tablespoon butter

1 medium onion, finely diced

1¼ pounds (565g) ground beef (preferably 80% lean)

1 pound (455g) ground pork

2 large eggs

1 tablespoon kosher salt or sea salt

½ teaspoon freshly grated nutmeg

¼ teaspoon ground allspice

Freshly ground black pepper

Sauce

> 5 tablespoons (2½ ounces, 70g) unsalted butter, cut into
> cubes
>
> ⅓ cup (45g) all-purpose flour
>
> 4 cups (1l) beef stock
>
> ¾ cup (180g) crème fraîche or sour cream
>
> 1 teaspoon Worcestershire sauce
>
> Salt and freshly ground black pepper

For Serving

> Warm noodles
>
> Chopped fresh parsley
>
> Lingonberry jam or cranberry sauce

1. Make the meatballs: In the bowl of a stand mixer, stir together the milk and the bread crumbs by hand. Let stand a few minutes so the bread crumbs can absorb most, or all, of the milk.
2. In a large nonstick skillet, heat the oil and butter. Add the onion and cook, stirring occasionally, until it's translucent, about 3 minutes. Scrape the onion into the bowl of the stand mixer with the bread crumbs. Wipe the skillet clean with a paper towel and set aside.
3. Add the ground beef and pork to the mixer bowl, then add the eggs, salt, nutmeg, and allspice and season with pepper. Fit the mixer with the paddle attachment and set the mixer on low speed. Increase the speed steadily to high and beat everything together for 1 minute.
4. Line a baking sheet with parchment paper. Form the mixture into meatballs, using 1 tablespoon per meatball and rolling them into rounds with your hands. Set them on the baking sheet as you form them. (Having a

bowl of lukewarm water handy to dampen your hands occasionally will make it easier to shape the sticky meatballs. If you can enlist someone to help, an extra pair of hands will speed up the process. So will using a spring-loaded cookie scoop with a 1-tablespoon capacity, if you have one.)

5. Make the sauce: In a Dutch oven or similar-size pot, melt the butter. Stir in the flour with a whisk and cook over medium-high heat, stirring frequently with the whisk, until the roux turns a gentle brown color, about 5 minutes. Add the stock and cook, stirring continuously, until the sauce thickens, 6 to 8 minutes.

6. Turn off the heat and whisk in the crème fraîche and Worcestershire sauce. Season with salt and pepper and cover the pot.

7. Coat the skillet you used to cook the onions with enough vegetable oil so there is a good film of oil on the bottom. Working in batches, fry the meatballs, being careful not to crowd them in the pan. (Unless you have a particularly huge skillet, you should plan to fry these in three or four batches.)

   As the meatballs cook, turn them with a spatula or by firmly shaking the pan so they brown evenly on all sides. When the first batch of meatballs are browned on all sides and cooked through, add them to the sauce. Wipe the skillet clean with a paper towel between batches and cook the rest of the meatballs, adding more oil to the pan, if necessary, and transferring the finished meatballs to the sauce.

8. Gently rewarm the meatballs in the sauce. Spoon the meatballs and some of the sauce over a plate of warm noodles. Sprinkle chopped parsley over the top and serve a spoonful of lingonberry jam alongside.

27

The new wooden floors had been laid, which, surprisingly, didn't take very long. Certainly nowhere near the amount of time the crew spent moving all my belongings, the formidable pile of boxes and suitcases stacked and shoved together in the middle of the room, down the stairs to the *cave* so they'd have room to lay the floors.

With the apartment emptied and the wooden floors in place, I got a glimmer of how it would look when it was all done. I was bowled over by the grandeur of the pristine, open space, with the polished wood floors. Seeing it all cleaned up for those brief few hours made me think that maybe I hadn't made a mistake at all. Despite the problems and delays, and doubt, it would all be worth it in the end. Someday, I'd have a beautiful kitchen in Paris. Now it was time to finish.

I arrived the next morning to find them covering up the gorgeous oak floors with heavy, black plastic tarps. They brought all my stuff back upstairs and stacked it back in the center, just like it was before, throwing the same dusty tarps back over everything, because they still hadn't finished the work in the *cave*. I felt sorry for the workers having to lug my things back up. Although it was probably me I should have felt sorry for, because it still didn't look like I was going to have a place to live for quite some time.

It seemed like every time I went over the apartment, I had to retape the tarps back together because the crew had a habit of using my boxes as sawhorses, a resting place for tools, dining tables for eating their sandwiches, and, curiously, as an occasional resting place for intimate items. In addition to someone's toiletry kit, one day I came across a condom, which fortunately was still in its wrapper. But from then on, I walked around a little more carefully, just in case there were any others. (That had been opened.)

The windows and door were en route, *en principe*, which was the only thing that was keeping me from falling deeper into the funk I was feeling. I was tired of overseeing a construction zone, and living out of a small box of hastily gathered clothes I had packed when I'd been told that they'd be finished soon. My outfits were as grungy as my apartment, and it wasn't worth cleaning them, because they'd just be dirty again, a day later.

I had stopped cooking or baking, two of the things that make me happiest and two of the main reasons I loved living in Paris. I also missed my friends. By 8:30 P.M., I was emotionally zonked from spending yet another day worrying if I had the right thickness of flooring or hunting down electrical outlets or organizing which cabinets I needed or wondering when the workers would start on the kitchen. (Or concerned what I might slip on, considering what I'd found underfoot.) But what worried me more, was when—and if—Claude and his team would show up again. After they had installed the floors and put everything back in place, a week went by without anyone showing up. It was almost as if they didn't want to finish. We were at the end of the fourth month, and the "twice as long as planned" part had come and gone.

The only person I saw on a semiregular basis was the electrician, who seemed to like being by himself, toiling with wires and pulling cords through walls. Maybe the meditative work of threading wires calmed his mind? A number of the other workers had run-ins with him, which perhaps was another reason he worked solo. His eruptive tirades notwithstanding, we sometimes talked like two normal people, rather than our usual positions of me cowering while he bellowed. I've worked with some quirky people in restaurants and can excuse a lot of *curieux* behavior if people are good at what they do. I once worked with a very competent line cook who liked to sneak up behind the other cooks and yank our elastic-waist chef's pants down to our ankles. Because of her, we learned to work with our backs against the wall. One adapts when the situation requires it.

Even when my back was against the wall, I was still impressed by what the electrician had done: wiring an entire apartment, hiding the wires in stone walls and running them through concrete floors. The new outlets in the kitchen and in my bedroom looked a lot safer than what had been there before. I still wasn't sure of the reasoning behind putting all eighteen of the electrical outlets in my office clustered in one corner of the room, but I didn't want to ask because I was afraid he'd start jackhammering that corner of the room apart. The cords for the USB ports were still dangling out of the walls, unfinished, but I didn't see any places where the American outlets would go. Figuring it wasn't a common request, he had probably overlooked them. So I delicately pointed out where I had stashed them for safekeeping, letting him know they were there when he was ready for them. He nodded in agreement, his eyebrows lowering in my direction. Then he went back to his work.

Spring finally arrived in Paris. That glorious time of year that's become synonymous with the city itself and entices people to visit. The warmer weather draws Parisians to the outdoor terraces to take advantage of the gradual, and much-needed, extra daylight as summer gets closer.

Beer and rosé replace the *vin chaud* and hot chocolate on café tables, and the first cherries, still crunchy—and pricey—arrive at the market, a hopeful sign that stands will be heaped with them soon. When the prices drop, and the quality improves, that's when I start bringing them home by the kilo. They are followed by Gariguette strawberries, each rosy-red berry topped with a perky crown of leaves, meticulously placed in their baskets so that each fragile berry doesn't bruise. Then, the cavalcade of summer fruit begins: fresh apricots, Charantais melons that you can smell from a few stalls away, and fuzzy white peaches from Provence, which I buy last so they don't get crushed in my market basket underneath the rest of my *beauté*, which means "beauty" but might sound like "booty," which is equally appropriate.

My strategy of having completion dates for the various phases of the construction handwritten in my calendar didn't work out as I thought it would. I was supposed to be writing my book (and enjoying the splendors of Paris, so I could write about them), but I was spending my time organizing what was starting to look more and more like an abandoned construction site, putting workers' tools in piles, sweeping up, and wiping up where sticky-damp paintbrushes had been left. I stuffed piles of trash into plastic garbage bags (wearing gloves, in case I came across any more "personal items") and did my best to keep closed the plastic tarps draped over my things to avoid yet another dose of plaster dust landing on the boxes and suitcases. The tarps were as effective as the handwritten completion dates.

Ever hopeful, I figured if the cabinets were in the apartment, the crew would be motivated to get moving on assembling and installing them. After waiting around for several more days and leaving a string of unanswered messages on Claude's voicemail to find out when the crew would be returning, I was startled when he suddenly picked up. I didn't know why, and didn't ask, but jumped at the chance to get a date from him when we could go to Ikea with his truck to pick up the cabinets.

I woke up on the agreed-upon morning, ready to go, and headed over to the apartment to meet him. The model of cabinet had been decided on, but I needed to go with Claude, who had the exact dimensions of the kitchen, to make sure everything would fit. I am confident piping *pâte à choux* and cutting *pâtes de fruits*, which require a little measuring, but a kitchen is a different story. An overage of *pâtes de fruits* I could eat, but I didn't want to eat the cost of the refrigerator, which I'd already paid for and was ready to be delivered, if it didn't fit in the cabinets.

When Romain and I got to the apartment, Claude and his sidekick, the electrician, were there and ready to go. We shook hands and I headed toward his truck, ready to jump in. Just as I reached for the handle of the truck's door, Claude off-handedly said, "*Um . . . Daveed . . .*" I stopped and turned to look at him, as he continued. "You go by yourself and order everything. We'll swing by later after you've gotten all the cabinets, to pick everything up when you're done." It was as if a brain surgeon had beckoned me from my gurney while I was headed toward the operating room, asking if I could take over his job. Then he'd stop by afterward, after I'd finished, to close things up.

I sighed. I didn't want to have another argument with Claude. A few weeks before, out of frustration, I'd managed to get him to come to the apartment for a meeting to sum-marize what still needed to be done and to agree on a firm date when they would finish. He arrived four hours late and I was fuming. As if nothing had happened, he came over to shake my hand with a big smile. Shaking hands is the way men in France traditionally greet each other, a holdover from the days when men carried weapons: it proved neither party was holding something dangerous. I now understand why they continue this tradition.

I'd heard a number of excuses for why things were taking so long, some more credible than others, which I wrote off. But I was getting desperate and no longer amused by a pleas-ant smile and a wave of the hand, accompanied by the usual *pas de problème* that everything would be fine.

Romain was with me, and the three of us went into the room that would be my office and slid the extremely ex-pensive sliding door closed behind us, which was earning its price by blocking his way out. We stood in the slim aisle around the perimeter of the room, circling more of my stuff piled in the middle. I was so mad I was shaking with rage, which isn't like me at all.

"Where the hell have you been?" I said, getting very close to him, a little afraid of how angry I was getting. His response was simply a Gallic shrug, a nonverbal shirking of blame, as he shifted back and forth, not looking either of us in the eye. He didn't offer an answer. We'd cornered him physically, me on one side and Romain on the other. As he shifted around, he was gradually moving toward the corner where the door was.

"Why didn't you at least call?" I said, wedging myself in the path between him and his exit. "We've been waiting hours and we wasted the entire day here, waiting for you.

Why didn't you at least call?" I stood firmly in front of him, waiting for an answer.

I do have to applaud him for his quick thinking, and the explanation he came up with on the spot: "Well . . . I went to the Gare du Nord to drop someone off this morning. I was on my way over here afterward, until I realized I had left my iPhone on a table in the train station, so I drove back to get it. But there was a demonstration blocking all the roads around the train station, so it took me a few hours to get back there to pick it up. So that's why I couldn't call and tell you."

After he told his story, I stood there in silence. I know seasoned travelers, and even savvy locals, who've been pick-pocketed at the Gare du Nord, no match for the nimble-fingered experts at that station, pilfering wallets, passports, and computers. An iPhone sitting unattended for more than a second would disappear faster than bottles of Champagne at your local *caviste* (wine shop) at 7:59 P.M. on New Year's Eve, since they all close precisely at eight P.M., no matter what night, or how profitable it is.

I've heard some doozies in my time, most concentrated during the past year, and I didn't know how to respond, except to press further.

"*Vraiment?* Really? You expect me to believe you left an iPhone on a table in the Gare du Nord for most of the day, and when you came back, it was still there?"

"*Exactement, Daveed.* That's exactly what happened," he said, with a look of great contentment that I was accepting his explanation.

I may be a pushover, but I'm rarely speechless. All I could manage was one word—"*Really*"—which came out with just the slightest suggestion that it was a question.

"Yes, *vraiment,*" Claude said with a broad smile, convinced of his story. "That's what happened." And that was that. We eventually let him go because I didn't have conclusive proof that the story wasn't true. But the story was verification of something I had suspected: I had a big problem. I just didn't realize how large it was.

THE TRUTH SERUM

Sérum de vérité

MAKES 1 (BADLY NEEDED) COCKTAIL

The truth can be subjective in France. That, coupled with a flair for drama, means I've heard some pretty good stories over the years. While the one that raised my eyebrows the most wasn't told during *l'heure de l'apéro* (cocktail hour), nothing makes stories—true or otherwise—flow better than a stiff drink.

France has an equally colorful history with liquor. Stories about why absinthe was prohibited in France have been going around for decades. One is that it had druglike properties and made people do psychotic things. (Note that I didn't find any empty bottles of absinthe in the apartment, which would have explained a few things.) Another is that batches of absinthe had become spoiled, yet were bottled anyway, and people who drank the tainted bottles fell ill. Whatever version of the truth you believe, or choose to believe, absinthe was banned.

Absinthe is now legal again, and while I'm not a huge fan of anise-based liqueurs, I love Izarra, an herbal Basque liqueur that's similar to Chartreuse, with a lively green color and just a hint of anise flavor—with a potent kick at the end. This is a pretty strong drink, and it may not get people to tell the truth, but it might inspire a few stories—true or false.

4 fresh mint leaves

1 teaspoon simple syrup (see below)

2 ounces tequila

¾ ounce fresh lime juice

½ ounce Izarra or Chartreuse liqueur

1. Chill a stemmed cocktail glass in the freezer.
2. Muddle the mint leaves with the simple syrup in a cocktail shaker.
3. Add the tequila, lime juice, and Izarra. Fill the shaker halfway with ice, close, and shake for 15 to 20 seconds.
4. Pour into the chilled cocktail glass.

NOTE: To make simple syrup, bring ½ cup (100g) of sugar and ½ cup (125ml) of water to a boil in a small saucepan. Reduce the heat and simmer, stirring frequently, until the sugar is dissolved. Remove from heat and let cool completely. Simple syrup can be stored in a covered jar, refrigerated, for up to one month.

28

The day we were scheduled to go to Ikea and get the cabinets, Claude was actually in my apartment with some of his workers . . . who were actually working, so I agreed that I would go in advance with Romain, since we needed to pick up some extra things for the kitchen, like knobs and inserts for the drawers, and he could meet us later to order the cabinets and bring them back to the apartment. With the logistics agreed upon, including an exact time for meeting a few hours later, Romain and I took off. I told Claude to call me if he was going to be late, asking him to hold up his phone to confirm that he had it with him. I was getting better at this.

It takes a lot to get me to lose my temper these days. Working as a chef, I had my moments, and was known to throw a skillet against a wall or a salad in the face of a line cook who was constantly nibbling on my *mise en place*. (Which shocked him, but it worked: he didn't do it again.) I'm tamer now, but still have my chops, evident when Claude showed up at the agreed-upon time at Ikea, with the electrician (and his phone)—but for some reason, without the kitchen plans that had the dimensions and measurements. If the roof hadn't been so high at Ikea, I would have hit it.

I lost it. I started yelling, using words I don't normally use—including some French ones I had learned during a transit *grève* (strike) that left hundreds of French people, and me, standing on a train station platform in the middle of the night, huddling together in the frigid air, for which none of us were dressed. We waited a couple of hours, *en masse*, while frequent announcements assured us a train was coming. Finally, the station agents left for the night, turning off the lights inside the station, as well as on the platform outside, plunging us all into darkness. I couldn't see anything, but could definitely hear how angry everyone was.

Months of frustrations—the sizable delays, the excuses, the mess, the ear-splitting electrician (who at one point caused a three-day *grève* by the other workers, who refused to come back), the fruitless search for hardwood flooring in a size that doesn't exist, and the four dimmer switch fuses Claude told me to buy at 550 euros each because he said I needed that specific brand (the mystified clerk told me that those were for medium-to-large factories, and handed me ones that were 49 euro a pop)—boiled over in the Ikea kitchen department.

This time Claude didn't even offer an excuse. He just stood there, impassively, saying nothing. The electrician stood back, shuffling and looking around. Neither one of them seemed bothered that the whole day had been wasted. We'd have to come back.

Although the French don't like to take blame—*c'est pas ma faute*—I'm not that French yet, because I was to blame for the situation. I should have been following Romain's advice all along, not paying for anything, making *them* wait and beg for payment. No one in France would dream of paying for anything until it was absolutely necessary, and certainly not without a lot of discussion and assurances being made before any payment changed hands. But Claude and his crew found the exception: me. The mutual suspicion between bosses and workers in France, I learned, was merited. I wasn't worried about getting boss-knapped—I'd already given them everything they wanted—but I started to feel like I was getting taken to the cleaners.

If we didn't come home with the cabinets that day, I probably wouldn't be moving into my apartment until the following year. Fortunately, I'd been lugging around my ever-expanding messenger bag for the past year and a half, everywhere I went, because I never knew when I'd have to suddenly produce one of the invoices or documents related to the apartment. My back and shoulder paid the price for that, but it was worth it: Based on notes and measurements in one of the many notebooks in my bag, we were able to estimate the dimensions to put in the order. Another *cata* (catastrophe in French slang) averted.

I had decided to go with wood counters because I like the warmth of wood in a kitchen and felt they'd soften the white cabinets and stainless-steel appliances. I wanted to order one large solid oak counter from a professional outfit I'd found that makes them for bakeries. When I introduced the idea at the start of the project, Claude had said not to bother. He told me to buy three of the narrow oak counters from Ikea and he'd glue them together to make one large one. Assuming he knew what he was talking about, I said, "Okay, that's fine. Let's just do that."

Naturellement, they were out of oak countertops, not just at that store, but at all seven of the other Ikea stores encircling Paris. I went with beech instead; another compromise I'd have to live with.

Once the list of cabinets had been compiled—and I must say, Claude's charm worked on the salesclerk, and she was extra helpful putting the list together—we headed downstairs to sort through the aisles where everything is ware-housed.

We ended up wheeling three enormous flatbeds of boxes out of the aisles and toward the register. At least Claude was right about knowing which parts and "elements" to get for the cabinets; there were plenty of them on the printed list we were handed, which gave me confidence that it'd all be fine, eventually. I was more than ready to get out of there.

When we arrived at the register, the fellow ringing up orders wasn't in a very good mood, either. He beeped every-thing through with his handheld scanner as we pushed our loaded-up carts through the aisle alongside his register. After the last blip, just as he was about to ring up the total, Claude interrupted, and announced from behind that he had some-thing for me, a gift card from another project, and said that I could use it to get a 500-euro discount off the purchase.

I had to admit that it was a very nice gesture, especially after I had gotten so mad at him for not bringing the plans. After all, we had been so friendly during much of the reno-vation, chatting over coffee and sharing lunch. He did a few things that annoyed me, but here he was, offering me a gift card as a makeshift apology, perhaps. My frustration sub-sided and I handed the plastic card over to the cashier.

The cashier waved the scanner over the card, which didn't beep, and he looked confused. Discounts often don't show up at the register in France, and sometimes you have to insist, so I did. He scanned the card a few more times, but still, nothing was happening. No beep, no luck. The discount wasn't showing up. He tried running the wand over it a few more times before lifting the card up closer to inspect it. He handed it back to me, saying that something was wrong and it didn't work, but he didn't know why. I looked over at

Claude, who shrugged, insisting that it should work, and told the guy to try it again. It didn't.

A discontented mob of people was now surging behind us, and I was sure I was about to learn a few more choice French words to add to my vocabulary. Unfazed, Claude said he didn't know what was wrong, prompting the cashier to call a store manager, drawing groans from the people behind us. I had become The Person You Don't Want to Be Behind at the Register, like those people who still write checks, which need manager approval. After a few more minutes of waiting, the manager arrived and took a look at the card. He scanned it himself, looked at it, tried it again, then handed it back to me and declared, "This card is exhausted—*épuisée, monsieur*—it has already been used. That's why it's not working. It's *totalement épuisée*." I knew how the card felt.

I looked back at Claude and his cohort, who started giggling like a couple of ten-year-olds. The cashier was clearly not as amused as they were, nor was I. He finished totaling the order and I paid him, both of us concluding the transaction in furious silence.

Perhaps the contractor was brighter than I thought, though. Maybe at the start of the day, he had known how the day would go, and that it would be better if we went in advance so we'd have to ride home in separate cars. It was a good idea, because I was glad not to be in the same vehicle with him.

———

Back at the apartment, some space in the never-ending mess got cleared so that we could unload the boxes of cabinets, stacking them in tall piles in the corner. Romain took me out for a hamburger and fries at Big Fernand, a new place that opened at the time when burgers were on the cusp of becoming *branché* (trendy) in Paris. This coincided with my renovation, and for some reason, we started going out for burgers more and more as the construction wore on and on and on. I consoled myself by chomping down on juicy patties of griddled beef with blue-veined Fourme d'Ambert cheese melting down the sides, slid into a soft brioche bun and accompanied with a paper cone of salty *frites,* not feeling self-conscious in the least for picking the whole thing up while everyone around me was eating theirs *à la française*, with a knife and fork.

Maybe it was the taste of home, a connection to the familiarity of things in America and how things worked there, that I was starting to miss. I had begun at zero in Paris, arriving with a few suitcases and no knowledge of French and settling into a tiny apartment, working my way up from there. But buying and renovating an apartment was a lot different from picking out cherries at the market or ordering a box of chocolates at La Maison du Chocolat. I was in way over my head now, in a foreign country, at the mercy of a language that wasn't my own, with people who spoke it a lot better than I did, and customs that I clearly didn't have the right command of. If anyone needed the comforting power of a juicy burger and a big mound of fries, it was me.

It's now estimated that 75 percent of the restaurants in France have a hamburger on the menu. People who don't live in France scoff at how *le burger* (and its *fromage*-topped cousin, *le cheese*) took off in the country. "I don't go to Paris to eat hamburgers!" they'll scoff, but you'll find few tourists in the burger places that have infiltrated Paris. The clientele are locals, and judging from how many of them line up for burgers day and night, a lot of people in Paris need comforting.

Or maybe they're just renovating.

———

A few days later, I went to the apartment with Romain to assess the state of things. We wandered around the empty space. No one had shown up to work and nothing had been completed since the cabinets had been unloaded. Romain had taken to making signs for tasks that needed to be done and taping them around the apartment, with can't-miss colored arrows like French *bandes dessinées* (cartoons, which in France are just as popular with adults as they are with kids), one pointing to an unfinished drain with a prominent note next to the arrow stating that it was *pas fini*. Another was next to the fuse box, which still sprouted unruly wires everywhere. *"Finish this door frame!"* an arrow affixed to a door said, and *"Une deuxième couche"* was to make sure they gave another coat of paint to a wall where a water stain was still visible. There were so many signs and arrows that the place looked like a cartoon, minus any humor.

While we were walking through the mess, one of the workers came by and was surprised to see us there. He stopped in to pick up some of his tools for a job he was working on with another contractor. (Judging from the amount of tools and other items that were lying around, I was starting to suspect my apartment had become a storage area for other projects . . . and maybe a *cinq à sept* or two, what the French call the five-to-seven-P.M. liaisons that involve other kinds of tools.) We started talking about the state of things with the young man, who said he wasn't happy working on the job because of the way the work had gone. He was upset they weren't finished yet and didn't know what was taking so long, which I certainly agreed with. I guess he had enjoyed the homemade cookies and brownies during those first few weeks of work, because rather than heading back out the door, he paused for a moment and looked at me, then said, "I think you should see this."

We followed him over to a section of the floor that he had stopped in front of. It was hard to see anything because of the black plastic tarps that had been laid down to protect the floors and were now bunched up and dirty with muddy footprints and ground-in plaster dust.

"*Regardez-le*," he said, pointing down and tapping his foot over something that seemed to be resting on the floor. He lifted up his work boot, then pressed it down again even harder. Something under there moved. I looked puzzled, so he lifted his foot up and pressed it down a few more times. I still didn't get it, so I moved in and stepped down where his foot had been. I noticed what he was talking about. There was a sizable bump, like a wadded-up piece of clothing or some other soft and pliable object trapped underneath the tarp. Romain found a box cutter, slit through the plastic, and pulled it open. Two of the brand-new floorboards poked up from below, standing almost sideways, buckled up six inches or so, creating an inverted V with the point rising upward. Somehow a couple of the boards had come loose. I figured they just needed to be pushed down and glued back in place.

But just to be sure those were the only boards that had come loose, we moved some of the boxes and tools to get a better look at other parts of the floor. Romain started slicing the plastic tarp open and pulling it back in various places. Everywhere he opened revealed more buckled floorboards, running the entire length of the apartment. I held my breath for a moment as I knelt down and ran my hands over the hard-won slats. The polished oak flooring, which had been as sleek as a never-been-used bowling alley when they laid it down, was now twisted out of proportion. I felt myself starting to tear up. I didn't understand what could have happened.

I reached down to touch the boards and was surprised by how warm they felt. I put my hand on the concrete underneath, which almost burned my fingers; it was scorching hot. The radiant heat had been turned on, and left on. When the crew had done their disappearing act, the covered wooden floorboards "steamed" under the thick plastic that was supposed to protect them, causing them to twist and warp, then pop away from the subfloor. The new floors were ruined. And they weren't the only thing that was steamed.

ŒUF À CHEVAL

MAKES 2 BURGERS

I was confused and a bit taken aback when I first saw *œuf à cheval* on a café menu; I had never had a burger made with *viande de cheval* (horsemeat). As my French improved, I realized the burger wasn't made of *Monsieur Édouard*, but was a beef patty with an egg riding "horseback" on top. (*À cheval*, rather than *de cheval*, in case you find yourself in the same situation.)

One of the best burgers to be had anywhere is at Prune in New York City. The genius is that chef/owner Gabrielle Hamilton replaces the fluffy bun with an English muffin, which crisps up nicely on the outside so the burger is less messy to eat and there isn't a big wad of bread to plow through before you get to the beef.

I once told Romain that I was going to make hamburgers on muffins *à l'anglaise*. He's heard me make a lot of blunders in French, but like those burgers made of horsemeat that I was avoiding, he didn't want a burger on a muffin. It wasn't until I explained that an English muffin is different from a sweet blueberry muffin that he was reassured.

French people wouldn't dream of picking up a hamburger with their hands, no matter what you put the burger on; they eat them with a knife and fork. I'll have to admit that I now eat them the French way, too, which is less messy, especially if there is an egg riding horseback on top and I try to stay out of messy situations, although I don't always succeed.

You'll need to get two skillets going at the same time to make these. For best results, buttered silicone egg rings make near-perfectly shaped sunny-side-up eggs.

8 ounces (230g) ground beef

1 teaspoon Worcestershire sauce

½ teaspoon kosher salt or sea salt

Freshly ground black pepper

Canola oil

Butter

2 large eggs

2 English muffins, split

1. In a small bowl, mix the ground beef, Worcestershire sauce, and salt and season with pepper. Shape into patties about 1 inch (3cm) thick.

2. In a cast-iron or other heavy skillet, heat about 1 tablespoon canola oil over medium-high heat until the oil is hot.

3. Place the burger patties in the pan and cook until well browned on the bottom, about 3 minutes.

4. In a separate skillet, heat some butter until it starts to foam. (If desired, butter two silicone egg rings and put them in the pan.)

5. Flip the burgers over. Crack two eggs directly into the skillet with the butter or into the egg rings.

6. Cook the burgers to your liking; they'll take 3 to 4 minutes if you like them medium-rare, or *à point* (to the point), as the French would say.

7. When the burgers are close to being done, toast the English muffins. Slide a finished burger onto each English muffin bottom. When the whites of the eggs are cooked but the yolks still quite soft, slide one on top of each burger, then lean the tops of the English muffins off to the side of each burger.

29

The message I left on the contractor's voicemail was urgent. The days of leaving polite messages so as not to make anyone upset with me were over. That ship had sailed—and it was now sinking.

In spite of the growl in my voice (that scared even me), my call was returned within minutes. He arrived half an hour later and assessed the situation, saying he would fix the floors—*pas de problème*. And sure enough, he showed up Monday morning with a floor sander. Apparently sanders are easier to come by than sandblasters.

Romain's studio was cozy, and he'd set up a little desk in a corner for me so I could work. It wasn't ideal, but I had to admit, it was charming to be in a Parisian artist's studio. It's not always easy to live in Paris, and sometimes the city seems to do its best to make things more difficult. Like New Yorkers, Parisians have a complicated relationship to their city. They appreciate the beauty and excitement, but as Romain told me, Paris is *dur* (hard). That things aren't easy—*l'administration*, the neighbors, the brusqueness, the fact that it's not a perfect place—is what he likes about Paris. One of the reasons we get along is that I see the many facets of Paris for what they are; they're especially evident because I'm coming from a very different culture. It took some time, but living in Paris awakened something inside me that changed not only my cooking, but the kind of person I am. Without realizing it, I'd become entrenched in France, and French culture, and France made sense to me.

There's a conviviality the French have, which you wouldn't notice if you didn't have the gruff supermarket cashier who gives you a hard time for only having a 20-euro bill to buy a liter of milk to compare it to. (Romain once asked one why she wasn't happy, and she replied with a deadpan "Happiness is relative, *monsieur.*") You need people like the man who tripped me while I was exiting the *métro,* hobbling on a cane after painful knee surgery, who turned around and scowled at me for being in his way, to appreciate the generosity of other people, like my pharmacist, who will spend fifteen minutes letting me know what the rash on the back of my neck could be, then follow up with questions about how my knee surgery went, giving me the name of a local *kinésithérapeute,* who makes house calls. The woman at my bakery will ask where I've been if I haven't been by in a while to get my baguette, reassured when I tell her that I am okay, I've been traveling. (And how I miss their baguettes while I'm gone!) There's the chocolatier who lets me bring guests into his kitchen in the basement of his chocolate shop, which is normally closed to the public, telling me that I'm the only one he'll let go down there. And the receptionist who offered to help me write a check because I was so flustered making sure I put everything in the right place that she felt sorry for me tearing up *chèque* after *chèque,* and took over. Afterward, she told me my accent was *très adorable*, before I blushed and went on my way.

I was used to cooking in a small kitchen in my previous apartment. But now in Romain's studio, I had one lone electric burner that didn't even get as hot as my floors, and a counter that wasn't wide enough to slice a baguette on. Any chances of me cooking or baking anything were going on the back burner for a while. (And how I would have killed for a back burner!)

But I wasn't thinking much about cooking or writing or blogging, or anything else. I could only focus on the renovation, and getting through it. It was my life now. Everything was going in the wrong direction. And now the floors had to be refinished, although at least I knew the heat was working.

It took a couple of days and hundreds of euros' worth of varnish to sand down the floors and refinish them. I didn't argue about paying for the varnish because I was worried Claude would find a way to blame me for the floor warping ("See? You bought the wrong size. I told you."), and I was tired of fighting. As long as the crew was there, and doing something on the apartment, I figured I'd do what I could to keep the peace.

The crew must have felt a twinge of *coupabilité*, because they started assembling and installing the kitchen cabinets right after the floors were redone. Since the kitchen was so important to me, I arrived each morning (with no treats for the crew) and stood in the middle of the room watching every move and making sure they got it right, because I knew I'd get blamed (and charged) if something went wrong. My adorable accent didn't seem to matter to them.

FRANGIPANE PLUM-RASPBERRY GRATINS

SERVES 4

As anyone who has remodeled a kitchen knows, during renovations, the toaster oven becomes your best friend. To some, it's unthinkable to cook and bake without a standard- or regular-size oven, but many Parisians (even those who aren't renovating) have countertop ovens, a grown-up cousin of the toaster oven that will roast a whole chicken or bake a cake, because their kitchens don't have the space for a full-size oven. And they do just fine.

Camping out in an artist's studio with a countertop oven that wasn't quite big enough to bake a whole cake or tart was making me nuts, so I came up with these moist, fruit-studded individual gratins to satisfy my craving to bake.

In a regular-size oven, I bake these in wider gratin dishes, what are sometimes called crème brûlée ramekins, which allow for more of the almond cream to form a golden brown crust, framing the mosaic of tangy plums and berries. If you don't have gratin dishes or ramekins, any shallow baking dish or low custard cups with a 1-cup (250ml) capacity will work.

> 4 tablespoons (2 ounces, 55g) unsalted butter, at room
> temperature, plus more for the baking dishes
>
> ¼ cup (50g) sugar

1 large egg, at room temperature

½ cup (65g) ground almonds (sometimes called almond flour)

A few drops of pure almond extract

1 teaspoon rum or kirsch

Pinch of salt

6 medium ripe plums, pitted and cut into eighths

1 pint fresh raspberries

Vanilla ice cream or sabayon, for serving

1. Preheat the oven to 350°F (180°C). Butter four shallow gratin or baking dishes (see Headnote).

2. In the bowl of a stand mixer fitted with the paddle attachment, beat the butter and sugar on high speed for 2 minutes. (You can also beat it energetically by hand in a medium bowl if you don't have a mixer handy—for example, if it's in a box somewhere underneath a mound of other boxes under a plastic tarp.)

3. Add the egg, then add the ground almonds, almond extract, rum, and salt. Beat until smooth.

4. Divide the almond cream among the four dishes and smooth the tops. Arrange the plums in concentric circles in the almond cream (this is the *frangipane*), pressing them down to embed them in the cream. Place the raspberries between the plums and gently press them into the cream.

5. Place the fruit-filled dishes on a baking sheet and bake until the gratins are browned across the top, about 25 minutes. Remove from the oven and serve warm, with a scoop of vanilla ice cream or sabayon. (A recipe for sabayon, which, like these gratins, is easy to whip up in any-size kitchen, can be found on my blog.)

VARIATIONS: You can use 12 ounces (340g) of sliced peaches, nectarines, fresh apricots, poached pears (blotted dry), or quartered fresh figs in place of the plums. Pitted cherries, blueberries, or blackberries can be used in place of the raspberries.

30

As they worked on the kitchen, we got word that the windows were arriving in a couple of days, so the old, decaying ones would finally be replaced, along with the front door. The appliances had already arrived and were wrapped in protective plastic, including the refrigerator, which was even more spectacular than I imagined. It would be perfect in my kitchen.

———

A few days after they'd assembled the base cabinets for the kitchen island, I came by one morning to find the countertops had been glued together and attached to the top of the island. Two open, and very obvious, gaps ran lengthwise down the island between the three distinctly different rectangles of wood.

Claude didn't see the gaps as a problem. "They'll disappear once they get filled with crumbs and old bits of food," he reasoned. I didn't like looking at the gaps in the wood, but the idea of them filling up with decaying food was even less appealing.

"That's ridiculous. You expect the gaps in a kitchen counter to be filled with bits of rotten food?" I said, as I ran my hands down the open seams, my fingers confirming the distinct grooves between the sharp counter edges. "You told me this would work, and it'd be fine. Does *this* look fine to you?"

He looked down at the counter with the long slits and crevasses running between the planks of wood and said, "Those are *your* fault. You were too cheap to buy a larger countertop. So that's what you get."

I had been writing this guy four- and five-figure checks for months, faster than any other client he'd ever had in Paris, I was sure. I had paid a lot to have the walls of the *cave* sandblasted with an actual sandblaster, and they ended up looking like they had been attacked by a flock of rabid pigeons, the handheld sanders leaving thousands of scratches and grooves rather than the smooth, polished stone surface I was expecting. The beautiful floors had warped and had to be re-laid and refinished. And it was he who had encouraged me to use his window supplier, which I assumed would be fine, because my acquaintance who recommended him told me so. (I later called her up in a panic because my project was so behind, thinking since they were friends she could prompt them to finish. "Oh, I'm so sorry" she said, her voice quiet for a moment, then adding, "He was working on a project for me, too," and went on to tell me how they had left the project one day, and never came back.) I guessed I was lucky they were still around, and I was hoping this would all work out fine in the end. They were close to being finished, and once they finished installing the cabinets and, finally, my new front door and windows, I'd be done with most of this ordeal.

When the gapped counter was blamed on me, I didn't know what to say. (Except, "Next time I do this, I'm install-

ing a video camera in the ceiling and recording *everything*.")
It had been his suggestion to glue the three counters together
for the island. He had also assured me that the height of the
island could be changed easily—*pas de problème*, which I
learned was actually *un problème*, or should I say *les prob-
lèmes*, because I'd already bought four kitchen stools.

It was fortunate that they'd ruined the floors (which may
sound absurd to you, but I was doing the best I could, given
the situation), because the sander they'd used to fix them was
still in the apartment, and they used it to sand the counters
down so the planks were closer to being even. I persuaded
them to use wood filler, instead of waiting for leftover food
scraps to fill in the somewhat reduced cracks. The counters
had been smoothed over, but my anger was anything but. I'd
been very forgiving of a lot of things up until this point, but
now I was what the French call *une soupe au lait*: a once-calm
pot of milk, warmed up on the stovetop, that was threatening
to boil over.

———

Romain bravely went back to Ikea, twice, because the "gues-
timates" for the cabinet measurement weren't close enough,
and there was a large space between the wall and the cabinets. Claude didn't see this as an issue—of course—so Romain wisely went back to Ikea, alone.

Through the many layers of stretchy film, the appliances
still loomed over the kitchen, and I was ecstatic that it was
close to being done. I stood back and admired the way the
protective plastic was pulled so taut around the 90-degree-
angled edges of the refrigerator, emphasizing the strength
of its clean, precise lines. The thrill of brand-new appliances

made me giddy, and it was a relief to feel positive and upbeat about something. I hadn't felt that way since Claude handed me that gift card, which should've been a warning.

Since accurate measurements didn't seem to be anyone's priority, I was anxious about whether the refrigerator would fit correctly, and obsessed about that as they installed the cabinets. But the three days that I stood in the middle of the kitchen watching while they assembled and installed the cabinets paid off, because the refrigerator slid precisely into place.

The sink had been installed, and *oh la vache* (holy cow), was it beautiful! I had my restaurant-style faucet that swiveled and a spray hose, which I'd had to buy on Amazon and ask my cousin to bring over on a visit, since I couldn't find one in France. (Next time I go into a professional kitchen in Paris and see one, I'm going to ask where they got theirs, because I exhausted every possibility in the country before turning to Amazon.)

I was eager to use my new sink to clean all the fruits and vegetables and greens that I would soon be bringing home from the nearby market, which I'd visited a few times to scope out. My new market was smaller than the seemingly never-ending Bastille market, but had several *producteurs* (fruit and vegetable farmers) and not one, not two . . . not even three, but *four fromagers* selling cheese.

My head must've been on all those French cheeses, because the one thing I wasn't paying attention to was how far from the sink the crew had attached the faucet. When the water line to it was attached, the lever to the faucet happened to be in the open position, and after a few lurching sputters of water came out, a steady flow suddenly burst forth, drenching and flooding the counter. The faucet had been set too far back and the spigot barely cleared the side of the basin. Water flowed all over the counter and behind the sink, rather than into it. *How could* that *have happened?* I might have wondered before. But by now, I was getting a clearer idea. I decided to just use the hose attachment, forget about the faucet, and keep thinking positive thoughts: *It's almost done. It's almost done. It's almost . . .*

The dishwasher slid into its spot next to the sink and the full-size oven went into its space underneath the island. However, I noticed that there weren't any electrical outlets on the island to plug the oven, or anything else, into.

"Those will cost extra," the electrician barked back when I asked where the outlets were. "From this point on, anything you want, you're paying for. You are getting *service minimum.*"

"But the outlets were on the plans," I said, standing my ground. I wasn't paying extra for them.

The petty bickering has increased steadily after those first few months, around the time the homemade chocolate cakes and café lunches tapered off. A few days earlier, the electrician had gone on a twenty-minute rant about needing two plain screws to attach the bathroom lamp. I wasn't sure what happened to the ones that came with the lamp, which were in the box when I bought it. Looking around the apartment— still filled with half-empty cans of paint and varnish, toolboxes left open with tools haphazardly piled back in, as well as bags of plaster-crusted cords, wires, and trash (often all mixed together)—I was extremely surprised that there weren't two screws somewhere in all of that. It didn't seem like something big enough to go off on such a bender about, so I offered to go to the hardware store at the end of the street to get two plain screws.

When I told the guy at the hardware store the story, he looked at me in disbelief, then laughed for what must've been five minutes before giving me a very generous handful of screws for free, as thanks for making his day. I brought them back to the apartment. In my brief absence, the electrician had attached the lamp to the wall. With two screws.

I now had confirmation that there were several loose screws in the apartment, but there wasn't a plug for my oven, and I wasn't going to live with an extension cord running across the kitchen, as was suggested. Again, I wasn't backing down.

After standing firm that the electrical outlets were on the plans, he let me know they weren't ... "*Non, elles n'étaient pas là.*" He stopped what he was doing and stood facing me, his hands defiantly on his hips above his tool belt, ready for another *bataille verbale.*

"Where are the electrical plans? Let's take a look," I said, knowing for sure that they were on there.

"I don't know where the plans are," he told me, without missing a beat, standing firmly in place. Nearly a decade and a half of living in France had taught me to photocopy every piece of paper that crossed my path, no matter how insignificant it may seem at the time. But somehow, it hadn't crossed my mind to make copies of the all-important electrical plans. Yet I knew the outlets were on the plans, and he knew that was where the electric oven was going to go, so I dug in.

He slowly walked over to me and put his face directly in front of mine. "*Non.* I'm not installing them for you. If you want outlets, they're going to cost you *extra.*"

I'd been a pushover for a while, but that was ending and I refused to go quietly without a fight. Thirty minutes later, my kitchen island had electrical outlets—three on both sides, attached with screws.

Word must have gotten out that I wasn't the easygoing guy I had been when we started, because everyone was a little nicer to me and had been showing up more frequently, which resulted in a kitchen that was nearly finished; they just needed to hook up the appliances. It made me realize I should have been more French and adopted a tougher attitude right from the start.

I'd already unpacked the boxes of durable white Pillyvuyt dinnerware that I use for my daily dining, salvaged from a bistro that had gone by the wayside, and my antique wineglasses, made of heavy glass with squat stems; they were probably meant for absinthe, but I found they worked just fine for rosé. I lined them all up in the cabinets, appreciating the extra row of separate cabinets that Romain had grudgingly accepted. There was plenty of room for my cookware: enameled cast-iron pots, madeleine sheets, *financier* molds, and a second ice cream maker (always good to have a backup, in case my first breaks down), all of which I would unpack when the rest of the kitchen was finished and those boxes were finally *libérées* from beneath the tarps.

The still-unopened refrigerator was surely the largest refrigerator in all of France, and I wasn't ashamed of being *très américain* because I really did need it for my work. (Or at least, that was my story.) After months of admiring the floor model in the store, I was eager to unwrap mine. I pulled off the protective plastic film, ripping it into shreds because I was too impatient to stand there and unroll the multiple layers, then stood facing it, admiring the sleek appliance, not truly believing it was finally in my kitchen, and really mine. I stepped over the plastic lying on the floor around it and grabbed both handles to pull the double doors open.

It took a second, but very soon, a warm, festering smell hit me. My eyes began watering as the stench hit them first.

Because of the excitement, my next inhalation was extra-deep, and the odor clouded my nose and my throat, then worked its way down my windpipe, threatening to come back up along with everything I'd eaten that day.

I didn't think it was possible to be knocked over by a smell, but the force of this one threw me back. It was as if someone had packed the *frigidaire* with dead fish, closed the doors, and left them for a few months to rot. The refrigerator was empty, but my eyes burned from the smell and I slammed the doors closed. The stink sent all of us racing out of the apartment, taking in as much fresh air from the outside as fast as we could. For the first time, the odor of cigarettes that hangs heavy over the sidewalks in Paris was a relief.

After I was certain my lunch was staying put, I went back inside. The smell had subsided and was mostly contained inside the stainless-steel colossus in the corner, the one that had betrayed me. I tried to figure out what had happened. Possibly it was a used refrigerator, left over from a demonstration at a trade show, and whatever had been inside (which I can confidently say was fish) had been left to rot. Some poor soul at the warehouse may have discovered them, taken them out, and wrapped the refrigerator up for storage. *C'est pas mas faute,* making it someone else's problem. If anyone has a better explanation, I'd like to hear it. Because the company didn't offer one when I called.

My lofty status as a VIP didn't have much effect on their representative. She didn't want to take responsibility, but after I informed her that she was *pas correcte*, she offered to send someone over to wipe it clean. I'm not the kind of person who goes online and calls out companies for crummy service, but as she continued to avoid replacing the refrigerator, I worked on a 140-character tirade. I was ready to hit the "Tweet" button when she finally agreed to make a special exception in this case and send me a new one. I deleted the tweet and refreshed my screen to make sure it was gone. Now it was time to clear a few other things from my cache.

SWISS CHARD GRATIN
(Gratin de blettes)

SERVES 6 AS A SIDE DISH

The faucet in my kitchen sink had to be *condamné* (condemned) due to being *mal placé* (badly placed), but the hose sprayer worked just fine. A few vigilant neighbors saw it and suspected I must still be harboring ideas of opening a restaurant or bakery, so I continued to let Romain do the daily check of the mailbox. The faucet may have been put permanently out of use, but the sink worked just fine. (I hoped!) I loved it, and its size was especially great for rinsing the cache of giant stalks of Swiss chard, some as large and wide as tennis rackets, I find at the markets in Paris.

Leafy greens tend to trap a lot of dirt, so be sure to wash the chard and spinach well. I usually triple-wash each. No matter how good your faucet—or hose sprayer—is, even one grain of sand is disconcerting to chomp down on, and you want to keep the focus on the creamy-smooth, vibrant-green chard puree.

This recipe was adapted from one by Susan Friedland, the editor of my first two cookbooks; her inspiration came from Richard Olney. Fortunately for her, she wasn't editing the book I was working on, which was woefully behind schedule.

2 pounds (900g) Swiss chard

4 ounces (115g/4 cups loosely packed) spinach leaves

1 tablespoon butter, plus more for the baking dish

3 tablespoons (total) olive oil

4 garlic cloves, thinly sliced

Salt and freshly ground black pepper

1 tablespoon all-purpose flour

¾ cup (180ml) whole or low-fat milk

Big pinch of cayenne pepper

½ cup (50g) dry bread crumbs

½ cup (45g) grated Parmesan cheese

2 teaspoons minced fresh thyme leaves

1. Bring a large pot of salted water to a boil. Strip the leaves from the chard stems. Chop the stems into 1-inch (3cm) pieces. Add the stems and simmer until tender, 5 to 10 minutes, depending on the thickness of the stems.

2. Coarsely chop the chard leaves, add them to the water, and cook for a few minutes, until tender. Add the spinach and cook for 30 seconds, until wilted. Drain the greens in a colander. Rinse the pot and wipe it clean.

3. Use tongs or a spoon to turn the greens in the colander to speed up the cooling. Once cool enough to handle, squeeze fistfuls of the greens in your hands to remove as much moisture as possible and put them in a medium bowl.

4. Preheat the oven to 375°F (190°C). Butter a 1½-quart (1.25l) gratin or shallow baking dish.

5. In the pot you used for the greens, heat the butter with 1 tablespoon of olive oil. Add the garlic and the greens and season with salt and black pepper. Cook over medium-high heat for a few minutes, stirring, to remove excess moisture. Stir in the flour and cook, stir-

ring, for 30 seconds, then remove from the heat. Stir in the milk and the cayenne.

6. Carefully transfer the greens and the liquid from the pot to a food processor. Process until it's as smooth as possible. Taste, and add more salt and pepper, if needed. Pour the gratin mixture into the prepared baking dish and smooth the top.

7. In a small bowl, toss together the bread crumbs, Parmesan, thyme, and the remaining 2 tablespoons olive oil. Sprinkle the crumb mixture evenly over the top of the gratin. Bake until the top of the gratin is nicely browned, about 35 minutes.

31

In addition to the electrical outlets and plans *manquants* (MIA), I was also curious about the USB outlets, which still weren't finished, along with the U.S. electrical outlets, which were entirely absent. There were cords with rectangular "male" USB plugs dangling out of the walls, which confused me. (Imagine an electrical cord with a two-pronged plug on the end of it, hanging out of your wall, and you get my drift.) As far as I knew, outlets meant something with holes that you plug things *into*. But perhaps the literal French had taken the "out" part of "outlet" too seriously?

When I'd asked about them early on, the crew said not to worry—*pas de problème*—the men weren't finished yet and brushed my questions away, saying they'd finish the outlets later. Later had arrived, and when I asked when those outlets were going to be finished, the electrician replied, "They're done. Those are them," pointing to the USB plugs at the end of 10-inch cords, dangling out of the wall.

I explained that normally one plugs their phone *into* an outlet to charge it. The plugs hanging from the walls would have been great if I wanted to plug my apartment into my telephone, which seemed bizarre. But at this point, anything seemed possible.

The electrician told me that kind of USB outlets you plug

something into *n'existe pas* in France. I took out my phone, did a Google search for *prise USB murale* (USB wall outlet), the kind you plug things into, and came up with 636,000 results. I scrolled through the first five pages of images of outlets, "*Ici . . . et ici . . . et ici*"—"here . . . and here . . . and here"—then stopped, assuming I'd made my point. He just shrugged and walked away. I wondered if it was too late to make room for a wine refrigerator, delivered fully stocked.

The refrigerator wasn't the only thing that was fishy around there. When the plastic floor tarps were finally removed, I discovered that the kitchen island was crooked. It wasn't parallel to the straight lines of the floorboards.

This was naturally my fault, because I had changed my mind about how high I wanted the island. Or at least that's what they told me, because I didn't remember that discussion. But I do remember enough from high school geometry to know height has nothing to do with how straight parallel lines are. The off-kilter island was hard to ignore. Yet somehow, they did. It needed to be fixed.

Claude went out to his van, then came back and handed me a *devis* for how much it would cost to straighten out the island. Because there was a lot of work involved—unhooking the stove, switching the electricity around, and a bunch of other things he told me that would have to be adjusted underneath—it would take two weeks and cost 1,000 euros. I wasn't up for another argument, but I didn't want to pay to have it fixed. Romain said I should just live with it and not spend any more money. In a few weeks, I wouldn't notice it, he promised. So I let it go. *Yes, I'll get used to it*, I said to myself— knowing very well that, no, I would never get used to it.

———

A truck with a metal flatbed clacking loudly behind it barely cleared the narrow corner to my street, and came to a stop in front of my building. I'd been waiting impatiently on the sidewalk for the arrival of the windows and door frame, and they had finally arrived. Claude told me the door would be available a day or two later and they could pop it in, and then we'd be all set: I'd have a front door, and could move in.

It was nearly summer, and the meeting of the owners was scheduled for the following week, where they'd vote on my water line. It wouldn't be long before I'd be able to shower and bathe and wear fresh clothes, so I could feel like a real person again. One thing I hadn't been prepared for, from the onset of the renovation, was the disorientation. Most of us have a daily routine; waking up in our beds, having coffee the way we like it, and going about our lives, which aren't controlled by having to use a Porta-Potty, sleeping on the floor, baking in a toaster oven, the pain (and uncertainty of) shaving with cold water and no mirror (yowch!), and brushing plaster dust off your clothes before you put them on in the morning. Things like that are inconvenient for a few days, or a few weeks. When they stretch out to five months, or longer, it wears you down in ways you don't realize, until you're back to your normal routine—or you're on the couch of *une psych* trying to sort out your life.

After years of taking a shower with a nozzle that barely dribbled enough water to get soap to lather, I dreamed of standing under a steady stream of warm water cascading from the shiny new showerhead. My first shower in the apartment would be at least fifty minutes long, and be a lot cheaper than the 130 euros I paid weekly to a no-nonsense lady who coaxed me back to reality on the couch in her office. *La psych* was also the only woman in France who didn't want to discuss chocolates or pastries with me.

The neighborhood I'd soon be living in was once known as the quartier of *métallos*, or metal shops. They're all gone now, and the spaces have been turned into lofts, offices, and artist studios; you don't hear much metal clanging around anymore, except for the early-morning pooper-scoop truck that makes daily rounds, sweeping up the land mines left by the previous day's pooches.

But now the truck with my windows on it was giving the impression the *métallos* had returned. It made such a racket that people on the block peered out of their windows to see what was going on. The metal window frames were stacked on their sides on the flatbed trailer, one on top of the other, and clanked and clattered as the trailer hopped over the wobbly Paris street on two rubber wheels. This was a landmark moment for the apartment, the last major step: replacing the door and windows would make the apartment not only a true living space, but *my* living space.

The driver stepped out of the truck and everyone did the obligatory rounds of shaking hands, then the crew got to work untying and lifting the metal frames off the trailer and moving them onto the sidewalk. As they were unloading the windows, I stepped in to take a look. The thick metal framework was impressive, and I was looking forward to how the new windows would brighten up the apartment, allowing in much more light than the dingy opaque windows that would soon be pryed off with crowbars. These windows would change everything.

I leaned in to get a closer look at them and saw little metal squares affixed to the tops of some of the windows, which were the knobs to open, close, and lock the windows.

Normally, I thought, you would put those at the bottom, or at least within arm's reach, so the windows can be opened, closed, and locked easily. With 10-foot-high ceilings, I tried to imagine how I was going to open and close the windows. My excitement began to wane as I knew I had to bring up the out-of-reach knobs, pretty sure of the reaction I'd get when I did.

So I took the tactic of starting off by making a few circumspect remarks about the windows, first offering up how amazing they looked, how exciting it was to have them, and how certain I was that they'd look great once they were installed. After I'd made sufficient remarks to elicit a smile of contentment from Claude, I kneeled down on the pretense of getting a closer look and touched one of the knobs, innocently inquiring, "Oh, hey, what's this? Is it normal to have the knobs . . . *here*?" Claude stood there, frozen for a moment in silence, caught off-guard. I could see him thinking about it, but he didn't come forth with an answer. Instead, he rubbed his chin, then began to pace back and forth around the window frames lying on their sides, thinking of something to say. I could feel him almost muttering, "*Non, non, non*" until all of a sudden, he cheered up. "*Daveed, c'est normal.* That's where locks normally are on windows."

"*C'est vrai?*" I said. "Really? Because every single other window, in all the other apartments in the neighborhood, have their locks near the bottom." (What I really wanted to say, if you'll pardon my French, was "*Are you f*cking kidding me?*")

I bent down to touch one of the locks to see how the levers worked. When I moved one to the closed position, as if locking the window, the metal latch dropped off and landed on the ground. I held it up so he could see the *normal* lock, the kind that falls off the first time you use it. I was sure it was going to be my fault for not asking for the *abnormal* kind.

I looked under the window frames and saw that a few of the other locks had fallen off, probably when they were unloaded. Claude didn't say anything about them when I pointed those out, too, but clenched his hands and raced down the street, enraged. I wasn't sure what was wrong as he angrily ran around the block, reappearing every few minutes, checking out the other windows in the neighborhood to prove his point, looking everywhere for ones with normal, out-of-reach locks. I wasn't surprised that he couldn't find any.

He eventually came back. Standing over the window frames lying on the sidewalk in a big pile, he rubbed his chin. Then he told me, calmly, "This is your fault."

I wasn't sure how that could be, since I hadn't done anything—except give him a very large check to pay for them. He followed up with the reason: "You changed your mind about which of the windows opened. That's why the locks were put up so high, and are now falling off."

I'd learned that a healthy sense of humor is necessary to live in a foreign country, especially at some of the more perplexing things that happen. But I could only stand there, rubbing the throbbing sides of my forehead, trying to massage all of this away.

When ordering the new windows, we needed to keep the design of them as close to the original windows as possible, since almost everything on the exterior of a building in Paris is historically protected. I'd planned for more of the window panes to open than in the original windows, but knowing how bureaucrats can be sticklers for details, I decided to have the same number of panes open as in the original windows—no more, no less—so there wouldn't be any problems. I'd made the decision early on, before they'd even started making the windows.

I didn't see how making some windows inoperable could be a reason why a window latch on a completely different window would fall off, or why they were placed at a height that was inaccessible to anyone but a *géant*. But somehow, I was the cause of all this.

I went back into the apartment, wondering which of those boxes my return ticket to San Francisco was in.

————

The installation of the windows took a few days. There was heavy cutting and sawing, accompanied by ear-splitting noises, as they pried loose and ripped out the old windows and frames, before fitting the new ones in. The new windows looked a lot nicer than the ones that had been there before, and indeed, changed everything when I saw how much more light flooded into the kitchen. Now I just had to wait for the door to arrive. While we were waiting, I unpacked the high chairs I'd bought for sitting around the kitchen counter.

After the sink, and a fish-free fridge, high kitchen chairs that I liked for the counter were another challenge to find. My requirements were pretty straightforward (or at least I thought so): clean lines, made of a natural material, no plastic, not ugly, and not from Ikea. That didn't seem all that outlandish, especially in a country known for high style. But you can't have the high without the low.

At one end of the spectrum (the lower one) were chairs made of clear Lucite or in colors like *pistache* (fluorescent green), *sanguin* (which, eerily, means "blood," but I assumed it was short for "blood orange"), and—*mais oui!*—aubergine. Some chairs expected users to be fine teetering on mono-legs, with just the suggestion of a back supplied by a very slight upward curve toward the rear of the seat. I sat in a few, and found it only possible to sit in them if you didn't move a centimeter to either side, or forward or backward. I assumed those were for households who didn't want their guests to linger. Curiously, there were a number of high chairs that had British flags printed on the backs of them, although none had American ones. I didn't feel slighted.

I had gone down the same dead end of rabbit holes when looking for kitchen chairs that I did for my sink. Unfortunately, no public schools, military bases, prisons, or places of *collectivité* in France seemed to have a need for attractive, high kitchen stools with reasonable backs. Two companies in France—Tolix and Niccole—make beautiful stools, but Romain nixed both because he said they were *trop présents*. I never knew that an object could be "too present" until I moved to France. (I also learned that food can be too tasty when I was tending the meat at a backyard barbecue in the suburbs of Paris, grabbed a beautiful bunch of fresh herbs from the host's garden, and dipped them in olive oil, ready to baste the meat with the fragrant bundle. The host saw what I was doing and bounded across the backyard, wine sloshing in his glass, waving his hands to stop because the meat was going to have *trop de goût*, too much flavor.) After searching for high chairs and finding out the majority of them were as *moches* as my private parts, I learned that *trop de goût* doesn't only apply to food.

One day I was rambling down a street near Les Halles and something caught my eye. It wasn't the billion-euro can-opy they were building to replace the universally despised 1970s steel structure (low taste), that looked like a series of whitewashed Wurlitzer jukeboxes shoved together and had replaced Baltard's historic glass-and-iron covered market (high taste). (The billion-euro makeover was also proof of how hard it is to find a good contractor in Paris. When the shiny new canopy was unveiled in 2016, there were substantial leaks, some with so much water pouring out of them that they were described as *chutes du Niagara*, or Niagara Falls.)

A glint of silvery gray flickered at the edge of my gaze as I passed a restaurant window. I turned toward it and moved closer, pressing my nose against the glass, excited beyond belief. I didn't *lèche-vitrine*, or "lick the window," the French phrase for window shopping. But I would have circled my tongue on the glass if it would've made an opening big enough to grab four of the chairs I saw inside.

The restaurant was closed, so I jotted down the name, and first thing the next morning, called them up. The owner was a nice guy who said he bought the chairs in quantity for his four cafés in Paris and would be happy to sell a few of them to me. I didn't ask where he bought them, but from the number of boxes I saw stockpiled in his basement, I discovered the reason I hadn't been able to find them in France: he had bought them all.

After he and Romain talked, and each learned about where the other was from, where their parents were born, what were the gastronomic specialties of their regions, which villages in his region had notable churches, what era they were built in, why the restaurant owner got into the restaurant business, and what his wife did, etc., I paid for four of the chairs, thanked him profusely, and loaded them into Romain's car. Now that the kitchen island was finished, I slid one out of the box and propped it next to the island, taking a seat. I slid myself forward, but my legs barely fit under the counter: I've never had a mammogram, but from what I've heard, my legs felt they were getting one.

Claude had calmed down after the window incident and was puttering around with one of the workers doing some finishing work on the cabinets. Because it was spring, I opened the new windows using a six-foot-long wooden dowel with a little teacup hook attached to the end. Claude had replaced the broken knobs with tiny levers, and it usually took me at least four or five tries to get the hook through the *petit pois*–size circular loop to open or close them. Opening the windows became a carnival game, with fresh air as my reward when I managed to hook one of the hoops to get it open, instead of a stuffed animal.

Claude was still impatiently waiting for the door company to call him and let him know when it was ready for pickup. I wasn't looking forward to bringing up the fact that the height of the kitchen island couldn't be adjusted, as was promised, but he saw my struggle to pull up to the counter with the chair and offered a solution. "We can cut down the legs of the stools, *pas de problème*," he said with a now rare smile, a sign that another request for payment—ostensibly the final one—was coming. That sounded like a reasonable solution at the time. (Like gluing together three separate boards to make one countertop had been.) And I didn't have a better option . . . except to fill the place with concrete and keep it as a shrine to how *not* to remodel an apartment in Paris.

Out came a handheld circular saw. Claude plugged it in and revved up the machine. With the kitchen chair lying on its side, he measured a couple of inches and cut the first leg down. After lopping off a piece of the leg, he moved on to the second leg. When that piece of metal dropped off, he rotated the chair, cut off a piece from the third leg, then moved on to the last one, which he lopped off, too. When done, he propped the chair upright and proudly stood back so we could take a look at it. The chair remained stationary for just under a second before it started slowly tilting to one side. It wobbled unsteadily before picking up some momentum and falling toward the back left corner. I sprung forward to grab it before it hit the floor.

I set the chair back upright, but it wasn't sitting right. As I tried to steady it, it rocked back and forth dramatically; something was wrong. I looked down and saw that one of the legs wasn't touching the ground and was a lot shorter than the other three. I realized that instead of cutting all four legs down equally, one leg had been cut twice, so it was several inches shorter than the other three. It would take a wobble wedge the size of a good-size triangle of Brie to stabilize it.

Claude wasn't fazed. He had a solution. "*Daveed*, if you have a friend that is larger on one side than the other, you'll have a chair that's perfect for them!" he said with a straight face.

The only times my friends are lopsided are when they've had too much *vin de maison*. In which case, a rickety chair would do more harm than good. But even if I found a friend like that in the future, I wasn't sure how sitting on a chair with one much shorter leg would work for my askew *ami*. When I blankly blurted out, "Huh?" because that wasn't the response I was expecting, Claude looked hurt. Since I clearly wasn't convinced, it turned into something that was my fault, of course.

"You should have said something while I was cutting the legs." It's true, I should have been paying more attention to that, and a few other things. Otherwise, I would have known how to properly install a radiant heating system, I wouldn't have a kitchen faucet that was better for washing the counter behind the sink rather than what was *in* the sink, and the sixteen electrical outlets in my office wouldn't all be clustered in the exact same corner. I wouldn't have useless USB cords dangling from my walls, my kitchen island wouldn't look like a six-year-old had installed it, I wouldn't need a ladder in my kitchen to open the windows after losing the game of trying to snag the tiny latch handles with the hook too many times, and I'd have a front door by now and be living in my apartment.

So for reasons that I can't explain, I ended up with four kitchen stools of four various heights. People sometimes think I exaggerate stories about my life in Paris, but now I have solid proof that they're real. Well, not that solid.

32

Summer finally arrived, the time of year every Parisian looks forward to, when you'll find most of the city clustered on blankets by the Seine each evening, picnicking on dried sausage slices ringed with cracked black pepper, Basque hams, pâtés, a few *crottins* of chèvre, a wedge of bleu d'Auvergne, and—always—a slab of Comté, accompanied by plastic cups of inexpensive *vin de table*, and butter—because it's not a French meal without it. (Hard-core *gourmands* will spread a layer on bread, before topping it with cheese, which startled me the first time I saw it. But I've come around.)

After the dark winter, Parisians bloom in the extra hours of daylight, which lasts almost until midnight. I was invited to lots of picnics but couldn't make it to any, because I was so worn out that I would crawl into bed at nine P.M., while everyone else was watching barges, and boats of tourists, float down the Seine while swilling rosé. I'd become a recluse, and even though burgers and fries took the place of market-based home cooking, I had lost a good deal of weight, skinny enough to wear those jeans that Frenchmen have no trouble fitting into. (If only I'd had time to go shopping, and had the energy to go somewhere in them, to show off.) It was hard being around people who were happily getting on with their lives while I felt trapped in mine. I certainly hadn't expected the renovation to go on this long, but at least the end was in sight. Once the door arrived, I'd move in and it would all be over. And soon I'd be hoisting glasses of wine with my friends on the edge of the river, watching the sun go down, too, working on filling out my standard-size jeans again.

———

Getting my front door was becoming as hard as understanding how a supermarket in France could run out of butter. Claude finally told me there was, naturally, a *rupture de stock*, and the door wasn't available. For a few days, I didn't worry about it, since he said the woman at the company told him that she'd let him know when it was available, which wouldn't be long. But after a couple of weeks had passed, I grew concerned. And so did he. Part of his concern might have had something to do with delay of his final payment, which was due when the job was finished. And he couldn't finish until the door was installed.

He told me that he had pestered them so much that the woman at the company had told him to stop calling. She'd be in touch when it arrived. So I waited, and asked him every few days if he'd heard any news. "*Non, rien, Daveed.* No news. But they'll have it soon, they said . . . soon . . ." I'd just have to wait.

When a month had passed, I offered to go to the door place with Romain, since he's unparalleled at dealing with obstinate bureaucrats and salespeople, charging in even before they finished responding if he doesn't get the answer he wants, circling back if they try to talk their way out of something. (The downside is that he does it with me, too.) Claude said forget it—he'd tried everything.

After six weeks had passed, it was getting ridiculous. In spite of France's reputation for businesses that don't put the customer first, I had been dealing with professional suppliers for over a year and almost every salesclerk and shopkeeper had been responsive and reliable. So I picked up the phone and called the door company to find out what was going on.

"*Bonjour, madame*, I'm calling to inquire about a door that was ordered for me, but hasn't arrived. It was supposed to take only a few days, but it's been several weeks. I'm wondering what the delay is?"

"*Un retard?*" Madame said, "*Désolé, monsieur.* Give me your name and I'll check on your order." I gave her my name and the address of the apartment. I could hear her rifling through some papers in the background before she came back on the line.

"*Excusez-moi, monsieur*, I don't have an order under that name. Could it be under another?"

"Perhaps it's under the contractor's name, since he ordered it?" I offered, giving her Claude's name. I heard more papers rustling, then she came back to the phone.

"*Désolé, monsieur*, but I have nothing under that name, either."

Hmmm.

"Perhaps you can try the name of his company?" She gave it another look, then returned to the line saying there was nothing under the name of his company, either.

"*C'est pas possible*," I told her. "There must be some mistake. The order was put in nearly two months ago and the contractor has called many times to find out where it is." Surely she remembered speaking to him—*non?*

"*Non, monsieur.* I never spoke to anyone with that name and have nothing under your name, his name, or the name of his company. *Désolé.*"

French employees don't like anyone questioning their authority. Even their superiors are afraid to question their authority. But at the risk of incurring her wrath, I had to ask again because I couldn't believe it: "*Vous êtes sûre?*"

"*Oui, monsieur, j'en suis sûre,*" she affirmed.

I thanked her and hung up the phone. When I told Romain about the conversation, he was as confounded as I was. Why would the contractor tell us the door was on order when it wasn't? It was so absurd that I was starting to find it funny; like I was watching a theatrical comedy, with no shortage of *merde*. We decided not to say anything about the call and see what would happen. It was time to have a little fun. When I saw Claude over the next few days I'd innocently slide into the conversation, "Hey . . . have you heard anything yet about the door? I can't imagine what's taking so long."

"No, it hasn't arrived yet," he said. "It's coming, though . . . it's coming. We just need to wait, *Daveed.* They promised me it's on its way." This went on for nearly a week, until one day Romain took the lead, asking if there was any news, and him saying, again, "*Oui . . . oui . . . ne vous inquiétez pas,* don't worry, it's supposed to arrive any day now. Soon . . ." which he made the mistake of finishing with, "I just don't understand what's taking so long."

And with that, Romain exploded. "The door isn't coming—because *YOU* never ordered it," he erupted. The color drained from the contractor's face. "We called the place a week ago and they said there was no order for it!" Romain stood in front of him and continued to let loose, pointing his finger and punctuating every word that came out of his mouth with it. I'd never seen him this mad.

Claude innocently denied that the door hadn't been ordered and said that everything was going to be okay, *pas de problème,* we just needed to wait. But Romain wasn't accepting that and didn't let up, before he went on to list every thing that Claude had done wrong. Everything he was saying, I wish I could have said. It's not just because his French is better than mine, but I'm not that type of person. Fortunately, he is. He was saying everything I had wanted to say, and should have said a long time ago. How Claude managed to stand there and continue to insist that the door was truly on order, was beyond me.

So I stepped in and said that we'd decided we were ready to drive out to the door place right then, all three of us together, and see where it was. "*Non, non, c'est pas nécessaire.*" Claude backed away from the idea, waving the idea away with a casual chuckle. "That's not necessary. It's not going to be there yet." But Romain was irate and stood there with his hands above his belt on his small waist, and continued to accuse him of not ordering the door.

Claude swore that the door would arrive in a few days. And sure enough, the door showed up forty-eight hours later, nearly two months after it had (supposedly) been ordered. When it arrived, the design of the door wasn't at all what I'd ordered, but I was happy to have a door with a lock and a key, and couldn't wait for it to be installed so I could close it with everyone else on the other side. Except Romain, of course. He could stay.

KOUIGN AMANN

MAKES 12

I may not be so good at challenging *people*, but I don't shy away from a *baking* challenge. For the four or five people who read my blog each week, shortly after I moved to France I posted a recipe for kouign amann, a caramelized pastry from Brittany with a ridiculous amount of sugar and butter folded in.

Back then, hardly anyone—in America but also in Paris—knew what a kouign amann was. A few years later, they were showing up not only at bakeries in the French capital, but in New York, San Francisco, and Salt Lake City, of all places. I figured if I could go through buying an apartment in Paris and renovating it, I could update my recipe to make individual kouigns, which became more popular than the slablike pastries found in Brittany.

Romina Rasmussen of Les Madeleines bakery in Utah was one of the first bakers in America to make kouign amanns. I was intrigued by the success of these relatively obscure French pastries, which she was making in the unlikeliest of places, and we became friends, bonding over cocktails at Le Mary Celeste on one of her trips to Paris, where she comes to get inspiration.

Through a series of witty e-mail exchanges that included photos of some of the duds, Romina took a look at my tests. As with any risks you take in the kitchen, or in life, you won't succeed unless you try, which means you'll likely endure a few failures. I made this recipe over a dozen times, trying American versus French flour, and muffin tins versus 3½-inch (9cm) low tart rings. I didn't want to insist you order French flour or tart rings from France (see Note), so I'm happy to say that the soft French flour made them fall apart (not unlike how I was falling apart during the renovation of my *appart*), and most broke as I tried to pry them out of the muffin tins.

Then I found the trick to getting the sticky little devils out of the tins in one piece: lining the bottom of each indentation with a circle of parchment paper did the trick. To do so, find a water glass that has the same diameter as the bottom of your muffin tin indentations and use that as a guide to trace circles onto parchment paper. Cut those out and fit the circles into the muffin tins after buttering and dusting them with flour.

A couple of other tips for making kouign amanns:

When rolling out the dough, speed trumps precision, at least in terms of measuring the size of the dough. If rolled too slowly, the butter can melt and the dough will get too sticky. So you don't need to slavishly follow the sizes I give for rolling out the dough into rectangles when turning and folding it, until you get to step 12, when the pieces are cut for the final pastries. As long as the dough is a workable-size rectangle, you'll be fine.

You're doing four "turns" of the dough—rolling the dough the first two times in flour, then refrigerating the dough, then rolling the last two turns of the dough in sugar. The sugar on the pastry may become syrupy if left in the refrigerator too long, so in step 10, make sure you let it rest no longer than 30 minutes.

Don't make this recipe on a warm or hot day. The butter

will ooze from the dough as you roll it, and all your hard work will be for naught, as I learned one afternoon when my dough fell apart trying to "beat the heat" on the stainless-steel counter next to my sunny window. (The upside is that the picture of those, once baked, gave Romina a hearty laugh that I heard all the way from Salt Lake City to Paris.)

Lastly, if making kouign amanns seems like too much of a project, you can order them from Romina's bakery via her website, lesmadeleines.com. And unlike ordering a door in Paris, you can choose your day of delivery and get confirmation. Too bad she didn't sell doors.

> 1 cup (240ml) tepid water
>
> 1 teaspoon sugar
>
> 2 teaspoons active dry yeast
>
> 2⅓ cups (325g) all-purpose flour, plus more for mixing in (if necessary), and dusting
>
> ¾ teaspoon kosher salt or sea salt
>
> 1 cup (8 ounces/225g) salted butter, chilled

Shaping and Rolling

> 1½ cups (300g) sugar, plus more for rolling and shaping
>
> Butter, at room temperature, for the molds

1. In a medium bowl, stir together the water, sugar, and yeast. Let sit for 10 minutes, until the yeast becomes foamy. Gradually stir in 2⅓ cups of the flour and the salt until the dough comes together. (You can also make this in the bowl of a stand mixer fitted with the dough hook.)

2. Turn the dough out onto a lightly floured countertop and knead the dough until smooth but still soft, about

3 minutes. If the dough is sticking to the counter too much, knead in 1 tablespoon of the remaining flour at a time just until the dough no longer sticks.

3. Butter a medium bowl and put the dough in the bowl. Cover the bowl with a kitchen towel or plastic wrap and let rise in a warm place until doubled, 45 minutes to 1 hour. Punch down the dough, cover, and refrigerate for at least 1 hour or up to overnight.

4. To roll the dough and make the first two turns: Put the butter in a sturdy plastic bag and whack it with a rolling pin to make it more malleable. As it flattens out, fold it over a few times. (I do it through the bag, without opening it, to keep my hands and rolling pin clean, because bakers are OCD.) The final time you flatten it, the butter should be a rectangle about 4 by 5 inches (10 by 12cm).

5. Scrape the dough from the bowl and put on a lightly floured countertop. Dust the top of the dough lightly with flour and roll the dough into a 10 by 16-inch (25 by 40cm) rectangle. It may be a bit unwieldy at this point, but will be easier to roll with each successive turn.

6. When it's rolled out to a rectangle, the two shorter sides should be on your left and right, and the longer sides on the top and bottom, as if you were looking at an envelope containing a letter. Brush excess flour off the dough.

7. Mentally dividing the dough into three equal parts, like the French flag, place the rectangle of softened chilled butter vertically in the middle of the center third. Use the heel of your hand to quickly smear the butter so it almost reaches the top and bottom edges of the dough.

8. Lift and fold the left third of the dough over the butter in the middle third, then fold the right third of the dough

over the middle. You'll now have a rectangle with the longer sides on the left and right. Turn the dough one-quarter turn to the right, so the shorter sides are on the left and right again.

9. Roll the dough out again until it's a 10 by 16-inch (25 by 50cm) rectangle, then fold it over in thirds again, as you did in the previous step. Drape a sheet of plastic wrap over a small baking sheet, leaving the wrap attached to the box. Place the dough over the plastic wrap and tear the wrap to a length that you'll be able to cover the dough with. Chill the dough for 1 hour. (At this point, you can chill the dough up to overnight in the refrigerator. Depending on the temperature of your kitchen, you may need to let it sit for a minute or two when you remove it, since the butter may be too cold and brittle, and will crack when you roll it.)

10. To make the final two turns: Measure out two ¾ cup (150g each) bowls of sugar. Sprinkle some of the sugar from the first bowl on the countertop. Unwrap the dough and as you roll it into a 10 by 16-inch (25 by 50cm) rectangle, sprinkle the dough and the counter-top with the rest of the sugar from the first bowl. When you finish, roll the pin over the dough to press in the sugar. Fold the dough again in thirds, as you did in step 6.

11. Make the final turn of the pastry by rolling out the dough as you did in the previous step, working in the second bowl of sugar. Once the rectangle is 10 by 16 inches (25 by 50cm), fold the dough into thirds for the final time. Run the rolling pin over the dough, wrap it, and chill it for 30 minutes. (Don't let it chill longer, as the sugar will get too watery, making it challenging to roll.)

12. Butter the indentations of a 12-cup muffin tin or 12 tart rings (see Headnote) liberally with softened (not melted) butter. Cut twelve circles of parchment paper to fit the muffin tins and line the bottoms of the muffin tins with the circles. If using tart rings, put them on two baking sheets lined with silicone baking mats.

13. Remove the dough from the refrigerator. Sprinkle some sugar on the countertop and sprinkle a small amount on top of the dough. Roll the dough out to 12 by 16 inches (30 by 40cm).

14. With the two short ends of the rectangle on your left and right, use a chef's knife to trim the edges of the dough so it's neatly squared off. Use decisive motions; don't drag the knife, but use a clean, sure cutting motion. Make two lengthwise horizontal slices, cutting across the dough into three strips, each 4 inches (10cm) wide. Then use the knife to cut the dough vertically, straight down the center, then cut each side down the center, so you end up with twelve 4-inch squares.

15. Working with one square at a time, grab a corner and pull it so the corner point is in the center. Do the same with the other three corners. Place the pleated dough in one of the muffin tin indentations or prepared tart rings, pleated-side up. Repeat with the remaining squares of dough. Drape a sheet of plastic wrap over the tin or baking sheets and let rise for 1 hour in a warm place. Twenty minutes before they are ready to bake, preheat the oven to 375°F (190°C).

16. Place the kouign amanns in the oven. Immediately reduce the oven temperature to 350°F (180°C). If using muffin tins, you may want to put a sheet of aluminum foil on the rack underneath the muffin tin to catch any drips or spillovers.

17. Bake the kouign amanns until they're deep golden brown on top, about 35 minutes. Remove them from the oven. If using tart rings, lift them off right away and transfer them to a wire rack. If using muffin tins, immediately run a knife around the outside of each kouign amann to loosen it and lift it out with the aid of a small flexible silicone spatula or a butter knife. Peel off the parchment and let cool on a wire rack.

NOTE: I did, ultimately, prefer baking the kouign amanns in the French tart rings, which I bought at E. Dehillerin in Paris. You can find them online, on Amazon (made by Matfer, or another company), or at jbprince.com. They're sometimes called flan rings and should be about 1 inch (3cm) high and 3½ to 4 inches (8 to 9cm) in diameter.

33

We gathered early in the evening for the meeting of the building's owners in the basement of a nearby church. Everyone took their seats in folding chairs arranged around a series of tables that had been pushed together for the AG. For snacks, paper plates held an array of candy from the supermarket: strawberry-flavored marshmallows emptied from a plastic bag, gummy green animals that were toothpaste white on the underside, and an occasional mini Carambar, the cavity-pulling sticky caramels that are popular with kids (and evidently some adults) in France. I rifled through the colorful confections, hoping for an *Ourson guimauve*, a chocolate-covered marshmallow bear—which are my favorites—but there weren't any.

Romain had told me beforehand not to talk during the meeting. I would likely be subject to *le bizutage*, a "hazing" that takes place when you're the new person, and he thought it best to keep quiet.

"But I'm the perfect co-owner!" I'd told Romain. I thought I was improving the building by replacing the decrepit, cracked windows with new ones, as well as solving the humidity issue in the basement. I didn't think much of it when friends in Paris talked about their co-owners' meetings as being difficult and often contentious. I had met an older couple who lived upstairs in the building and asked them if they were going. They made the same face I do when the bakery clerk asks if I want a *croissant ordinaire*, made with margarine, rather than a *croissant au beurre*.

Non, merci.

Nonetheless, I didn't anticipate any problems. But the meeting hung heavy on my mind, because if I didn't get permission to attach my water line to the main of the building, I was sunk, and I didn't want to shower in the half-bathroom, hosing myself down with a *douchette anale* for the rest of my life. Nevertheless, I patted myself on the back for having them put a drain in the floor and install the awkwardly named personal hygiene hose, good insurance in case things went south.

A long list of things to be discussed at the meeting was part of the heavy packet of paperwork that arrived via registered mail a week before. My water line connection was at the end of the list, #27. Even before we got to the first order of business, there was an extensive discussion about the exorbitant costs for registered-mailing the inch-thick agenda of paperwork. That seemed excessive to me, too, and I wanted to say, "Can't this be sent as a PDF?" or "How about we just stack them in the entryway to the building and each owner can pick theirs up?" But since I was the new person in the group, I heeded Romain's advice to *fermer ma boîte à Camembert*, as they say, and kept my cheese box shut. The discussion went on for an hour, the final compromise being to have the agenda printed on both sides of the paper. *Voilà*—on to item #2 . . .

Parisians eat late, often sitting down for dinner at nine P.M. or so. As the hours rolled by . . . eight P.M. . . . nine P.M., other issues provoked similarly lengthy debates. The discussions were happening in rapid-fire French, making it hard for me to keep track of what was going on. One of the advantages of being an Anglophone is the ability to zone out the discussion around me, which I did. Which, unfortunately, meant my thoughts became squarely focused on one thing: dinner. But I wasn't the only one.

Around 9:45 P.M., the woman sitting next to me finally couldn't take it anymore, either, and pulled a Big Mac out of a McDonald's bag, purchased hours before, and began to eat it. For the first time since I can remember, a burger from *chez McDo* looked good to me, even one that had been made hours ago and was now stone-cold.

The rest of us picked at the imitation-fruit-flavored marshmallows, until the plates were almost empty. I wanted to add to the agenda, as item #28, that I'd cater the next meeting and offer up a selection of tapenades, some nutty mountain cheeses, rounds of creamy chèvre, wooden bowls of Lucques and Picholine olives, an assortment of thinly sliced hams, and perhaps a few pâtés, as well as baskets of hearty bread and bottles of a fruit-forward Côtes du Rhône to wash it all down with. But I didn't.

If we ever meet in person, I might tell you what happened some time after ten P.M., once the twenty-six items on the agenda had been discussed and everyone turned their attention on me, the new guy. But let's just say that Romain was correct (and *correct*), and I hope that never happens to me again. When everyone was finished with me, it was time to vote on my water line. Jacked up on sugar, after what had just happened I was even more nervous about what was coming next.

As if the previous ten minutes had never happened, without one word of dissent everyone voted "*Oui*" on letting me hook up my water line to the main of the building. The French can be frighteningly brusque one minute, then completely forget about whatever it was and be absolutely charming the next. Clearly I wasn't as evolved as they are, but it didn't matter: I was soon going to be able to take a proper shower at home, with a full-body showerhead.

Afterward, we all filed out into the night. One young woman surprised me by coming up and introducing herself. She lived upstairs, and I quickly apologized for any noise or disruptions during the last few months. She was very nice about it and said not to worry, and after chatting on the street for a few minutes, with a "*Bonne soirée, Daveed,*" she went back to her apartment. The French can take a while to warm up to people they don't know. But when they do, the friendship is genuine and sincere. You can't ask for better friends, and maybe the other neighbors would turn out to be just as friendly as she was.

A few days later I knocked on her door and handed her a bottle of Champagne. She was beyond thrilled and said, "If you want to do any more remodeling—go ahead!" followed by a laugh and a smile as she took the bottle. I laughed, too, with the worst behind me. No more work needed to be done. The door had been installed, and now the water line just needed to be hooked up so I could finally have a *douche chaude*, a hot shower, rather than a *douche froide*. But I hadn't had my last one quite yet.

PALETS BRETONS

MAKES 8 LARGE COOKIES

It used to be that using salted butter in desserts was a *faux pas*. But in Brittany, where they eat so much butter that they salt it to extend its life, they make good use of the locally made *beurre salé*, considered the best butter in the world.

Like contractors, getting bakers to change something can be a tough task. The mantra to use only unsalted butter when baking has been drilled into us for a long, long time, and I'll admit I was guilty of promoting the gospel of unsalted butter myself.

When I moved to France, I found that salted butter adds a rich complexity to cakes, pastries like the kouign amann (page 299), and *palets bretons*, thick, crisp, buttery biscuits that—to use a cliché that would confound the French—are like shortbreads on steroids. They'd wonder why you were adding drugs to cookies. (And rightfully so.) But don't worry, they're very addictive even without any habit-forming substances mixed in.

The salted butter should be extremely soft before you mix it in—as the French say, it should be *en pommade*, "as soft as paste." If your kitchen isn't warm, find a place that is to let it soften (but not melt), so it'll meld easily with the eggs and sugar.

> 7 tablespoons (90g) sugar
>
> 2 large egg yolks
>
> 6 tablespoons (3 ounces, 85g) salted butter, cut into cubes, at room temperature
>
> 1 cup (140g) all-purpose flour
>
> 1½ teaspoons baking powder, preferably aluminum-free
>
> ½ teaspoon baking soda

1. In a medium bowl, whisk together the sugar and the egg yolks until light in color, about 30 seconds.
2. With a flexible silicone spatula, mash in the butter

until it's completely incorporated and smooth, with no lumps.

3. In a small bowl, whisk together the flour, baking powder, and baking soda. Stir the dry ingredients into the butter mixture.

4. Use your hands to form the dough into a *boudin* (sausage) as wide as the bottom of the wells of your muffin tin. If you need to, you can roll it on a lightly floured countertop to get it into the right shape. It should be about 5 inches (12cm) long.

5. Wrap the roll in plastic wrap and give it a few more rolls on the counter to smooth it out, doing your best to make it as even as possible. After rolling it, I find that pressing it inward on both ends, like an accordion, helps to coax it into a more uniform shape. Chill the dough for 1 hour. (The dough can be made a day or two ahead and kept refrigerated at this point.)

6. Preheat the oven to 350°F (180°C) with a rack in the center position.

7. Slice the dough crosswise into disks slightly wider than ½ inch (1.25cm) each, and place them, cut-side down, in the wells of a nonstick muffin tin. (No need to butter the molds. The cookies should come out easily after baking.)

8. Bake the cookies until they are light golden brown across the top, 11 minutes. Let cool in the pan, then remove the *palets* from the tins, using a butter knife to aid their release.

34

After outfitting the basement with a dehumidifier, which a Parisian friend told me she relied on to keep the humidity in her place in check, I moved into my apartment. Apparently humidity is a common issue in subterranean Paris, which shouldn't be suprising, considering all the aging pipes and waterways that run underneath the city. So there I was, rolling a dehumidifier home from the BHV department store over the bumpy, crowded stone sidewalks of the Marais. Tourists looked at me funny, but locals seemed to nod in recognition, probably having done a similar *promenade* themselves.

While a few members of the crew worked on hooking up the water line, I unpacked boxes and did my best to clean up all the dust that had found its way into everything. Thankfully, I was able to "shower" by hosing myself down while squeezed in between the toilet and the little hand sink in the half-bathroom. I was finally home.

I have to admit, though: after all the challenges I'd had to overcome to get there, it was a little anticlimactic. And I wasn't *quite* there yet. Someone offering me a bottle of Champagne to welcome me would have made for a smoother arrival. Instead, Romain and I had pizza with a few close friends, accompanied by a bottle of supermarket red, which we opened with a screw (I still kept plenty of those on hand, just in case) and a hand drill, since my wine opener was buried in one of the boxes I'd yet to unpack. It felt like an uneventful landing (which I should be thankful for—the purchase and renovation had been eventful enough), but I didn't need to lie awake at night and worry if anyone was going to show up that day (or week), or wake up and face the mess my apartment had been for the last six months, having taken three times longer than anticipated, and costing over three times as much—which is going to be my new Parisian platitude. There would be no more conflicting stories, or accusations that I was responsible for lopsided chairs, a crooked counter, and windows that would never close quite right. But I was home.

With two ovens, plenty of kitchen cabinets, the right number of electrical outlets, and a brand-new, unscented refrigerator, the kitchen was done. I unpacked my cookware, putting the pots and pans on the stainless-steel shelves I had installed just next to the stove, so they were within easy reach, and started stocking the cabinets under my *spéciale* kitchen island with all the French salts, spices, vinegars, and olive oils I'd collected from Italy and Provence so they'd be within easy reach when I made my first homemade *salade verte*, something I'd missed during my time without a kitchen. And best of all, I got to use my gleaming trophy: the French farmhouse sink—though I made sure to only use the hose, not the spigot. I forgot to tell one of the guests who came for dinner that first night about the faulty faucet, and wish I'd thought to put out some water-thirsty *serpillières*.

Claude and the crew were working in the basement, connecting the water line. In the meantime, I was making do with the *douchette* in the *demi*-WC, carefully hosing myself down with the hand sprayer. Fortunately, I've lived in France

long enough to know that shower curtains are optional
(hence the abundance of *serpillières* in French bathrooms,
too), so I'd become more adept at taking curtainless showers
than when I was a tourist and soaked entire hotel bathrooms,
and part of the bedrooms, when I showered. Of all the decisions that I made during the entire renovation, putting a
drain in that floor was the best of them. Because it was going
to be a longer time than I ever imagined until I got to use the
actual shower.

I don't like going into dark, damp underground spaces.
Basements, lit by bare bulbs that cast frightening shadows
and are covered with sticky cobwebs, creep me out. So I let
the crew do the plumbing work while I listened from upstairs
to them pounding and jackhammering and breaking rocks.
I kept busy, liberating my clothes, kitchen items, and office
supplies from suitcases and boxes. Everything needed to be
washed or wiped clean. After my ninth load of laundry, I
knew that I could never live without a dryer again. I hadn't
come across my book manuscript and notes yet, but figured
those were buried under one of the many stacks of brown
cartons that I would eventually get around to opening.

Every few hours, Claude and whoever he was working
with would come upstairs, their clothes damp with sweat and
errant water, muck clinging to their work boots, to report on
the progress. I'd long stopped offering them treats or even a
glass of water, but remained cordial. I'd also switched back
to using *vous* with them, verbally keeping a polite distance.
That was my biggest mistake in the renovation. In a society
that still clings to the remnants of a monarchistic hierarchy,
I will always wonder, if I had kept them at a distance—acting
like the boss, and treating them like workers—would the
renovation have gone differently? I can't say.

I, the optimistic American, thought everyone would nat-

urally want to do their best, just like all the cooks and chefs
I've worked with over the years did. Claude and the crew took
advantage of that. I should have started off on another foot,
one I should have put down more often than I did. Or at least
used it to provide a well-placed kick in someone's *derrière*.

————

Two days after work started on the water main, Claude came
upstairs and knocked on my front door. He had the usual
innocent look on his face, but wasn't smiling. Which didn't
matter at this point, because we both understood that it no
longer worked on me.

"*Daveed*, I have something to tell you."

"Oh, really?" I said, and wanted to add, "Once, just this
one last time . . . please tell me something was done right."
But I didn't. Something was up.

"The water pipe is hooked up, but water from your bathroom isn't flowing downward toward the water main of the
building. It's not going to work. We're going to need to install
a water pump in your bedroom to evacuate it."

I looked at him long and hard, and just stared. My head
started to feel like wet concrete was filling it, the brunt of it
piling toward my forehead. The idea of a water pump had
come up at the start, which would have mitigated the need
for permission to hook my water line to the main of the
building. But the idea of a noisy machine in my bedroom
pumping shower and waste water through the room wasn't
appealing to me. I'd spent months agonizing over whether I
should spend the money and call a special meeting, or just
wait. Once I decided to go with the new water line, I had
to hire an architect to draw up plans for the pipe to present

to the neighbors, supply documentation of insurance, and persuade the president of the building, the head of the *syndic*, and the architect for the building to come to the apartment and explain it to them. Once they said it was okay to proceed, and they signed off on the thick *dossier* of paperwork, I sat through the meeting with the other owners before getting the final approval.

I didn't say anything to Claude. I had nothing left to say. He had built the bathroom. He had laid the pipes, knowing that they would need to be angled enough so the water would drain downward to the water main. That was his job.

I continued staring at him, trying to keep it together. Everything that had happened in the apartment, that I had internalized or chalked up to my bad decisions on how I could have behaved, or what I should or could have done, had become moot. He didn't say anything after that, and I didn't have anything left in me to respond. I'd let so many things slide that weren't installed properly or didn't work, and this wasn't just another one: it was the last one.

Oh, and by the way, it was going to cost me another 2,750 euros for the pump and the installation. So if he could get a *chèque* for that . . .

I took a hard look at him. All of a sudden, a blinding white flash of anger surged through me, and with all my force, I grabbed him by the collar, lifted him up, and shoved him out the door, slamming it behind him.

Then I started shaking, partially from outrage and anger, but also because my exhaustion had made me do something so uncharacteristic of me. This final blunder, another one that I'd have to pay for, had pushed me over the edge. I couldn't believe this was happening.

When I called Romain right after to tell him, he couldn't believe it, either. So he called Valérie, an architect friend of his, and she offered to come over the next night with Daniel, a contractor, to check out the plumbing configuration and see if I really did need a water pump. The next evening, the four of us sat around the kitchen island looking a bit like chess pieces, not just because of our different shapes but because the irregularly hacked-off chair legs had us sitting at different heights. Although the crooked counter was still driving me nuts, it was the water line I was concerned with. I explained the issue to them and they were there to give me a second (and third) opinion as to whether it was necessary to have a water pump.

I had learned from having a few architects in the apartment that, unlike me, architects in Paris love going into basements and *caves*, where the "bones" of buildings are. Unlike American structures, buildings in Paris are hundreds or thousands of years old, and no one loves French history more than the French. Go underground, and you can actually see the layers of Paris's history, each built on top of the one before it. (Which I was now contributing to as well.)

Valérie barely hid her enthusiasm. "I'd like to see the basement first, to see what's going on," she said eagerly. I grabbed a flashlight and the weighty ring of keys to the locks on the basement door, each suggesting a different era (and level of security), and led everyone to the basement. We carefully wound our way down the crumbling dirt staircase and through the Napoléon-height tunnels, to where my pipes led. Valérie stopped suddenly when she saw them.

"Oh . . ." she said, gasping a little when she saw the pipes. "*Non, non, non,*" she continued, shaking her head, punctuating her concern. "This is *not good*. Not good *at all*. Look what they've done here!" she cried, pointing at the leaking brand-new pipes, in the process of being buried in fresh concrete. But that wasn't the worst of it: They had also done something that Valérie said could compromise the structural integrity of the entire block of buildings in my neighborhood. If I had to apologize for that to the neighborhood, I'd need a larger mailbox for all the crumpled-up letters.

Valérie was serious, but Daniel found it amusing. "*La vache!*" he laughed. "Don't those people have any pride in their work? What were they thinking?" he said to no one in particular. I couldn't answer that. The people who could answer weren't there.

We trudged back upstairs from the dank basement, and Valérie and Daniel went to get a look at how the water lines had been connected in the bathroom. Valérie shrieked, "Look! Look there! They didn't put them high enough. The water can't possibly flow downward. Why on earth would they *do* that?" she asked. (Once again, the right person to answer that question wasn't present.) I bake cookies and brownies for a living, but you don't need to be an engineer, or a scholar of physics, to know that water flows downward.

While she looked around, trying to figure out if there was a way to get the water to evacuate without a pump, Daniel walked around my bedroom, running his hands over the vaulted walls. Because there was a thermostat on one, he was puzzled as to why there weren't any radiators. "What's this connected to? Where is the heat for this room?" he asked.

"It's radiant heat, installed under the tiles, which will be nice in the winter," I offered up with confidence. I knew it worked well because I had turned it on after it had been installed and it heated up the room so it was nice and cozy. I was looking forward to stepping out of the shower and drying myself off while my feet were warmed by the luxuriously toasty floor.

"Mind if I take a look at how it was hooked up?"

I didn't mind at all, and he took some sort of gadget from

his tool kit to check things out. I wasn't sure what he was doing.

"Well . . . *alors* . . ." he began. "Just to let you know, there is a very good chance that you're going to be electrocuted if you step onto this floor with wet feet. You have a *fuite d'électricité* [electrical leak] passing through the material under the tiles. You're lucky the shower hasn't been hooked up yet." I was glad to be alive and all, but how could it have been installed wrong? Claude told me he had the same heating in his apartment and was very familiar with it, one of the main reasons I had let him install it. The heat felt fine to me when I turned it on, and I didn't understand how there could be a problem.

"Do you mind turning on the entire system? Let's check it out," Daniel instructed me, which I did. Because it was now summer, and warm out, I hadn't turned on the heat after they repaired the wood floors. We gave them a little time to warm up, then the four of us walked around touching the floors in various places with our hands, feeling them for heat. None of us could feel warmth coming through the floor in my office, and none in the kitchen. The floor in the adjacent living room area, however, felt like it was heating up. One thing that *was* rising was my anxiety at not having heat in key areas of the apartment. Fortunately, I had taken a lot of pictures during the construction, including when the heating coils were being laid down before they were covered by the flooring, and pulled them up on my phone.

Daniel's brown eyes bugged out as he leaned in closer to the illuminated screen. "Look . . . look . . . right . . . *there*," he said, tapping his finger at the bottom of one of the pictures of the kitchen. "Right there . . . that's why there is no heat. There are no heating coils there." Sure enough, the floor was a maze of heating coils everywhere—except if you looked carefully, you'd spot grimy pieces of Styrofoam resting over parts of the floor, ones that had no heating coils underneath. The foam boards made sure that wasn't obvious.

That explained why my apartment only had heat in some places, but not in others. I described to Daniel how we discovered the floors had warped and I could feel the heat then. So it should be working in the other places—right?

"Well, that explains it," Daniel started in, delivering more bad news. "The heating system got overloaded when that happened, and at that point, it died." I was shocked, although, fortunately, not literally. How could it be fixed?

"You need to tear up the floorboards, jackhammer the subflooring, replace the coils, then replace the wood floors. That's how." The French don't mess around delivering bad news. That's how it is. *C'est comme ça.*

The heat did work in the living room area, which would warm part of the kitchen, but that was it. At this point, the water pump was becoming a minor issue. The more we all walked around the apartment, the more both Daniel and Valérie found things that were wrong. I thought the project was finished. But it wasn't done with me yet.

35

Daniel was now taking a much closer look at everything in the apartment, opening drawers and cabinets, checking outlets with a voltage meter, pressing his hands against the walls, and taking the kitchen and bathroom fixtures through their paces. (Yes, I warned him in advance about the kitchen faucet, which elicited an extra-deep laugh.) When he was in the half-bathroom, he peered up at the ventilator in the ceiling. "Where does this lead?" he asked, swiveling his head around to see where it might go. When I proudly showed him the new hot water heater just a few feet away in the kitchen, in a cabinet next to the fuse box, he started rubbing his forehead and shaking his head.

"*Non, non* . . . now . . . now, this is really bad. Up here"—he pointed to what was supposed to be the ventilation—"look, *Daveed*, see how this is hooked up?" I looked up. "You've got CO_2 being pumped into your apartment. You're going to die." He said the last part of that phrase with a hearty laugh of disbelief, which I didn't find as amusing as he did.

After he inspected the new hot water heater, which fortunately was fine (until it had to be replaced a few months later with a larger one, because its size wasn't adequate for the apartment), he opened up the cabinet next to it, where the new fuse box was. Removing the flashlight from his belt, he shined it at the wiring behind the switches to get a closer look. *"Aïe!"* he cried sharply, calling me over to take a look. He wasn't laughing anymore.

"I need to bring my electrician in here to see this. But look . . . look at these." I didn't see anything wrong when I peered in. But then he aimed his flashlight at the back of the box, where all the wires were.

"Look in the back. See there? All those wires. . . . *ils fondent* [they're melting]. The fuses are underpowered and they can't handle the wattage going through them." He estimated that the contractor saved about one euro ($1) on each of the fuses, buying cheaper ones. So because he wanted to save twenty-five bucks, I had wires that were melting. Looking the fuse box up and down while moving his flashlight over the gray wires, which were drooping rubber at their bottoms from the heat, he continued, "This fuse box needs to be completely rewired, and if you don't change these fuses and wires, you're going to have a fire."

When he walked over to the windows to look at them, he looked with curiosity at the window levers that were lying at the base of a few of them. More of the boxy metal knobs had fallen off, startling me whenever one dropped without any warning, hitting the stainless-steel counter with a loud "ka-*plunk*." When I had shown Claude how the metal levers were continuing to drop off one by one (and scaring the heck out of me when they did), he replied, *"Pas de problème* . . . I'll just glue them back on, *Daveed.* They'll stay put. Don't worry." The white glue he showed up with to reattach them was the kind you bought for your kids' elementary school art project, not six-foot-high industrial metal windows.

"These windows will never close right, no matter what," Daniel said, inspecting the frames. "They're *torsadées.* They should have been returned to the company who made them before they were installed," which Valérie nodded in agreement with. *Torsader,* meaning "to twist," was a new word for me, and although he used it to refer to the window frames, I was thinking it could be applied to a number of other things that were, or had happened, in the apartment.

All along I had been worried about silly lopsided chairs and unusable USB plugs dangling from the walls. Valérie wasn't happy that we hadn't called her to come in earlier to take a look, while the work was going on. But how could I have known? The contractor had come with a good recommendation and had been doing this for over a dozen years. Daniel and Valérie both said they'd seen *pire* (worse) in Paris, which I think was meant to make me feel better, but I didn't see how *pire* was possible.

After two years of working on purchasing the apartment, then renovating it, in one evening I'd learned enough to realize that I'd made a huge mistake. I had been in over my head right from day one, not understanding the intricacies of purchasing an apartment in a foreign country, with all those new terms and concepts, and customs, to understand. I was sideswiped by a real estate agent, and tangled for months with a contractor on the renovations. I clearly had had no business moving to a foreign country, let alone buying an apartment in one. My head had been in the stars. And now everything had been ruined—all that I had invested in Paris, not just financially, but emotionally, was in this apartment, and it was a complete *désastre.*

LEMON-YOGURT CAKE
Gâteau au yaourt et au citron

I used to tell people, "If you want to be comfortable, stay home." But I *was* home, so now that point was moot. I blame myself for a number of things that have happened to me here. Some of them can probably be attributed to cultural misunderstandings, and miscommunication as I verbally (and mentally) toggled between French and English, but no one can hold me responsible for the proclivity of the French to borrow terms from English, which vexes the Académie Française, an institution founded in 1635 to protect the French language.

Many of the words that get borrowed from English are action-oriented words, usually assigned to concepts that are not considered French (including the concept of being "action-oriented"), adding an *–ing* to the end: *le fooding* (adventurous eating), *le jogging, l'e-banking* (unfortunately, e-banking came into being after I dealt with the banks when I was buying and remodeling my apartment), *le scrapbooking, le sitting* (hanging out on a sidewalk curb, common practice among teenagers), *le coaching,* and *le marketing,* which, contrary to popular belief, does exist in France. The idea of "snacking," though, is thought not to. But it does, in the form of *le goûter,* the afternoon treat that tides you over until dinner. It's often for the kids, but I indulge in it myself.

The French not only have guardians for protecting their language from outside influences, but their sense of order also gets perturbed when classic pastries are tweaked. When I went to pastry school and we made *pâtes de fruits,* I suggested balancing their sweetness with a few drops of lemon juice. Even though it would have taken someone with an extremely discerning palate to taste three drops of lemon juice added to a very large, bubbling cauldron of puree, the chef instructor replied without even considering it, *"C'est pas possible,"* and told the class, "Adding lemon would mean they wouldn't be raspberry fruit gels anymore, because they would have lemon in them." The logic was hard to argue with. And that was that.

Even though the classic French yogurt cake isn't glazed, I went rogue and added a lemon-flavored one to mine. But to make the pedants happy, I've renamed it Lemon-Yogurt Cake, which is great for *le snacking*.

Cake

    Butter, for the pan

    1¼ cups (250g) granulated sugar

    Zest of 2 unsprayed or organic lemons

    ½ cup (120g) whole-milk plain yogurt, preferably Greek

    3 large eggs, at room temperature

    ⅓ cup (80ml) neutral-tasting vegetable oil

    2 teaspoons pure vanilla extract

    ¼ teaspoon salt

    1½ cups (210g) all-purpose flour

    2 teaspoons baking powder, preferably aluminum-free

Glaze

    1 cup (140g) powdered sugar

    2 tablespoons fresh lemon juice

1. Preheat the oven to 350ºF (180ºC). Butter a 9-inch (23cm) round cake pan and line the bottom with parchment paper, cut to fit.

2. In a medium bowl, rub the granulated sugar and lemon zest together with your fingers until the sugar is moist. Whisk in the yogurt, then the eggs, oil, vanilla, and salt.

3. In a small bowl, whisk together the flour and baking powder, then mix the dry ingredients into the yogurt mixture using a flexible spatula, just until there are no visible traces of flour.

4. Scrape the mixture into the prepared cake pan and bake until the top is golden brown and the center feels set, 30 to 35 minutes. Remove from the oven and let cool completely.

5. Make the glaze: In a small bowl, stir together the powdered sugar and lemon juice until smooth. The glaze should be thick and not too liquid, just runny enough to spread. If necessary, add more sugar or lemon juice.

6. Remove the cake from the pan, peel off the parchment paper, and set it on a serving platter. Spread the glaze over the top of the cake, encouraging some of it to gently drip down the sides. The cake will keep at room temperature, under a cake dome, for 3 to 4 days.

36

People tell me I'm lucky to live in Paris. But I didn't have any lucky *astres* (stars) to thank. I was responsible for making it happen, but I was also to blame for the mess I was in. Being French, Daniel and Valérie didn't attempt to soften the blow.

Sitting with them around the counter in my new kitchen, I'd decided to move back to the United States. Paris had lured me from San Francisco with pastry shops and chocolates lined up in pristine glass showcases, baskets of crusty breads at *boulangeries* on every corner, and caramels *beurre-salés* made with the exquisite salted butter from Brittany available everywhere, even at the supermarket. (Which someone should have informed whoever catered the meeting of the building's owners.) And then there were cheeses, fatty pucks of Camembert with their barnyard funk, and Roqueforts with strains of sharp green mold running rampant through the wedges. I was hooked.

But now I couldn't remember the last time I'd visited an outdoor market. Without a kitchen, I had lost my desire to cook and bake. I didn't want to go into a chocolate shop in my grungy work clothes covered with dirt, and peruse chocolates. I had become a phantom to my friends, not having seen them for months. I'd been *bouleversé* (bowled over) by the purchase and renovation, and now I was listening to Daniel and Valérie rattle off a list of everything that was wrong with the apartment and we hadn't even gotten to the reason why they came in the first place: to determine if the water could be evacuated without a pump moving sewage through my bedroom.

———

Valérie was a well-connected architect and came from one of France's most esteemed families. She recommended a plumbing company that turned out to be the Hermès of plumbers. (In terms of both quality and price.) She gave me the number to call and told me to use her name. If anyone knew if it was possible to correct the *raccordement* (connection) for the water, it was them.

Sitting around the kitchen counter, dazed from the barrage of bad news, I blurted out to Daniel that the crooked kitchen island was really driving me nuts. The whole kitchen seemed off-kilter, and no matter what, I knew I'd never get used to it. I told him that I understood it was a big deal to fix, as it apparently was quite a bit of work to realign it.

"*Ah, oui?*" said Daniel. "Let me take a look," which he did by getting down on his hands and knees, peering at the cabinets, then under the baseboards. He stood up, hitching his pants back up, and said, "Do you have a screwdriver?"

"Hold on just a minute," I said, grabbing one and handing it to him. He got back down on the floor to tinker with something underneath the cabinets in a few places. After a couple of minutes, he had me, Romain, and Valérie each grab one side of the island. "*On y va . . .* let's go—everybody lift."

Which we did, and I was surprised at how the island had come loose so easily. "Okay. Now let's turn it."

We all raised the counter in unison, just enough to move it so it lined up straight with the floorboards. "Is this where you want it?" Daniel asked, while holding up his end.

"Uhh . . . why, yes, that's right," I said, *bouleversé* that it happened so fast.

We all set the counter back down, and he went back underneath with the screwdriver. When he was done, I stepped back to look at the kitchen island, which was now perfectly aligned with the rest of the kitchen. It had taken less than five minutes. (And he didn't hand me a bill for it, either.)

I shook hands with Daniel and thanked him profusely before he left. Valérie got ready to leave just after he did. As she slipped on her coat, she stopped and looked me in the eye—to make sure I understood what she was about to say (she probably already sensed that I was a pushover, maybe because of my accent)—and stressed, "Whatever you do, *do not let that man back in your apartment!*" And she wasn't talking about Daniel, whom I later hired to correct the *malfaçons* (defects) and oversee the rest of the work.

―――――

Valérie also recommended a lawyer, and I telephoned his office the next day to make an appointment. I'd spent so much time in a discombobulated construction zone that it was a relief to walk into a sumptuous waiting room with ornate wood carvings and framed mirrors hanging on the walls. The *salle d'attente* made the posh tea salon at Ladurée look like the cafeteria at Walmart. Glass sconces bathed everything in a Sauternes-like golden glow; I wouldn't have been surprised if the prone-to-elegance Louis XIV came strolling out from behind one of the doors. I took a seat, sinking into one of the plush tufted chairs where I planned to spend the rest of my life.

Lawyers hold a special position in France, as they are the only ones who could possibly figure out all the complicated laws in the country. It's no surprise that most French lawyers have prematurely gray hair.

And like all lawyers in France, this one also had crazy hair. His bushy gray locks swirled in thick swoops around his head and seemed to defy gravity without the aid of any hair products. I imagine French lawyers are so busy memorizing all those dates that most don't have time to get a proper haircut. But no matter how unkempt their hair, French lawyers are always well dressed. And like anyone in France whose job involves enforcing rules, they aren't always popular.

I hauled each and every file, bill, record of payment, and photograph over to his office and laid them all out on the gilded baroque conference table. I did my best to explain what had happened, backing it up with paperwork and pictures. My goal was to simply recoup the money I had spent to get everything fixed. *C'est possible?*

"*Désolé,* Monsieur Lebovitz. This isn't America," the lawyer told me, pushing back a swoop of salt-and-pepper hair that continued flopping over his forehead as he spoke. Traffic rumbled faintly outside on the Boulevard Saint-Germain-des-Prés. I silently admired his windows, particularly the latches to open and close them with, and how they were within reach and still attached to the frames.

Oh, how I wanted to hear from the lawyer that he was aghast and shocked at what had happened. And, yes, it was a terrible thing and he was going to do whatever he could to make it right. The results-oriented, American part of me wanted to hear that I'd been wronged and something could be done about it.

"Monsieur Lebovitz," he continued to explain from across the table, "this is France. It would take at least five years of legal work and cost a lot of money to get anything back, if you even can. You are clearly right, but in the end, you would probably lose because you are the *propriétaire*, and owners always lose."

He did pause to think about something for a moment, then added that because so many people had bad experiences with contractors, maybe that could perhaps work in my favor. People dislike contractors more than bosses or owners, he pondered aloud.

Yet in summation, he said that I should forget about it, get the work fixed, and be done with it. However, being France, there was, of course, paperwork that I had to fill out to get the contractor (whose calls I had ignored for the last couple of days, while I figured out what to do) to sign that he was "renouncing" the project, stating that he would not be coming back, and I could get the *malfaçons* fixed by someone else. The second option was that I could allow him to come back and fix everything. Valérie's words echoed in my ears. That wasn't going to happen.

————

It had been years since I'd had a vacation. Those four- to ten-week paid vacations that everyone envies about France are for salaried people who work for companies, or are part of the one-third of the population that works for the government. Writers may be as highly esteemed and celebrated in

France as pro football players are in America, but we don't get vacations. (Or seven-figure salaries.) I was *épuisé*. But it was urgent that I fix the problem with the configuration of the water pipes. A vacation would have to wait.

The word *Lavillaugouet* brings a smile to everyone in Paris who hears it. No, it's not a proposed law in France for giving paid vacations to writers, unfortunately. Mention Lavillaugouet to any architect, reputable contractor, lawyer, or freaked-out apartment owner, and they'll break out into a broad, knowing smile of reassurance. Ch. Lavillaugouet has been in the business of *assainissement*, water drainage, since 1872, and I'm not the first person they've saved in Paris.

I'm sure they've seen worse during the last hundred and fifty years, such as in 1910, when the Seine flooded Paris and the water rose 28 feet above the normal level, submerging the city for a week. Parisians paddled boats through the *métro* stations and makeshift footbridges were set up over water-filled streets so pedestrians could cross. I didn't want to go down in French history books as being the cause of the next deluge.

Contrary to any less-than-stellar customer service experiences I've had over the years, they could not have been more attentive or helpful on the phone. I explained what had happened, who had recommended them to me, and knowing that the French can't resist drama, I said the situation was dire. That was the magic word and they said they'd be there first thing the next morning.

Their truck pulled up in front to my building as scheduled, with big, blocky black letters painted on the front: SERVICE D'URGENCE, and the guys hopped out. I brought them to see the handiwork of my soon-to-be-former contractor.

"*Oh la la!*" they said, sticking out their necks and rocking their heads from side to side. "*Oh la la la la!* Look at this . . ."

The first guy prodded the other, and both leaned in closer to get a better look at what they were seeing.

The work area was a picture-perfect scene of chaos and disorder; a still-life of tools, sludge, water-saturated clothes wadded up in corners, badly cut scraps of metal tubing, and a steady flow of water trickling out of freshly installed pipes, semi-embedded in concrete.

"*Bien sûr*, we can fix this," they said, with the sound of water gurgling from the joints in the background, calming my fears that the situation couldn't be salvaged.

"First, we'll clear this mess up," the foreman said, surveying the disarray, then added, "but I'd like to know one thing first: How could anyone work like this?" I couldn't answer that.

He continued, "We'll redo all these pipes, changing the joints and gaskets so they're not leaking. We'll get this mess fixed up so it's perfect, *sans problème*. And if you'd like, we can also install a flap; in case there is a plumbing problem in the building, your apartment won't become awash with sewage from the other apartments in the building." That flap added a few hundred euros to the cost, but I thought it was a good investment because I was in the *merde* now and didn't want to be there—in a more literal way—in the future.

It was August and everyone was on vacation, except for writers, as well as my new favorite people in Paris: the workers who showed up to fix the problem. Unlike other contractors, they gave me a definitive finish date, and from the thoroughness and professionalism of the contract I signed, I knew they meant it. I wanted to hug them, but stuck to shaking hands—and *vouvoyer*'d them—when they arrived to start the work.

After a week of them toiling underground, I braved the crumbling stone stairs leading down to the basement to see how everything looked. It was immaculate. They'd cleaned everything up, hauled away all the debris, and in place of the previous mess was a gleaming, perfectly laid (and bone-dry) water pipe. Until now, I never knew a water pipe could bring so much joy. Here I was, spending all my time in Paris, my attention on French éclairs and almond-stuffed croissants, crusted baguettes, salted Brittany butter, and chewy *pâtes de fruits*. Who knew a water pipe could bring the same joy?

A few days later, one of their plumbers came over to look at the plumbing lines inside the apartment. When I explained that I was told I needed a pump to evacuate the water if I wanted my bathroom to be functional, he looked at me, scrunched up his face, and said, "*Quoi?* You don't need a pump at all. The water line is fine. It just needs an additional joint to raise it a little, so the water can flow downward. That's all. What was your contractor thinking?" Which was a question I kept asking myself.

After about half an hour, the shower and the rest of the bathroom plumbing worked. I was good to go.

37

Tired—and admittedly jealous—of seeing pictures of friends on social media, relaxing on beaches holding cocktails with glistening blue waters stretching out far beyond their sandaled feet, Romain and I decided to go south for a week to a small island off the coast of Provence where our friends have a house overlooking the Mediterranean. The island is quite remote; there isn't potable water and cars aren't allowed, so it's not everyone's idea of the ideal vacation in Provence. But there are lovely beaches, and because it's France, there's cell phone reception. And because it's Provence, there's rosé.

I had made the decision not to check my messages during the week, turning the ringer off to *profiter* from the solitude the remote island offered. No dust, no doctors, no bankers, no architects, no lawyers, and, best of all, no contractors. Sitting on a beach flipping through magazines, rather than plumbing catalogs, with a bottle of wine never far from my glass once again made me inexplicably happy to be in France. My only thoughts were about what our next meal was, which was the bouillabaisse Romain and I had most evenings at the restaurant owned by the fisherman who cleaned his catch each morning, after anchoring his boat, standing in the waist-deep water by the dock. Normally I would have been terrified of the *murène*, a very-much-alive, vicious-looking eel, whose jaw the fisherman opened to show me rows of sharply pointed teeth. But I'd seen much scarier things in my recent past, and looked forward to dining on him later that evening.

Each morning started with breakfast on the terrace overlooking the sea, drinking *café au lait* and eating the country bread made by the baker on the island, who only worked three months out of the year. It was my idea of paradise. (The breakfast, and the idea of working only three months a year.) I found myself forgetting what had happened, thoroughly refreshed and ready to make a new start.

That is, until a few days later when my phone vibrated. The screen said it was Claude. I didn't know what to do. A few days on the island had turned my life back around. Years of stress melted away as I tuned everything out and planted myself on the beach, gazing up at the blue skies, with my only concern being, *How could I re-create the cream-filled* tarte tropézienne *they served for dessert at the bouillabaise restaurant?*

It was probably the first time in history that a client ignored a message from a contractor, rather than the other way around. Or I guess I should say, from my ex-contractor. (Whose name we vowed never to speak again.) I went back to flipping through magazines, sitting on my beach chair overlooking the soothing sea a few feet away, dreaming of another *tarte tropézienne* for dessert—and trying not to think of what was going to happen when I got back.

―――――

Daniel had given me a bid to fix the *malfaçons*, and I was confident he would do them correctly. He told me his least-favorite thing to do was fix things others had done wrong, but he was so mad about the state my apartment was in, he took the job.

The plumbing problem had been solved. It cost quite a bit more than I'd spent on straightening the kitchen island out, but I didn't have to worry about a Wikipedia entry about how *un Américain* destroyed an entire *quartier* of Paris. Now it was on to fix the other problems. I stopped searching for my return ticket to San Francisco.

One day while Daniel was working, I heard laughter coming from downstairs. I wasn't used to hearing happy sounds in the apartment, and it made the place finally feel more like home. Daniel was a nice guy who didn't argue or play games: he came and he worked, which you never realize is such a big deal until you're up against someone who doesn't. I didn't have to walk on tiptoe around the electrician who worked with Daniel, a Lebanese fellow who left me a package of his favorite chickpeas to try (which was nicer than the packet of condoms someone else left behind), and his family's za'atar seasoning blend. *Quelle différence.*

———

Fall was turning the corner to winter. The skies over Paris were still bright and clear, but as the days passed, each breeze brought in another blast of colder and colder air. Whereas last year at this time, the gloves were just coming off (in a *notaire*'s office), now the gloves were being pulled back on, along with overcoats, scarves, and caps. Café terraces emptied as Parisians moved inside to warm themselves over a *p'tit café* or *chocolat chaud*, which I now had the luxury of time to enjoy, too. I felt like I was part of Paris again, able to savor the simple pleasures that make the city the place I wanted to call home. Having my own apartment made me feel like I finally belonged here.

The radiant heating worked fine in the main living area of the apartment, bolstered by strategically placed space heaters. Daniel gave me an electric wall heater he had from another project for the downstairs bedroom and bathroom. I made sure he installed it far, far away from the shower, or anywhere that could get wet.

We'd already aligned the kitchen island and Daniel closed off the CO2 coming into the apartment, but he couldn't fix the far-away faucet by the kitchen sink. He did note that there was no drainpipe attached to the overflow hole, so I had to be careful when filling the sink. I forgot to give Romain that memo, though, and one day I heard a shout of panic as a flood of water came pouring out from the cabinet underneath when he was filling the sink to wash dishes. (Which he automatically jumps into when I'm testing recipes and they pile up. Another reason he's a keeper.) Like the radiant heat downstairs and the CO2 diffuser, the overflow hole was another thing in the apartment that had to be *condamné*. I had amassed an impressive number of wine corks since moving in, and one plugged in to the overflow hole of the sink effectively, and economically, did the trick.

The electrician removed all the melted wires and replaced the fuses and wiring behind them, so the electricity hummed along nicely, and safely. He got a kick out of the USB plugs hanging out of the walls, so at least they served some purpose.

Daniel had looked at the window locks and knobs and said there wasn't much he could do except replace all the windows—for twenty-two thousand euros. So like the four kitchen chairs that are still four different heights, I was going to have to live with the whims of the windows.

When I went downstairs to see what was making Daniel laugh so hard, I saw that he'd pulled off the board covering the water filtration system Claude had installed. I was happy to not have to contend with the "plaster of Paris"—the calcium in our water that grinds hot water heaters, coffeemakers, irons, and dishwashers to a halt. The only liquid I go through more bottles of than wine is white vinegar. Installing a filter for your entire apartment solves the problem, so I had taken Claude's advice and decided to go for the same water filter he had at home, the one Daniel was standing in front of, in hysterics.

"Oh, this is really funny . . ."

"Really? What's so funny about a water filter?" I asked, looking at the tubes and filter fixed to the wall.

"Look!" he said, pointing to the filter holder. "This . . . this . . . it's upside down! The whole system was installed upside down. It's doing *rien*!" The filter was facing the wrong direction, so it did nothing—*rien*. I couldn't believe it either, but I found myself laughing, too.

TROPÉZIENNE VERRINES

SERVES 6

I had dreamed about sharing a *tarte tropézienne* recipe for a long, long time. In *My Paris Kitchen*, the book I had begun around the same time I started my renovation, I finally tackled it. It's a classic French pastry, popularized by a bakery in Saint-Tropez, near the island where we spent our dreamlike vacation. Like a number of things in my apartment, it took several tries before I got it right. A freestanding *tarte* with several elements—a custardy filling, orange-scented syrup, and brioche dough—needed to be carefully tested and measured, since readers understandably get anxious when they finish a recipe and have half a cup of filling left on the counter.

It wasn't until later that I realized the same flavors could be combined more easily in individual glasses, which the French call *verrines*. Like *thé glacé* and *salades César* served in jam jars (*à la Brooklyn*), *verrines* caught on like wildfire in France a few years back, but got overused to the point of silliness. Yet proof that I'm as openminded as the next Parisian, I got over my aversion to them and adopted the concept to make an easier version of the dessert, with a lot less fuss.

The idea came from my tester in America, Cindy, who went rogue and assembled the pastries in mason jars with screw-on lids, which she said made them easy to transport to a picnic. So you can be *très* Parisian, or *très* Brook-*leen*, if you want to do the same.

Normally I like to use fresh orange juice when I cook and bake. But store-bought juice has a more concentrated orange flavor, so I use it here. If you want to use fresh, tangerine juice is a better option, if available.

Orange Chiffon Cake

- 1 cup (135g) cake flour (not self-rising)
- 1 teaspoon baking powder, preferably aluminum-free
- ¼ teaspoon salt
- 3 large eggs, separated
- 2 tablespoons water
- ¼ cup (60ml) neutral-tasting vegetable oil, such as canola or sunflower

¾ cup (150g) sugar

Zest of 2 oranges

1 teaspoon pure orange or vanilla extract

Orange Curd

2 large eggs

2 large egg yolks

⅓ cup (80ml) orange or tangerine juice (see Headnote)

2 tablespoons fresh lemon juice

½ cup (100g) sugar

Pinch of salt

8 tablespoons (4 ounces/115g) unsalted butter, cut into cubes, at room temperature

Zest of 1 orange

Grand Marnier Syrup

¾ cup (180ml) water

⅓ cup (80ml) sugar

¼ cup (60ml) orange juice

¼ cup (60ml) Grand Marnier, Cointreau, or triple sec

1 cup (250ml) heavy cream

4 to 6 navel oranges, peeled and cut into *suprêmes* (after peeling, use a paring knife to cut the segments away from the membrane)

Additional orange segments, candied orange peel, or berries, for garnish (optional)

1. Make the cake: Preheat the oven to 350°F (180°C). Line the bottom of an 8-inch (20cm) square cake pan with parchment paper. Do not grease the pan.
2. Into a small bowl, sift together the cake flour, baking powder, and salt. Set aside.

3. In the bowl of a stand mixer fitted with the wire whisk, or by hand in a medium bowl, whisk together the egg yolks, water, vegetable oil, ½ cup plus 2 tablespoons of the sugar (130g), the orange zest, and orange extract. Whisk on medium-high speed until very light and fluffy, about 5 minutes. Stir in the dry ingredients.

4. In a separate bowl (one that's clean and dry), whip the egg whites until they start to hold their shape. Whisk in the remaining 2 tablespoons sugar and whisk until the egg whites are stiff but not dry.

5. Fold one-quarter of the egg whites into the beaten yolk mixture, then fold in the remaining whites, just until no streaks of egg white are visible. Do not overmix. Scrape the batter into the prepared pan, smooth the top, and bake until the cake springs back in the middle when you touch it, 25 minutes. Let cool.

6. Make the orange curd: In a medium saucepan, whisk together the eggs, egg yolks, orange juice, lemon juice, sugar, and salt. Add the cubes of butter. Heat the mixture over medium heat, stirring continuously with a whisk, until the butter has melted. Cook, stirring continuously, until the mixture thickens to the point where it looks like it's about to jell but hasn't boiled. (It will take a few minutes—perhaps as few as 2½ to 3 minutes, but then it happens quickly, so be vigilant.) When it reaches this point, scrape the curd into a bowl and stir in the orange zest. Cover and chill thoroughly.

7. Make the Grand Marnier syrup: In a small saucepan, combine the water, sugar, and orange juice and heat over medium-high heat, stirring, until the sugar has completely dissolved. Remove from the heat, stir in the orange liqueur, and let cool to room temperature.

8. Assemble the verrines: In the bowl of a stand mixer fit-

ted with the wire whisk, or by hand in a medium bowl, whip the heavy cream until it holds soft, droopy peaks. Fold the orange curd into the whipped cream.

9. Cut the cake into thirty-six 1-inch (3cm) cubes. (You won't use all the cake. The rest can be snacked on, or frozen and used for another purpose.) Gather six tumblers or wineglasses (or jam jars) with at least a 1-cup (250ml) capacity.

10. Put a generous tablespoon of the orange curd cream in the glass. For the next layers, for each verrine, dunk three squares of cake in the orange syrup and make a layer of them in each glass. Put 5 or 6 orange segments on top of the cake and press the ingredients in each glass down to "meld" them together.

11. Add a generous 2 tablespoons of the orange cream to each glass, on top of the orange segments, then top each with three cubes of cake dunked in the syrup. Press down again, then divide the remaining cream among the glasses and smooth the top. Refrigerate until ready to serve. (The verrines are best made at least 4 hours ahead, which gives time for the ingredients to meld together.)

12. To serve, top each verrine with a few orange segments, a few strips of candied orange peel, or sliced strawberries or raspberries. (Since this is not a traditional Tropézienne, you've got some leeway.)

VARIATION: In place of the orange segments when layering the verrines, use hulled and sliced strawberries tossed with a little sugar. Figure four strawberries, sliced, per verrine, plus a few additional ones for garnish.

38

By January, everyone in Paris had returned from their Christmas break, which even writers take. Unlike summer, the winter holidays are meant to be spent *en famille*. The previous week, we'd had our annual holiday dinner with Romain's parents and siblings, who lived in the nearby Marais. As per the custom—or at least our custom—we started with platters piled up with freshly shucked oysters from Brittany accompanied by thin slices of rye bread smeared with butter embedded with crystals of sea salt, along with flutes of Champagne. For the main course, his dad presented a juicy leg of lamb, perfectly cooked *rose*, and I made a *bûche de Noël* for dessert in my new oven, since I finally had one large enough to hold a jelly roll pan to make the sponge cake. Parisians buy their *bûche de Noël* from their local *pâtisserie*, but I was especially proud this year to be able to make the dessert for the family dinner in my new kitchen, a fitting way to put everything that had happened behind me and start the new year off on the right foot.

I never found the cookbook notes and recipes I'd been working on. After unpacking the last of the boxes, the ones holding my testing notes were nowhere to be found. I'd caught the crew using some of the boxes of my personal possessions as sawhorses or worktables, and perhaps they didn't think the piles of papers inside were of value (my publisher felt otherwise), and tossed them out when they got covered in dust.

But I was used to starting all over again. I had moved to Paris to do so, barely knowing anyone, not speaking French, with no idea how my life would turn out. As I immersed myself in French culture, and the city, I found much to like about where I had planted myself: fresh bread on every corner; open-air markets; chilled oysters sold by the crate, stacked up on sidewalks in the lead-up to Christmas and New Year's; and lots and lots of chocolate. So once again, I took a deep breath and moved on.

It didn't take me long to warm up to my kitchen. I was using my new ovens to dive into working on recipes for the book, which I decided to end with the *bûche de Noël* recipe; it seemed fitting. Having a big counter meant I could keep my laptop nearby. Losing my notes and book-in-progress made me realize it was best to get things off paper and onto my computer—and into the cloud. (And not a cloud of dust.) Although my kitchen started off looking rather sparse, with lots of uncluttered surfaces and open space, most of it was soon overtaken by baking ingredients, miscellaneous cookware, a stand mixer, cake pans and tart rings, cookbooks filled with bookmarks, and flea market finds that I could no longer fit into the already-packed two rows of cabinets. (I know I should have lobbied for a third.) I reserved a space on the kitchen island for my computer so I could toggle between writing and baking at the same time. Even though I didn't have built-in USB ports (just plugs), I was happy to have the extra electrical outlets, which had been worth fighting for. I never got to the bottom of why they didn't install the American outlets, so if you're from the States and decide to renovate an apartment in Paris, get in touch. I have a few extras—as well as a few words of advice.

My life-changing sink with the sprayer made doing dishes (almost) a pleasure, and having a double-sized refrigerator, ridiculously huge by Paris standards, made sure that at the market I could load up on everything I used frequently: slabs of butter sold *en baratte*, lopped off a rounded slab; ripe peaches; crème fraîche; berries; milk; eggs; and apples and pears; as well as room to store all my doughs, custards, and even *verrines*. I also discovered it had an ice maker, which, after living in France for so long, I had forgotten even existed. It made Romain happy, too. In an ice-adverse country and culture, I somehow found the one person who likes ice in his drinks.

Between the radiant heat and space heaters in the main room, I was able to keep comfy while working in the winter. And I loved the kitchen light! *La lumière* is a premium in Paris, and I was fortunate to have it streaming into my kitchen.

Everything was back to normal, and I began having friends over for dinner again. Being a good host, I immediately offered them a drink—a glass of white wine, perhaps, although *les cocktails* have become fashionable in Paris, and I've started shaking up more potent libations now that I had buckets of *glaçons* in my freezer. (No more having to use the French plastic bags with special grooves you fill with water and freeze; when you want ice, you squeeze out each pill-size oval, one pellet at a time.) I do have to keep in mind that French people aren't as accustomed to hard liquor as Americans are, so thank goodness for having chairs that are level.

As I learned with my ice maker, I've never appreciated level chairs as much as I do now.

I had almost overcome my fear of opening the mailbox, and later that winter, I brought in my mail and slid open the envelopes, starting with the one from EDF, the French electric company. I unfolded the paper inside and took a look at it. I stared at the paper for a minute, not sure of what I was reading. Maybe I was making a mistake. It was for €3,535.00. (What gave me hope is that the French use commas for longer numbers, while in America, we use periods. So I was hoping maybe the bill was for €35.35 ... or even €353.00, which wouldn't have been as bad.)

Paris is famously expensive, but €3,535 for two months of electrical service was, as they say in Franglais, *too much*. French friends agreed that an electric bill for €3,535 was pretty high, but one suggested that it was because I used my ovens often. (None of the bakeries in Paris would still be in business with electric bills like that.) Another offered that it was because I wasn't putting my computer to sleep when I walked away from it. And a few others were certain that the energy used by my *très américain* dryer was responsible for such a preposterous total. The man on the phone from EDF agreed, saying that a small factory doesn't use that amount of electricity.

"*Et alors,*" he continued—there was the matter of €3,535 that I owed, and did I want to do a *prélèvement*, so they could take it out of my bank account, which he could do right now?

Hyperventilating, I called Daniel, who came back over and took a look at the fuse box. The new fuses his electrician had installed hadn't melted, which was reassuring. But he looked at the electrical meter, which was going crazy, the dials turning around and around and around at a wild clip.

Something was using an incredible amount of electricity. I thought maybe the previous contractor (we still weren't saying his name) had hooked up everyone else's electricity in the building to my electrical meter, which would not have surprised me.

I looked at my checkbook, imagining writing another enormous check, and wondered if this was going to be my life in Paris from now on—problem after *problème*, check after *chèque*.

Daniel brought me bad news, again: there was another *fuite d'électricité* because of the faulty installation of the heating coils, which was draining electricity faster than I could replenish my bank account. And so began the third year of the project. I couldn't imagine ripping up all the floors, laying down new heating coils, then replacing them, again. So I've become more French than I thought because I found myself agreeing to go backward. I sighed, shrugged, and decided to *condamner* the last bit of radiant heat and have him install traditional hot water radiators. Which required replacing the new hot water heater with a newer one.

And while you can't always fight city hall (although the one in Paris had been startlingly efficient in approving my residential conversion), the electric company is another matter. After some concerted negotiations—thanks to Romain's vigorous, and tenacious, debating skills—they agreed that my bill was implausible and offered to lower it by one-third, which I could pay in installments. The first of which they said they'd be happy to take over the phone, which they could take care of right now if I just gave them my bank account number.

After that was over, I had Daniel take out the thermostats left over from the old heating system, which were still attached to the walls, and patch over the holes. He didn't quite understand why that was so important to me, but when I told him I wanted to *cacher la misère*, he understood.

CHOCOLATE SOUFFLÉ

I've been obsessed with chocolate ever since I found a chocolate soufflé recipe in my mother's copy of *The Settlement Cookbook* when I was a kid. I didn't know quite what it was, but I whipped it up anyway in her Mixmaster and baked it in a Pyrex measuring cup since our kitchen lacked a proper soufflé mold.

I'd never had anything so good, and thus began a lifelong affinity with France, and French cuisine. There are a number of things that brought me to Paris, but one that keeps me staying is the love of chocolate I share with the French. (As well as a mutual wariness of contractors.)

Chocolate soufflé remains one of my all-time favorite desserts, and even though I now have a variety of porcelain soufflé molds in my kitchen here in Paris, I prefer to bake a chocolate soufflé in a shallow baking dish. Some can barely wait to get past the crust, to dive into the warm, tender pool of dark chocolate underneath, but I like the fragile, cocoa-colored crust just as much as what hides beneath it. It's a balance between the tough, and the tender, and one rarely exists without the other.

I've also replaced the squares broken off the dull bar of baking chocolate that my mother kept in her pantry with better chocolate. The French chocolate I keep on hand melts into a glossy brown puddle and fills my kitchen (even as large as it is) with that familiar smell that means something good will soon be coming out of my oven.

Édith Piaf famously sang, *Non, je ne regrette rien* ("No, I regret nothing"). Although I have my share of regrets, using good chocolate to make a soufflé is never one of them.

2 tablespoons butter, cut into cubes, plus more for the baking dish

8 ounces (225g) bittersweet or semisweet chocolate, chopped

3 tablespoons strong coffee or espresso (or water)

⅓ cup (45g) cornstarch

2 cups (500ml) whole milk

5 large egg yolks

6 tablespoons plus 3 tablespoons sugar

Generous pinch of salt

7 egg whites, at room temperature

1. Butter a shallow 2-quart (2l) baking dish.
2. Set a large bowl over a pan of barely simmering water (do not let the bottom of the bowl touch the water). Melt the butter in the bowl. Add the chocolate and coffee and stir gently until the chocolate has melted and the mixture is smooth. Remove from the heat and set aside.
3. In a medium bowl, mix together the cornstarch and ¼ cup (60ml) of the cold milk until the cornstarch has dissolved. Add the egg yolks and whisk until smooth.
4. In a medium saucepan, combine the remaining 1¾ cups (420ml) milk, 6 tablespoons of the sugar, and the salt and heat over medium-high heat until the mixture is warm. While stirring continuously with a whisk, gradually pour the milk mixture into the yolks. Scrape the milk and warmed yolks back into the saucepan and

cook over medium-high heat, stirring continuously with the whisk, until the mixture comes to a boil.

5. Reduce the heat slightly and continue to stir with the whisk until thick and shiny, 15 to 30 seconds. Remove from the heat and scrape the mixture into the bowl of melted chocolate; stir until smooth. Let sit until it's just slightly warm.

6. Preheat the oven to 375ºF (190Cº) with a rack in the center position.

7. In the bowl of a stand mixer fitted with the wire whisk, or by hand in a medium bowl, whisk the egg whites on medium speed until frothy. Increase the speed to high and when the egg whites start holding their shape, whisk in the remaining 3 tablespoons sugar, 1 tablespoon at a time.

8. Fold one-third of the egg whites into the chocolate mixture, then fold in the remaining egg whites just until no streaks of whites are visible. Transfer the soufflé mixture to the prepared baking dish and bake until the top just feels set when you touch it in the center, about 25 minutes. Most soufflé aficionados like theirs on the less-cooked side. Avoid opening the oven while the soufflé is baking, so begin checking it closer to when it should be done.

9. Serve portions of the soufflé on plates, making sure everyone gets some of the nice crust along with the moist interior, with a scoop of vanilla or coffee ice cream, or very cold crème anglaise. Although chocolate soufflé is traditionally served hot from the oven, after it cools for 10 minutes it settles into a moist, warm, mousselike dessert. It's also not bad the next day, at room temperature—for breakfast.

Epilogue

I ended up not leaving Paris, but it took me a few years to feel *correct* again. I was in over my head right from the start, and didn't grasp the language or the culture enough to take on such a daunting project. But regardless of the cultural hurdles and differences, it wasn't France, or the French, who were at fault. It was me. (I'm not French enough yet to deflect blame by pointing out I wasn't responsible for being in a situation that I wasn't ready to embark upon.)

Fortunately, I had Romain, who didn't think buying the apartment was a good idea in the first place, but gamely went through the apartment search and renovation with me. And now he loves the place. So I guess I can take credit for something that (eventually) turned out right.

Baking again, writing about France, and cooking *la cuisine française* in my new kitchen eventually helped me remember why I had moved to Paris, and why I wanted to stay. I love being able to run down the street to buy a freshly made baguette for breakfast from a boulangerie where the clerks now know me. And I love walking home, holding the bread by the thin sheet of paper the clerks wrapped around the middle, *pour des raisons d'hygiène*. (And yes, I even own a skimpy Speedo now, so I can take a dip in the public pools, even though I've developed a *p'tite brioche*, or "little tummy," from eating too much brioche.)

I became friendly with more food purveyors in my neighborhood than just bakers, from the cheery women who sell cheese, to the guys who offer over a dozen kinds of tiny salad greens, at my local outdoor market. I always stop in the little café down the street where a ruggedly handsome man makes me a post-market coffee, which I sip while we chat. And then there are the people in my building, whom I've come to know and have invited over for drinks, or dinner, on occasion. I think a few were disappointed that I didn't open a bakery in the space, but I do hand them cookies, cakes, and ice cream from time to time, which keeps our relationship sweet.

I had paid my dues to the city, sometimes in a series of installments (thanks to Électricité de France); sometimes the cost was more than financial. In addition to my shirt, I had nearly lost my mind.

All of it had been a shock at the time. (And not just because of the faulty electricity.) The kaleidoscope of Paris had shifted for me. The elements were the same, but I moved them around and saw another side of the city. Searching for sinks, flipping through toilet catalogs, and even trying to get a handle for a stove—it all made me feel a little more Parisian, and regardless of a few bad *pommes* I'm forever grateful for the people who did come through for me, the ones who made things right. I'm not sure I would have had that same experience anywhere else. They saved my life. Literally.

Paris was always Paris, and the French were . . . well, the French. But because of what happened—*j'avais mûri*, I had "ripened," as they say.

Living abroad, I learned and acclimated to different ways of doing things. Sometimes it's learning not to touch the produce at the market. Other times, it's going into a situation expecting the worst, instead of the best. In France, one uses *système D*, a way to *démerder*, or get out of the *merde*, by being resourceful and determined to get the job done, by whatever means you can. Whether it's changing the mind of a banker by offering up a little drama, or straightening out an off-kilter kitchen island by (finally) finding the right person for the job, the impossible becomes possible.

I learned to adapt. I'm no longer surprised at people crumpling up papers and shoving them back in my mailbox, or at being sent home by a bureaucrat to get a piece of paper, which they'll wave away when I wait in another long line to give it to them.

I'm amused, rather than bothered, by someone who does his best to slide past me in line. And when the pastry chef hands me a new chocolate he's come up with, that's *trés forte*, I know he's offering me a taste because I share his passion for very dark chocolate, not because he's trying to sell me something.

The French, who often get a bum rap for being soft, are tougher than we give them credit for.

I don't know if I'll ever make the full-on transition to *being* French, in spite of my folders bulging with nearly a decade and a half of electric bills (and now, three substantial binders of construction *devis*, *factures*, and *bons de livraison*). But I've learned some important lessons anyway. A few years later, there are still *malfaçons* in the apartment, which irk me, but I've learned to live with them—and now, I laugh about them, too. Flaws are part of life, and nothing is perfect, even if it appears that way from afar. I look at my experience from a distance now, and focus on the greater picture rather than the details. And I'm keeping my distance from my mailbox, too.

Acknowledgments

Thanks to Dianne Jacob, Miranda Junowicz Bothe, Paule Caillat, Emily Cunningham, Marc Desportes, Susan Friedland, Mara Goldberg, Jeannette Hermann, Steve Horton, Mohammed Issa, Hélène Le Cheviller, David Leite, Romina Rasmussen, Élisabeth de Rothschild, Lauren Seaver, and Carolyn Touquet. My appreciation to Cindy Meyers for testing the recipes and her valuable feedback.

At Crown Publishing, thanks to Domenica Alioto for being such a diligent editor, helping me put the story (and keep my head) together, and being exceptionally understanding of such a *spécial* author. And to her assistant, Claire Potter, for additional advice and support. *Merci beaucoup* to proofreader Benjamin Hamilton and production editor Ada Yonenaka. And publisher Aaron Wehner, for making sure I was in a good home.

To my agent, Bonnie Nadell, for feedback on the proposal and beyond, and to Austen Rachlis, for taking care of the details.

And to Romain Pellas, even though you don't always understand me—somehow, you do.

Author's Note

In some instances, for the sake of continuity, events have been condensed for clarity. Most names have been changed in this book. The only person whose name didn't get changed was Romain's, since there's nothing about him that I would ever want to change.

I've mostly used the euro as currency since it seemed incongruent to talk in U.S. dollars when mentioning purchases in France. Although the dollar sank to an all-time low while I was in the process of buying the apartment, at the time of the publication of this book it had stabilized to roughly the equivalent of the U.S. dollar, give or take 10 percent. (In my case, it always seemed to be "take.")

Lastly, the story and descriptions in this book are a snapshot of a certain time in Paris. Paris changes frequently, so some of the incidents, social and business customs, and places mentioned in the book may not be the same as they are today.

Index of Recipes

cuisine (Version

chaud.

élec

LAVE VAISELLE

Plan travail

Four